D1230352

The Politics of Monetarism

The Politics of Monetarism

Its Historical and Institutional Development

GEORGE MACESICH

Rowman & Allanheld
PUBLISHERS

ROWMAN & ALLANHELD

Published in the United States of America in 1984
by Rowman & Allanheld, Publishers
(A division of Littlefield, Adams & Company)
81 Adams Drive, Totowa, New Jersey 07512

Library of Congress Cataloging in Publication Data
Macesich, George, 1927–
    The politics of monetarism.

    Includes index.
    1. Money. 2. Monetary policy. 3. Quantity theory
of money. 4. Chicago school of economics. I. Title.
HG221.M124 1984   332.4   83-24766
ISBN 0-8476-7344-8
ISBN 0-8476-7345-6 (pbk.)

84 85 86 / 10 9 8 7 6 5 4 3 2 1
Printed in the United States of America

In Memory
of
My Parents

Contents

Tables and Figures

Preface

This book provides a systematic interpretation of "money" within the framework of political economy. The basic framework is Quantity Theorist or Monetarist and reflects the evidence provided by recent studies and history.

It draws upon and attempts to fit into a consistent picture the continuing discussion on monetary policy and monetary reform, classical and neoclassical monetary theory, the ideas and vision of Keynes and his followers, and the contributions of Milton Friedman, Anna J. Schwartz and the Monetarists, recent empirical studies, and recent contributions to the theory of bureaucracy. None of these is treated exhaustively, but only, as it were, drawn upon in painting a picture of the ease with which "money" slips into the political arena. Thus, in approach the study is basically integrative. Its principal conclusion is that discretionary authority facilitates monetary manipulation for political ends, thereby increasing uncertainty and casting in doubt money, the monetary system, and indeed the monetary authority itself.

This book is directed to the general economist (rather than specifically to the specialist), to students of economics, and to laymen. I hope that it may have some influence in moving them toward that consensus of views of the need for defined monetary guides within lawful policy systems. Only in this way can the uncertainty and undesirable political implications of discretionary actions by government and central banks be curbed. The work presupposes some acquaintance with the literature in its area and the tools of economic analysis. Although some mathematical notation is used and a simple economic model is employed as a general framework of analysis, the book should be understandable to anyone with a knowledge of elementary mathematics. The study deals with its subject in a comprehensive way, thus making it useful to intermediate and advanced students of economics and allied fields.

I am grateful to Marshall R. Colberg and Anna J. Schwartz, Walter Macesich, Jr., Dimitrije Dimitrijević, Branimir M. Janković, Rikard Lang, and Dragomir Vojnić for useful comments and suggestions.

1

Money and Political Economy

The Issues

Past monetary policies have been a major cause of economic instability throughout the world. A contributing factor to the poor performance of monetary policy is the ease with which "money" slips into the political arena to become a singularly important political issue. Discretionary authority facilitates monetary manipulation for political ends, thereby increasing uncertainty and casting in doubt money, the monetary system, and indeed the monetary authority itself. This raises fundamental questions regarding public policy constraints on the monetary system as well as the ideas and economic philosophy underlying past and current monetary policies. The purpose of this study is to consider "money" and specifically the quantity theory of money within the context and framework of political economy. Emphasis will be on American experience, although observations from other countries will be drawn upon.

These issues are as important today as they were at the turn of the century when Irving Fisher (1867–1947) was prompted to write, "It has seemed to me a scandal that academic economists have, through outside clamor, been led into disagreements over the fundamental propositions concerning money." He attributed the "confusion in which the subject has been thrown" to "the political controversies with which it has become entangled." Indeed, writes Fisher,

> It would seem that even the theorems of Euclid would be challenged and doubted if they should be appealed to by one political party as against another. . . . Since the quantity theory has become the subject of political dispute, it has lost prestige and has even come to be regarded by many as an exploded fallacy. The attempts by promoters of unsound money to make improper use of the quantity theory — as in the first [William Jennings] Bryan Campaign — led many sound money men to the utter repudiation of the quantity theory. The consequence has been that, especially in America, the quantity theory needs to be reintroduced into general knowledge. [1]

In the modern world the quantity theory of money and its implications for policy, and indeed monetary theory and policy in general, are still enmeshed in political controversy, though perhaps more complex and involving more fundamental issues than in Fisher's time. As in Fisher's time there appears to be a puzzling choice between real and spurious solutions. The various "solutions" have come protected by strong political, economic, and ideological interests. In part, the difficulties seem to arise from the economic circumstances, theory and methodology of the interwar and postwar periods. Thus group interests and group ideologies remain involved in the discussion, with the Federal Reserve and other central banks joining the banking community and national governments with immense opinion-making resources in a long-standing involvement in these issues. Finally, some themes in the literature of monetary controversy may be interpreted as involving puzzles fundamentally vexing to the human mind, since they have provoked discussion over the centuries with no evident improvement in the general level of comprehension. Monetary problems are thus as fascinating as they are perplexing, combining as they do a rich mixture of technical economics, political repercussions, and even the psychology of symbols and beliefs.

Milton Friedman, for instance, writes, "The Federal Reserve System is criticized by some for being slavishly monetarist; by others myself included for not following a monetarist policy. How come? 'Monetarism' has two very different aspects: as scientific analysis and as prescription for policy. Monetarism is a new term for an old empirical generalization known as the quantity theory of money." These statements according to Friedman are ideologically neutral. "In the scientific sense," writes Friedman, "Karl Marx was a monetarist and so are the bankers in Russia and China today."[2] In effect, monetarism can not be immobilized with the charge that it is "just so much ideology." If so, why the disagreement over money and monetary policy? In good part, for reasons given by Irving Fisher earlier. The disagreement is between, on the one side, Monetarists or Quantity Theorists urging a policy system based on rules and nondiscretionary intervention into the economy. Its principal policy corollary is that only a slow and steady rate of increase in the money supply—one in line with the real growth of the economy—can insure price stability.[3] On the other side of the issue are people whose preference is administrative discretionary intervention to maintain aggregate demand in the economy.

Essentially, the central issue in the disagreement is over defined versus undefined or discretionary policy systems. On this score the major opponents of the Monetarist position are modern Keynesians and central bankers whose position is that defined policy systems are inferior to administrative discretion. In effect, the modern Keynesian position and that of central bankers does not involve a search for optimal decision rules for monetary (and fiscal) policy. Their preference is to place "the political economist at the President's elbow."[4] Central bankers are more or less in accord since it is consistent with their view that the conduct of monetary policy is an "art" not to be encumbered by explicit policy rules. If this is correct, the controversy is indeed ideologically driven and does involve money in political considerations.

The modern Keynesian approach is, in effect, the economic branch of the political interventionist position whose defining principle is the extensive use of government power without definite guides or policy systems.[5] It has important allies in central banks with whom it shares many banking school ideas. Its opponents, including Monetarists, are those seeking lawful policy systems and limitations on the undefined exercise of power by government.

Culbertson puts it well when he writes,

> A basic difficulty with undefined policy systems . . . is that since the policies to be followed are uncertain, they may prove to be disastrously inappropriate. Such policy systems are risky. The intellectual difficulty of the proponent of discretionary policy formation is a real one. If the policy matters, then certain correct choices must be made, which implies that power must reside in those particular men who will make the correct decisions — but in a context in which the correct choices themselves are asserted to be incapable of being defined (since it is the basis of rejection of defined policy systems). Inevitably, it seems, the approach implies the existence of an elite or priestly class that promises to accomplish the indefinable.[6]

For the discretionary outcome it does matter which economist sits at the elbow of which President after all.

The Monetarist position is that a "political economist" is really not needed at the President's elbow, given a well-defined policy system. In his *Counter Revolution in Monetary Theory, First Wincott Memorial Lecture* (London: Institute of Economic Affairs, 1970), Milton Friedman summarizes the Monetarist view on the relationship between the money supply and the price level as follows:

(1) There is a consistent though not precise relation between the rate of growth of the quantity of money and the rate of growth of nominal income.

(2) This relationship is not obvious to the naked eye largely because it takes time for changes in monetary growth to affect income, and how long it takes is itself variable.

(3) On the average, a change in the rate of monetary growth produces a change in the rate of growth of nominal income about six to nine months later. This is an average and does not hold in every individual case.

(4) The changed rate growth in nominal income typically shows up first in output and hardly at all in prices.

(5) On the average, the effect on prices comes about six to nine months after the effect on income and output, as the total delay between a

change in monetary growth and a change in the rate of inflation averages something like twelve to eighteen months.

(6) Even after allowance for the delay in the effect of monetary growth, the relation is far from perfect. There's many a slip " 'twixt the monetary change and the income change."

(7) In the short run, which may be as much as five or ten years, monetary changes primarily affect output; over decades, on the other hand, the rate of monetary growth affects primarily prices.

The Monetarist view as summarized in Friedman's *Counter Revolution,* in effect, questions the doctrine advanced by John Maynard Keynes that variations in government spending, taxes, and the national debt could stabilize both the price level and the real economy. This doctrine has come to be called the *Keynesian Revolution.*

The battle between neo-Keynesians and Monetarists has been waged for almost a half century. It has long since moved into the policy area. The critics of monetarism declare that the proposed monetarist cure for inflation can work only by imposing excessive burdens and huge losses in real output and prolonged losses on the economy. The Monetarists respond that the burden must be borne because there is no other way to restore the economy to price stability or economic stability.

The acceptance of monetary policy by modern Keynesians, for instance, does not mean that they accept the principal Monetarist tenet regarding the importance of the money supply. Indeed, along with central bankers they strongly oppose the measurement of monetary policy by the money supply, whatever its definition. They apparently prefer to use interest rates and other credit market conditions as measures of monetary policy. Such a view is, in effect, similar to the defunct views of the banking school which takes "sound credit conditions" as its guiding principle, rather than the money supply. Although many variants of the theory are possible, they typically take as a principal autonomous and explanatory variable some measure of credit conditions, amount of credit or bank credit, credit availability, credit terms or interest rates. These measures are as important to central bankers today as they were almost two hundred years ago.

No doubt modern Keynesians do not consider themselves heirs to the banking school tradition. Their strong rejection of the concept of the money supply, however, is similar as in the banking school view. It is curiously intense and implacable.[7]

For instance, John K. Galbraith attributes the lack of "success" of monetarism in the United States and Great Britain to difficulties at three levels.[8] There is, according to Galbraith, first, the difficulty as to what is "money"; there is, second, that what a central bank elects to call *money* cannot either in quantity or velocity be controlled; there is, third, the certainty that efforts at vigorous control will substitute for the problem of inflation the alternatives of high unemployment, recession or depression, and disaster for those industries which depend on borrowed money. In effect, monetarism, which places its sole confidence in stabilizing the growth of some "esoteric monetary aggregate" to the exclusion of other concerns is a prescription for calamity.[9]

These critics are distressed that monetarism which began with the slogan, "Money matters" and manifested a healthy skepticism to early Keynesian views has over the years blossomed into all-out opposition to such discretionary Keynesian stabilization policies as compensatory use of fiscal and monetary measures. So, too, it is upsetting to such critics to hear Monetarist charges that a discretionary and interventionist stabilization policy causes more problems than it cures.

Critics charge that Monetarists have never really provided a convincing theoretical foundation for their policy prescriptions. There is not, so the critics argue, a clear conceptual basis for a sharp distinction of "money" from its substitutes and for ignoring systematic and random variation in velocity. Apparently, the empirical evidence presented by Monetarists is insufficient.

Monetarists, moreover, are charged by their critics with converting long-run equilibrium conditions into short-run policy recommendations. Thus "natural rate theory" argues that no permanent reduction of unemployment can be gained by accepting inflation. Anti-inflationary policies produce protracted social costs in lost output and unemployment. These costs are not fully addressed by Monetarists. This is not surprising, so the critics argue; given their free market ideology, they will not entertain wage or price controls or income policies as alternatives or complements to anti-inflationary monetary restrictions.

Milton Friedman identifies monetarism with the quantity theory he freed of dependence on the assumption of automatic full employment, the focal point of Keynesian ridicule of traditional quantity theory. It is also in his University of Chicago monetary workshop during the 1950s, and in which this writer had the privilege to participate as a graduate student, that studies on inflation and the role of money in inflation received considerable attention. Friedman's work changed professional thinking on matters pertaining to the role of money.

Harry Johnson has described changes in monetary theory as owing much to Friedman's efforts which made "monetary economics exciting and concerned with crucial issues."

> More fundamentally, the Friedman analysis gave a central place to expectations about future price movements and to Fisher's distinction between real and money rates of interest — in contrast to Keynesian analysis which always started with the assumption of stable prices — and in so doing steered theory and empirical research and monetary economics towards concepts and methods far more

appropriate to the inflationary-cum-necessary development of the past decade
than Keynesian economics was capable of providing.[10]

It is, in fact, unfair to present Friedman as just another ideologue who lets
his politics dominate his economics. To do so is to distort the actual situation. Indeed, Karl Brunner writes:

> The remarkable fact is that many of Friedman's political or policy views were
> guided by a strong commitment to a relevant empirical use of economic analy-
> sis. His "politics" emerge to a major extent as a consequence of his economic
> analysis. Analysis led him to a series of quite radical questions bearing on
> many of our social institutions, or more specifically, on the prevalent views of
> stabilization policies. The proposal for a monetary rule was not motivated by
> any "laissez-faire" preconception—but evolved from his appreciation of the
> unpredictable variability of monetary lags.[11]

Indeed, Keynesian emphasis on the basic instability of the private sector
and the stabilizing function of a stable government sector is a central idea
which Brunner correctly notes is turned on its head by Friedman on the basis
of his work with Anna Schwartz on the Great Depression. Their argument is
that it is essentially the stable private sector which operates as a shock
absorber to the shock imposed by an erratic and unstable government sector.
This inversion has generated a considerable amount of intellectual and political heat but little resolution.

A case in point is an illustration reported by David Cobham[12]—in
attempting to sort out whether "monetarism" is politically right-wing, left-
wing, or neither. The beginnings of an answer, writes Cobham,

> are provided, curiously enough, by a criticism of Milton Friedman made by
> Samuel Brittan, himself a monetarist journalist who could hardly be described
> as left-wing. In an "open letter" to Friedman in the *Financial Times* (December 2,
> 1976), Brittan criticized him for not distinguishing between "Friedmanite eco-
> nomics and the personal opinions of Professor Milton Friedman" on the
> grounds that ". . . your eminence as an economist does not deprive you of your
> right to express your views as a citizen on those gray areas which are halfway
> between academic analysis and personal opinion. But there is danger that your
> expression of what is purely speculative or personal may discredit the more
> securely established parts of your analysis."

In other words, writes Cobham, "Friedman's economics do not logically
imply his politics; monetarists do not have to '. . . denounce the whole welfare state . . . or . . . suggest that the developments of the last 70 years in
Britain and Chile alike have been predominantly in the wrong
direction. . . .' "

There may well be a "fallacy of association," as some argue, one perhaps
more accidental than systematic that can be attributed to equating
monetarism, conservatism, and a "free market."[13] The evidence reported
upon by a recent study, however, indicates that monetary theory cuts across a

wide spectrum of economic systems and a variety of ideologies.[14] This is consistent with Friedman's observation that in a scientific sense monetary theory and more specifically the quantity theory is ideologically neutral. It is perhaps the "fallacy of association" along with differences in interpretation of theoretical and empirical evidence generated for the most part from U.S. experience that is the source of misunderstanding between monetarists and their detractors.

It is, moreover, erroneous to attribute to money and monetary policy an all-embracing power and thus make discretionary interventionism desirable. Milton Friedman is quite explicit on this issue when he writes:

> I stress nonetheless the similarity between the views that prevailed in the late twenties and those that prevail today because I fear that, now as then, the pendulum may well have swung too far, that, now as then, we are in danger of assigning to monetary policy a larger role than it can perform, in danger of asking it to accomplish tasks that it cannot achieve and, as a result, in danger of preventing it from making the contribution that it is capable of making.[15]

Indeed, Monetarists argue that the monetary authority can control only nominal quantities and directly the quantity of its own liabilities.[16] By manipulating the quantity of its own liabilities, it can fix the exchange rate, the price level, the nominal level of income, the nominal quantity of money; it can also influence directly the rate of inflation or deflation, the rate of growth of the nominal stock of money, and the rate of growth or decline in nominal national income. The monetary authority cannot, through control of the nominal quantities, fix the real quantities such as the real interest rate, the rate of unemployment, the level of real national income, the real quantity of money, the rate of growth of real national income, or the rate of growth of the real quantity of money.

This does not mean, as Monetarists are quick to point out, that monetary policy does not have important effects on real magnitudes. Indeed, when money gets out of order, important repercussions are felt throughout the economy. As this study underscores, monetary history provides ample evidence on this score.

In spite of the empirical evidence advanced by Monetarists supporting the limitations of monetary policy and the ideological neutrality of monetary theory, "money" is used, however erroneously, to promote goals of ideology and social philosophy. Given the optional and political determination of a country's monetary system, this is not surprising.[17] Constraints imposed by the rules of the international gold and specie standard on national monetary sovereignty have been eroding since the interwar collapse of the international monetary system.[18] Fumbling attempts to reimpose monetary constraints through international monetary reform in the years since World War I have served the cause of discretionary intervention and imposed tasks on the monetary system which it has been unable to attain.

Attempts to reimpose monetary constraint have not been successful in good part because the contemporary world differs radically from that of the pre–World War I era. The revolutions of the nineteenth century were aimed at assuring political and economic liberty by breaking through the outworn controls of a preceding age of regulations. For the most part the revolutions of our time have been protests against the philosophy and institutions of the system of individualism based on natural rights. They have aimed at the opposite values of social control, and they have created myths and utopias of individual liberty. The impersonal forces of the market on which classical (and neoclassical) economists relied to bring about a maximum of production and distribution of income which, if not equitable, would at least be effective in maintaining high production, tend now to be displaced as political ideals by such objectives as full employment and various social safety-net programs.

Inevitably these objectives imply intervention and regulation. And the only mechanism presently available for such intervention and regulation is the national state and its bureaucracy, including the central bank. As we shall discuss in this study, the penchant by bureaucracies for discretionary authority as a means of self-preservation and expansion is well known. The evidence for this is to be found on every hand, moreover, and nowhere is it more conclusive than in expanded activities of central banks in domestic and international monetary affairs. Intervention and regulation, however, can take place within constrained policy systems. It does not call necessarily for the granting of important discretionary authority to the state bureaucracy, although extension of intervention has also promoted discretionary authority.

Few monetary problems can ever have been so ingeniously contrived to maximize difficulty as that of granting discretionary authority to central banks. Such authority granted central banks over domestic monetary policies, and undertaken for various and often illusive goals, constitute a formidable reinforcement of nationalism in the economic sphere as well as create an important source of instability. At the same time, discretionary authority serves well the central bank whose preference function may well differ significantly from that of the public in general. They are indeed an economic arm of the political interventionist position, while admirably serving their own bureaucratic goals and interests.

Central banks are, of course, subject to political pressures to which they typically respond, in the absence of explicit constraints, by manipulating money and monetary policy as a matter of bureaucratic survival. They are, after all, creatures of the nation state. Their independence is more myth than fact. Their alliance with political elements in government is understandable as our theory of bureaucracy suggests. However, their attempt to carry out seriously the various goals assigned, e.g., low interest rates, price stability, economic growth, employment and balance of payments equilibrium, through the exercise of discretionary policies is more likely to cast doubt on their own credibility and that of money and the monetary system itself. This is in fact what has happened in the United States and elsewhere. Subsequent demands for monetary constraints and reform are thus understandable. Whatever may be thought of the wisdom or practicability of such intervention and use of discretionary authority by central banks, the fact must be recognized that the nineteenth-century integration of market processes has been impaired by the emergence in every country of a greater measure of state intervention, particularly in monetary affairs. Indeed, Milton Friedman and Anna J. Schwartz report that "government intervention in the exchange markets since the 1930s has been more potent in disunifying the markets than improvements in transportation and communication have been in unifying them."[19]

Recognition of these drastic changes in the monetary system from a largely constrained specie standard to an unconstrained fiduciary standard by the public has been slow. Since the mid-1960s, however, a pronounced awareness of these changes is registered by lenders and borrowers. This, according to Friedman and Schwartz,[20] is suggested by the close relation for the first time in a century between interest rates and the rate of price change.

Proposals for Reform

Alarm and concern over the drastic changes in the monetary system has prompted all sorts of reform measures. They range from proposals to impose constraints on the monetary system within prescribed policy guidelines to calls for reinstituting interest rates and credit market conditions as guides to policy reminiscent of the banking school. Many are taken from the dust bins of history with little if any modification.

Money and the monetary system, however, are not a junkyard of political and economic system parts. These institutions have evolved along with general economic ideas and political economy. Attempts to resurrect no longer existing bits and pieces of systems to shore up or reform the monetary system is an exercise in futility. The pre-Socratic philosopher Heraclitus sums it up well with his remark that we cannot step into the same river twice.

In any case, we do not have to go to the past since a well-implemented and -executed monetarist rule will serve to constrain money and the monetary system within a defined nondiscretionary and lawful policy system. Money and monetary theory is ideologically neutral. This does not mean that it must be the same in all countries or throughout history, though the evidence tends to support the view that "money does matter—that any interpretation of short-term movements in economic activity is likely to be seriously at fault if it neglects monetary changes and repercussions."[21]

Recent proposals for return to some form of the gold standard as a constraint on the domestic and international monetary system have not met with notable success.[22] This is not surprising. What is often lacking in these proposals is an appreciation and understanding of the fact that the gold standard was more than a monetary standard. It cannot be understood, as it cannot be operated successfully, except as part of a socioeconomic, political, and philosophic system in which it was developed. This system no longer exists for reasons we discussed above.

There is, moreover, a tendency on the part of some gold advocates to idealize the gold standard and to overlook some of its more troublesome aspects. Thus between 1815 and 1914, there were twelve major crises or panics in the United States which pushed up interest rates, created severe unemployment, and suspended specie payments (conversion of the dollar into gold) in addition to 14 more minor recessions.[23] To be sure, between 1879 and 1965—a period when America was on some sort of gold standard (the dollar's final links with gold were not cut until 1971 during President Nixon's administration)—the consumer price index rose by an average of only 1.4 percent a year. On the other hand, the severe bouts of inflation were followed by deep deflation in which prices actually fell. For instance, in the 1921 world recession, when production actually fell for only a few months, there were 30-40 percent cuts in manufacturing wages in some countries in the period 1920-1922.

An alternative proposal, pushed from theory to practice by F. A. Hayek, is that governmental monopoly in the supply of money be abolished and that the provision of money be left to an unregulated market.[24] Hayek contends that with private provision of money, money users would receive a better product, and the problems of business cycles would be ameliorated. Pre-1860 American monetary experience with multiple private currencies which this study examines sheds light on the feasibility of Hayek's proposal. At that time, moreover, the ultimate constraint on the American monetary system was the specie or gold standard. Hayek's proposal on this score is not clear.

Another reform proposal is to opt on the national level for a fiduciary monetary standard within a "monetary constitution." This is essentially a Monetarist proposal. It is suggested by Leland Yeager and James Buchanan and incorporates a Friedman-type rule on the rate of monetary growth.[25] On the international level, fully flexible exchange rates would replace the existing "dirty-float" system of exchange rates.

One merit of these proposals for constraining the monetary system by a monetary constitution and rule is their implicit recognition that the nineteenth-century integration of market processes has been impaired over the past several decades by the emergence in every country of a greater measure of state intervention and particularly the discretionary nature of such intervention in the monetary sphere. Moreover, the degree of intervention varies from complete central planning, such as in the Soviet Union and other

East European countries through various modifications of the social service state, to national economies still operating for the most part on a basis of private enterprise.

The fact is that in every country there has been an increased degree of intervention, and, in all, the instruments of intervention are primarily national. The flexibility of exchange rates could well deputize for the varying degrees of price flexibility in internal price structures brought about by state intervention. Such a flexible system also takes into account varying political, economic, cultural, and indeed historical conditions of the world community of nations, thereby avoiding conflict over sensitive issues of national sovereignty. The International Monetary Fund has become neither the constraining influence on national monetary systems, nor the international central bank that some of its founders hoped it would.

The ease with which money slips into the political arena is aptly demonstrated in recent Congressional attempts to have the Federal Reserve change its policies. Echoing banking school arguments, a call for reform by 31 Democratic senators, led by Minority Leader Robert C. Byrd, introduced legislation in August 1982 that would direct the Federal Reserve Board to abandon the monetary policy it has pursued since October 1979.[26] The measure, called the *Balanced Monetary Policy Act of 1982* and subtitled A Democratic Recovery Initiative," would direct the Federal Reserve to give up priority to meeting yearly targets for short-term interest rates instead of to controlling the money supply, the presumed focus of its current policy. According to Senator Byrd, the aim would be to return interest rates to their "historical levels" of roughly one to four percentage points above the inflation rate. Indeed, Byrd cites the October 1979 Federal Reserve decision — to focus on the money supply as its operational goal rather than controlling interest rates — as "one major cause" of the 1982 deep recession.

Little chance for the passage of the Democratic bill was given at the time, owing to the month or so that remained before Congress adjourned for the election campaigns. Nevertheless, Senator Edward Kennedy (D-MA) indicated that the bill might at least serve as a shot across the Fed's bow, perhaps encouraging it to "abandon this academic, experimental monetary policy" it has been following for almost three years.

Not to be outdone by the Democrats, the Republicans came forth with an alternative proposal, the Kemp-Lott bill (Representatives Jack Kemp, R-NY, and Trend Lott, R-MS). As in the Democratic proposal, the Kemp-Lott bill would direct the Federal Reserve to abandon concentration on the money supply and move to a greater concentration in targeting interest rates. According to its sponsors, the Federal Reserve had already moved in this direction in July and August 1982, when it reduced the discount rate and took steps to cut the federal funds rate, i.e., the interest rate on overnight loans between banks.

At the same time, the promoters of the Republican proposal would direct the Federal Reserve to include other factors in determining interest rate policy, including employment, economic growth, stable prices, and stable exchange rates. The priority, however, is to be given to price stability, and any threat to it would require the Federal Reserve to refrain from pushing interest rates. In effect, the bill is so phrased as to blunt criticism that it seeks lower interest rates and economic growth at the expense of increased inflation.

In other words, the Kemp-Lott bill would direct the Fed to opt for price stability in the event of conflicts among the stated goals of low interest rates, unemployment, growth, and exchange rates. In this sense the Republican bill does differ from the Democratic proposal. In both instances, however, the results are likely to be an increase in the exercise of discretionary authority by the Federal Reserve Board and away from consideration of nondiscretionary rules within a lawful policy system. If either proposal is seriously adopted by the Federal Reserve, the net effect is likely to be a repeat performance of the Fed's indifferent past record.

Chairman Volcker's skeptical view of interest rates as a guide to policy does not mean that the Federal Reserve is now in complete agreement with the Monetarist position. Monetarists are also critical of the Federal Reserve's experiment with monetary control, as noted in Friedman's comments. Since the experiment began in October 1979, the volatility of money growth, short-term interest rates and exchange rates have been raised beyond previous levels and, Monetarists argue, more than necessary. This suggests that something is indeed wrong.[27] It indicates that risk may be excessive.

To be sure, argue the Monetarists, the failure is not complete.[28] Money growth has been reduced and inflation cut in half. The cost of reducing inflation, however, is much greater than necessary. Indeed, the cost is the direct result of the Fed's failure to adopt procedures that control monetary growth effectively. It is this that imposes an excess burden on the economy by raising interest rates and slowing the recovery.

According to Monetarists, the way out is for the Fed to increase its credibility by sticking to an announced policy of disinflation and improving its procedures. One necessary procedural change is for the Fed to move to contemporaneous reserve accounting, which has long been proposed but not implemented. It is expected to go into effect on February 2, 1984. Meltzer, for instance, argues that the current monetary procedures are unreliable and costly; they should be abandoned. Instead of focusing on M1 (currency and checking deposits in public hands) and M2 (M1 plus saving deposits and money market funds aimed at individuals), the Federal Reserve, according to Meltzer and other Monetarists, "should announce a disinflationary path for the growth of its assets and liabilities. It should remove the remaining self-imposed restrictions and faulty seasonal adjustments that make monetary control more difficult and less reliable. A growth path for Federal Reserve assets and liabilities means that the growth of either total reserves or the monetary base (total reserves plus currency) becomes the target. Either of these targets is difficult to miss, so control would improve, credibility would increase, and risk premiums would gradually return to normal levels."[29]

These Monetarist measures are not advanced as a cure-all for the troubles in the monetary system. They do, however, represent correct steps with minimal institutional change. Moreover, they are in keeping with objectives of those seeking defined guides within lawful policy systems. Since these measures would also constrain central bankers in their exercise of discretionary monetary authority and thus limit the practice of their "art," these measures are not likely to generate much enthusiasm on their part—especially since central banks as a result would become smaller and less influential bureacratic institutions. Nonetheless, the uncertainty and the undesirable political implications of discretionary actions by government authorities including central bankers would be curbed.[20]

Notes

1. Irving Fisher (assisted by H. G. Brown), *The Purchasing Power of Money: Its Determination and Relation to Credit, Interest and Crisis* (New York: Macmillan Company, 1913), p. viii. For the impact of political factors on money, see also Milton Friedman and Anna J. Schwartz, *Monetary History of the United States, 1867–1960* (Princeton: Princeton University Press for National Bureau of Economic Research, 1963) and Milton Friedman and Anna J. Schwartz, *Monetary Trends in the United States and United Kingdom: Their Relation to Income, Prices, and Interest Rates, 1867–1975* (Chicago: University of Chicago Press, 1982), e.g., agitation over silver; Anna J. Schwartz, "Empirical Findings of the Study of Monetary Trends in the U.S. and U.K." in *Proceedings and Reports*, Vol. 15, ed. George Macesich (Florida State University), pp. 1–8. See also George Macesich, "Sources of Monetary Disturbances in the U.S., 1834–45," *Journal of Economic History*, September 1960, pp. 407–34, and George Macesich, *The International Monetary Economy and the Third World* (New York: Praeger Publishers, 1981). For a different view on a number of these issues dealing with a monetary history, see James Tobin, "The Monetary Interpretation of History," *American Economic Review*, June 1965, pp. 464–85.

2. Milton Friedman, "Defining 'Monetarism', " *Newsweek* 12 July 1982, p. 40. See also George Macesich and H. Tsai, *Money in Economic Systems* (New York: Praeger Publishers, 1982) and George Macesich, *Monetarism: Theory and Policy* (New York: Praeger Publishers, 1983), as well as the bibliography cited in these studies. Friedman writes, "Personally I do not like the term 'monetarism.' I would prefer to talk simply about the quantity theory of money, but we can't avoid usage that custom imposes on us" in "Monetary Policy: Theory and Practice," *Journal of Money, Credit and Banking* February 1982, p. 101. This study takes *Quantity Theorist* and *Monetarist* as identical terms. It is my understanding that Karl Brunner coined the term *Monetarist* or *Monetarism.*

3. Milton Friedman, "The Role of Monetary Policy" in *The Optimum Quantity of Money and Other Essays*, ed. Milton Friedman (Chicago: Aldine, 1969), p. 99. See also George Macesich, *Monetarism: Theory and Policy.*

4. John M. Culbertson, *Macroeconomic Theory and Stabilization Policy* (New York: McGraw-Hill Book Company, 1968), p. 545.

5. Ibid., p. 535.

6. Ibid.

7. Ibid., p. 534.

8. John K. Galbraith, "Up for Monetarism and Other Wishful Thinking," *The New York Review of Books*, 13 August 1981, pp. 27–32.

9. E. A. Birnbaum and P. Braverman, "Monetarism—Broken Rudder of Reaganomics," *Wall Street Journal*, 23 July 1981. See also Benjamin Friedman, "The Theoretical Nondebate About Monetarism" (Discussion Paper No. 472, Harvard Institute of Economic Research, Harvard University, Cambridge, April 1971); George Macesich, *Monetarism: Theory and Policy*. In reply to critics of monetarism, Dallas S. Batten and Courtenay C. Stone, "Are Monetarists an Endangered Species?" (Federal Reserve Bank of St. Louis *Review*, May 1983), pp. 5–16, write:

> This paper has assessed the claim that monetarism, in the scientific sense, has failed, by testing four key monetarist propositions to see whether they can explain economic events over the past three years [1979–82]. Contrary to recent rumors of the death of monetarism, we have found that the four propositions tested were as valid and as useful over the past three years as they had been over the past 20 years. Moreover, when compared with the predictive behavior of two well-known nonmonetarist econometric models, we found that a simple monetarist analysis worked equally well in explaining the economic patterns of spending, output, and prices over the past three years. Rumors of the death of monetarism have indeed, been exaggerated. [Ibid, p. 16]

10. Harry Johnson, "The Nobel Milton," *The Economist*, 23 October 1976, p. 95.
11. Karl Brunner, "The 1976 Nobel Prize in Economics," *Science*, 5 November 1976, p. 648.
12. David Cobham in *Lloyds Bank Review*, April 1978, and reprinted in T. M. Havrilesky and J. T. Boarman, eds., *Current Issues in Monetary Theory and Policy* (Arlington Heights, Ill.: AHM Publishing Corp., 1980), p. 566. See also Macesich and Tsai, *Money in Economic Systems*, and Macesich, *Monetarism: Theory and Policy*.
13. Walter W. Heller in "What's Right with Economics," *American Economic Review*, March 1975, p. 5, writes:

> These associated claims are not lumped together in any inexorable logic—in part they seem to be an accident of both, as in the case of the Chicago twins of monetarism and *laissez-faire* rules. A belief in the supremacy of monetary over fiscal tools could quite logically go hand-in-hand with avid interventionism. But this escapes the jaundiced eye of the outside observer who takes the ideological lineup as further evidence that economics is riven to its core.

14. Macesich and Tsai, *Money in Economic Systems*.
15. Friedman, "The Role of Monetary Policy," p. 99.
16. Ibid. See also Macesich, *Monetarism: Theory and Policy*, chap. 5.
17. For a discussion of these issues, see Culbertson, *Macroeconomic Theory*, chap. 19.
18. Macesich, *International Monetary Economy*, chap. 2.
19. Friedman and Schwartz, *Monetary Trends*, p. 626.
20. They write:

> A sharp break has apparently occurred in recent years in the relation between price change and interest rates in both the United States and the United Kingdom. Since about the mid-sixties, a close relation between interest rates and the rate of price change has emerged for the first time in the century we study. Gibson has been replaced by the original Fisher. Nominal returns become more variable than real returns, nominal returns on nominal assets are as variable as nominal returns on physical assets. Lenders and borrowers apparently have been able to predict price changes more accurately and to adjust the terms of lending and borrowing accordingly.
>
> This break has been noted by other investigators. Like Benjamin Klein, we are inclined to attribute . . . the break to a recognition . . . of the . . . change in the monetary system from a largely specie standard to a fiduciary standard. [Ibid., p. 631]

21. Milton Friedman, "The Quantity Theory of Money—A Restatement," in *Studies in the Quantity Theory of Money*, ed. Milton Friedman (Chicago: University of Chicago Press, 1956), p. 3.
22. See, for example, a useful summary by M. D. Bordo, "The Classical Gold Standard: Some Lessons for Today," *Review*, Federal Reserve Bank of St. Louis, May 1981, pp. 1–16; R. M. Bleiberg and J. Grant, "For Real Money: The Dollar Should Be as Good as Gold." Editorial commentary in *Barron's* 15 June 1981; L. E. Lehrman and Henry S. Reuss debated issue "Should the U.S. Return to the Gold Standard?" *Christian Science Monitor*, 21 September 1981; *The Economist*, 5 September 1981, pp. 11–12, the report of the U.S. Gold Commission studying greater

role for gold in U.S.; see also Martin Bronfenbrenner, "The Currency-Choice Defense," *Challenge,* January/February 1980, pp. 31–36:

> The gold clause was relegalized by Section 463 of the U.S. Code in October 1977. Little publicity has been accorded this change; few people know about it; any rush of gold clauses may lead Congress to reverse its 1977 action. On the other hand, that action may be a straw in the wind; it has friends in Congress; extension of the legal tender privilege to other currencies and thus freer competition between currencies may be closer in the U.S. market than anyone realizes. [Ibid., p. 36]

See also Anna J. Schwartz, "The U.S. Gold Commission and the Resurgence of Interest in a Return to the gold Standard," *Proceedings and Reports,* vol. 17, 1983 (Tallahassee: Center for Yugoslav-American Studies, Research and Exchanges, Florida State University, 1983). Dr. Schwartz was Executive Director of the U.S. Gold Commission.

23. *The Economist,* 19 September 1981, pp. 17–18.

24. F. A. Hayek, *Denationalization of Money* (London: Institute of Economic Affairs, 1976).

25. See, for example, Leland B. Yeager, ed., *In Search of a Monetary Constitution* (Cambridge: Harvard University Press, 1962); James Buchanan, "Predictability: The Criterion of Monetary Constitutions," ibid, pp. 155–83; Milton Friedman, "Should There Be an Independent Monetary Authority?" ibid, pp. 219–43; Friedman and Schwartz, *Monetary History;* Milton Friedman, *A Program for Monetary Stability* (New York: Fordham University Press, 1959). See also Robert E. Lucas, Jr., "Rules, Discretion, and the Role of the Economic Advisor," in *Rational Expectations and Economic Policy,* ed. S. Fischer (Chicago: University of Chicago Press, 1980), pp. 199–210; T. J. Sargent and N. Wallace, "Rational Expectations, the Optimal Monetary Instrument, and the Optimal Money Supply Rule," *Journal of Political Economy* 83, 1975, pp. 241–54.

26. "Democrats in Senate Seek Federal Policy Shift," *Wall Street Journal,* 4 August 1982, p. 3.

27. See Milton Friedman, "An Aborted Recovery?" *Newsweek,* 23 August 1982, p. 59. Friedman, evaluating the 32 months' experience from October 1979 when the Fed changed, presumably, from interest rates to the money supply, writes:

> Monetary growth (M1) over short periods has become very erratic: annual rates of 2 percent for six months, over 11 percent for a year, negative growth for six months, over 15 percent for three months. . . . We shall not have a healthy and lasting recovery along with steadily declining inflation until the powers that be recognize the importance of curbing the erratic ups and downs in monetary growth and take effective steps to ensure reasonably steady growth in the quantity of money along a gently declining path.

28. See also Allan H. Meltzer, "The Results of the Fed's Failed Experiment," *Wall Street Journal,* 29 July 1982, p. 18.

29. Ibid.

30. On the other hand, some economists do protest and argue that discretionary monetary policy might contribute to economic stability by such institutional reforms as lengthening the terms of office of members of Congress, improved economic education on the part of the public at large; and that, after all, public policy can benefit from past mistakes. While they may be correct someday, thus far the available evidence in support of their argument leaves much to be desired. For a discussion of political pressures on the Federal Reserve System, see Edward J. Kane, "External Pressures on the Operations of the Fed" in *The Political Economy of International and Domestic Monetary Relations,* ed. R. E. Lombra and W. E. Witte (Ames: Iowa State University Press, 1982), pp. 211–32 and the discussion of Kane's paper, pp. 233–36.

2

Interaction of Economic and Interventionist Ideas

The Approach

It is useful to approach the study of contemporary problems historically. This is especially important to our discussion of interventionist and discretionary policies as they impinge upon monetary issues. One reason is that many of these questions and issues have been set for more than two hundred years by a school of thought to cope with the problems of England in the period of great change since the seventeenth century. Their contributions to economic thought are notable and deserve serious study.[1]

For instance, John Locke (1632-1704) prepared the way for a scientific study of political economy when he set forth his exposition of a society based on natural rights of individuals. Among these rights property loomed large; Locke was a philosopher of the middle-class revolution of 1688. He represented the views of men who founded the Bank of England in 1694. The fight against the divine right of kings was won, and the new social order was dominated by the right of individual property.

Conditions of economic instability at the beginning of the eighteenth century promoted examination of the connection between money and output. The most outstanding contribution in addition to that of John Locke was made by John Law (1671-1729). In essence, Locke and Law focused on the obvious fact that total monetary receipts must equal total monetary payments. They contended that increases in the quantity of money and in the velocity of circulation not only raised prices but expanded output. Their policy prescription was to increase the quantity of money. Their presentation of policies was designed to create a favorable balance of trade.

Richard Cantillon (1697-1734) focused on the processes by which variations in the quantity of money lead to variations in prices and output, thereby providing useful insights into monetary dynamics. He also recognized what many would later point out — that the nominal quantity of money is beneficial to trade only during the period in which it is *actually increasing*. Once a new equilibrium is reached, output will return to its original level at a higher price level. This process of *increasing* the quantity of money, however, cannot last indefinitely because the process leads to an adverse balance of payments and so to an outflow of money. How to buy the benefits of the inflationary process without generating balance of payments problems is a monetary policy goal conflict resolution familiar to contemporary society.[2]

In the 1760s David Hume (1711–1776) linked the general level of prices to the quantity of money in the now classic quantity theory of money and the price-specie flow mechanism of international trade theory. The larger the supply of money, argues Hume, the higher the price level was likely to rise; higher prices, in turn, tend to make exports less competitive in foreign markets and imports more competitive in home markets. A drive to enlarge the stock of money would be self-defeating because the accumulation of specie (gold and silver) would produce effects that would later erode the favorable balance of trade. Moreover, attempts to check such deterioration in the balance of trade by controls of one kind or another would be damaging to the national interest, since it would deprive the country of the benefits of international specialization and division of labor.

Henry Thornton (1760–1815), in *An Inquiry into the Nature and Effects of the Paper Credit of Great Britain* (1802) dealt with the same general topic Hume had treated in *On Money*. Thornton, however, considered not gold and silver but bank credit, by which he meant bank notes. These were the main circulating medium in terms of value in Britain in his time.[3]

England was the center and testing ground for many of the ideas put forward by economists. In economic theory, as distinct from economic policy, the classical doctrine steadily won its way. This is especially true in the case of the United States, as we shall discuss. But it was essentially the same character as English commerce. As we shall see below, Continental European preoccupations with economic strategy, misgivings as to the moral consequences of the enterprise, historical criticism of economic institutions, and socialist theories of more equitable distribution and more humanistic production did not prove a fertile ground for English ideas.

Indeed, Walter Bagehot (1826–1877) of *The Economist* put it well when driven to explain the "obvious reasons why English Political Economy should thus be unpopular out of England." His explanation is a double one: in effect, it is difficult for most people to understand that political economy is an abstract science; moreover, it is particularly difficult for those whose economic development is less developed than in England and hence more remote from the assumptions of political economy.

Though rigorous and complete within the assumptions of their theory, many English writers excluded important aspects of economic policy that are clearly revealed in earlier thought, and have never ceased to be influential in practice.[4] Ethical considerations are not expressly taken into account. Nor are the complexities of international politics. Social policy, and particularly the welfare of general workers, though not ignored did not represent any special problems to society. The controversial issues of past and contemporary economic policy are largely from these ethical, political, and social factors.

By the second half of the nineteenth century, if not earlier, concern focused on the economic, social, and political problems cast up by rapidly industrializing European and American societies. It was a concern that by the early years of the twentieth century had in practice if not in satisfactory theory most of the elements of the interventionist economic position which Keynes articulated later in theory. How revolutionary the Keynesian revolution was in these aspects is suggested in the brief survey presented in this chapter.

Classical Contributions

The moral dilemma between individual and social benefits with which social philosophers and moralists wrestled is resolved by Adam Smith in his analysis of the market economy. His system of natural liberty, free markets, free men, and competition lead to an orderly increase in wealth of the nation. The free competitive play of individual selfishness is shown by Smith to be the source of economic growth, social order, and general welfare. Individualism does not lead to chaos but to order and prosperity.

Smith did more. In *Wealth of Nations* (1776) he provided economics with an analytical framework. The idea is of a competitive self-adjusting market equilibrium following a path of growth and affluence. At the same time, *Wealth of Nations* is a philosophical treatise concerned with fundamental problems of order and chaos in human society. Smith provided what came to be, especially in England and the United States, the orthodox approach to economic problems and policy which is very much alive in the twentieth century.

Critics seize upon two limitations to Smith's analysis of the free market. One is the distribution of income, which if highly unequal will signal the market to provide more for the rich and little for the poor. If the distribution of income is wrong, so too will production be wrong, however efficiently the market works to produce the goods and services. It is this very problem, in fact, that the early socialists raised and that Karl Marx (1818–1883) later developed into a theory for the breakdown of capitalism.

The second criticism, closely related to the issue of economic justice, concerns private property in land and capital. Smith's support for the institution of private property as both natural and necessary to the preservation of economic incentives is good liberal doctrine. The fact is, however, that he supports it only in advanced societies. In primitive societies, only labor is considered a factor of production and is thus rewarded by wages. Conversely, in advanced societies rent on land and profit on capital are also part of the costs of production. Since rent and profit as costs of production are really the products of social organization, and not natural phenomena like human labor and the motive of self-interest, Smith's idea of an equilibrium of natural forces in the market is compromised.

These shortfalls provide socialists, among others, an opening to argue that only a return to labor is natural. Accordingly, only when the full value of output is gained by labor through social ownership of the means of production (land and capital) would the natural state of society be regained. Economic justice would be served since the entire product of society would go to its producers, and society's demand would not be distorted by unearned income.

Thomas R. Malthus (1766–1834), David Ricardo (1772–1823), Jeremy Bentham (1748–1832) and Jean Baptiste Say (1767–1832) contributed enormously to the body of ideas now called *classical economics*. Writing at the close of the eighteenth century and during the turbulent early years of the nineteenth century, they promoted economics to a "science." These were the years of political, social, and technological revolutions that wiped away the vestiges of feudalism and the old aristocratic order. Much was expected of the American and French revolutions by English intellectuals and others. Some attribute the success of the American revolutionaries to the support of English liberals. Political reform in England was at the time a pressing issue. Even the French Revolution was looked upon favorably because it would bring democracy to France and so peace to both countries.

The disappointment was all the greater when the wars with France began and continued for almost two decades. The Napoleonic period dashed all hopes for liberal political reforms in England. The Establishment concerned itself with holding the line and rooting out the "radicals." The suspension in 1795 of the Habeas Corpus act for five years; in 1799 the Anti-Combination Laws, prohibiting any combination of workers or employers for the purpose of regulating conditions of employment — for the most part these laws were directed and enforced more against labor than management. Suppression ruled these turbulent years.

Nevertheless, problems created by rapid change brought about by the war years demanded attention. The most obvious concerned the poor displaced by the economic, political, and social turmoil of the period. Their numbers increased as a result of demobilization following the Napoleonic Wars; enclosures of common land, displacing many farmers from their small plots, served to promote the growth of cities already overburdened with problems of poverty. Reaction against the French Revolution assured that the problems of the poor would receive little priority from conservative policymakers, particularly if solutions required political and social reforms. Still, something had to be done.

A solution of a sort was given by a religious minister, Thomas Robert Malthus. It is a solution consistent with the preservation of the *status quo* and one calling for minimal government intervention. Government, argued Malthus, can do little in any case since the problem of the poor is moral. The problem has its origins in two propositions. One is in the food supply. The other is in the sexual proclivities of man. The result is Malthus' principle that "the power of population is infinitely greater than the power in the earth to produce subsistence for man."

In effect, "misery and vice" hold population in check. If the supply of food increases, there is a corresponding increase in population until brought back to subsistence level, at which point population increase will stop. Wages tend toward the subsistence level which is the *natural* wage. Any increase in wages above the natural or subsistence level causes the population to grow and subsequently for wages to decline. If, on the other hand, the price of food increases, wages would be forced up to maintain the subsistence wage. Moreover, increasing relief to the poor would mean taking resources out of the hands of those willing to invest, thus increasing output.

The implications for the poor are ominous. Relief payment simply raises the wages of the poor above subsistence and so results in more people. No increase in food production takes place as poverty continues unabated. Not a very happy state of affairs, but one for which the government and the conservative establishment are not to blame. Nature must be allowed to take its course.

For David Ricardo, capital accumulation is the mainspring of growth. Economic policy is to be directed to facilitating and promoting such accumulations. His model is based on the belief that economic freedom leads to maximum profits, which are the source of investment capital, and in a competitive economy lead to profit-maximizing investments. Business is to be encouraged since it leads to maximum economic growth.

The political and social issues in England following the Napoleonic wars turned in part on whether the country should become more heavily industrialized or preserve a balance with agriculture. The issues involved among others the role of England's landed aristocracy in the country's social and political system. The contest was drawn in Parliament on the so-called Corn Laws and the import of grain into England. Existing laws protected English agriculture against foreign competition without at the same time resulting in "significant" price increases for food.

As a result of war-created increases in demand for agricultural products, English farmers enjoyed considerable prosperity. When peace finally came, British farmers and landed interests pushed for the enforcement of the Corn Laws as a means for preserving their prosperity. All sorts of schemes were put forward for promoting agriculture as England's leading industry.

All this was anathema to the British business community which saw high food prices and high wages, reduced profits, decreased exports spelling general ruin for British industry, and demanded nothing less than repeal of the

Corn Laws. Ricardo and other economists entered the debate on the side of business interests and against those of agriculture. Ricardo, in effect, argues that it is the landowners and not farmers as such who benefit if the price of wheat is raised by tariffs. The high price of wheat enables an extension in the amount of land under cultivation which would not normally be profitable. The result is that in the older wheat-growing areas, landowners would raise rents to take advantage of the higher prices received by farmers. Consequently, a larger proportion of the nation's income would go to landowners, who would use these additional resources not for productive investment but rather for "luxury expenditures."

Moreover, additional capital and labor would be drawn from industry to enlarged agricultural production stimulated by artificially high food prices. The net result would be to distort the nation's productive pattern, retarding the country's *natural* development of industry. Ricardo noted that high food prices would require high wages and thus high costs of production in industry. Since England must sell the products of industry throughout the world, higher costs would reduce business for English exports and so reduce the level of output of industry. Profits would be reduced, thereby slowing capital accumulation and economic growth owing to both a lack of incentive and resources out of which to invest.

If left alone, a country's economy will achieve maximum growth possible, according to Ricardo. It is, therefore, important that business be left alone to pursue profits; thus would the nation maximize the amount of saving and capital accumulation so necessary for growth. Government intervention would simply make the process of saving and accumulation all the more difficult. Ricardo, in effect, reinforced the theoretical and ideological underpinnings set in place by Adam Smith. Business interests are indeed well served by Ricardo's analysis.

The facility with which the international economy is integrated into Ricardo's model served to reduce all economic phenomena to fundamental relationships among factors of production. It demonstrates that the international division and specialization of labor is advantageous to all nations and that protection of domestic producers serves simply to damage the country imposing such protection. Free trade is beneficial internationally as well as domestically. The famous law of comparative advantage is used in support of the free trade doctrine. Moreover, capital will seek out countries where the returns are highest, provided such nations assure political stability and offer protection for private property rights. All of this remains very much part of contemporary international trade theory, if not practice.

The realization of the full benefits of free international trade made necessary a sound international monetary and financial system. We shall have more to say on Ricardo's views on the issue later. Suffice it here to note that he insisted that the domestic monetary system should be regulated so as to minimize any disruption in the international division of labor. Ricardo adopts a "bullionist" position, arguing that the domestic money supply should be directly tied to the country's gold supply. Such an arrangement assures that a country suffering a loss of gold through an unfavorable balance of trade automatically contracts its paper note issue. Contraction in the money supply thus tends to depress the country's general level of prices, which in turn encourages the desired adjustment in international accounts. The deficit country's exports become more attractive to foreigners while imports compete less successfully in home markets as the price of home-produced items decline. Ricardo, in effect, sets out in its essentials the classical theory of the gold standard.

The monetary idea that money used as a standard of value consists of bank notes redeemable in specie or bullion and that coins circulate at their value as bullion is central to the body of classical ideas. This money is assumed to be convertible into gold or silver bars and to be freely exchangeable either as coin or as bullion between countries. Its value is fixed at its bullion value, and the rate of exchange between two currencies is easily calculated by comparing the intrinsic value of the precious metals which would automatically adjust to the "needs of trade" in each country.

Moreover, there is nothing that governments can do about this. If they issued paper money beyond the amount that the public would accept in the belief that these notes could at any moment be converted into gold, the surplus issue would be cashed and the government would have to redeem it with gold and silver from its reserves. If the notes are made inconvertible, their value would fall and the price of gold — indeed of all commodities — as measured in the paper money would rise in proportion to their overissue. This is Ricardo's argument published in his pamphlet (1810) entitled *The High Rise of Bullion: A Proof of the Depreciation of Bank Notes*.

The conclusion drawn by classical theorists is that governments must accept the fact that the only true money (gold and silver, or *specie*) is beyond their control. All the elaborate government devices for increasing national supplies of specie are self-defeating. Money accommodates itself to the "needs of trade." If governments issue inferior monetary substitutes, their value will depreciate. There is no place, therefore, in the classical theory for discretionary interventionist monetary policies designed to maintain full employment, balance of payments equilibrium, or to combat inflation or depression.

It remained to be demonstrated that a free market would also achieve full employment of all resources including labor and capital. That this in fact appears to be the case is demonstrated by Jean Baptiste Say (1767–1832) in his *Treatise on Political Economy*, which first appeared in 1803. The principle is *Say's Law of Markets*. According to Say, there can never be a general deficiency of demand or a glut of commodities throughout the economy. While there may be given sectors or industries in which overproduction may occur, along with a shortage in others, this is only a temporary situation. The fall in prices in one area and their rise in other areas will provide incentives for businessmen to shift production and thereby correct the situation.

Say pointed out that people produce in order to exchange their products for other products. Production thus creates its own demand. It is therefore impossible for production in general to outrun demand. Say's Law of Markets dominated economic thought on the level of economic activity until the concept was challenged by J. M. Keynes in the 1930s.

Jeremy Bentham (1748–1832) and such "philosophical radicals" as James Mill, David Ricardo, and John Stuart Mill agitated for political reform, democratic government, and majority rule. The utilitarian political philosophy that dominated the "radicals" called for nothing less than a social system based upon full democratic participation and majority rule. According to Bentham and his utilitarian followers, this is the only way that a social system can maximize its total welfare and distribute it as widely as possible.

Bentham differs significantly from the classical liberalism of the eighteenth century which emphasizes individual freedom as the end goal of public policy. He sees potential conflict in the idea that only individual action can create welfare. It is possible, for instance, that the action of one person in pursuit of his own interest may injure another and so reduce his welfare. After all, argues Bentham, human society is organized by man-made institutional arrangements. Conscious action can create social forms that enable men to live better. In effect, classical liberalism establishes by way of Benthamite utilitarianism a place for interventionist liberalism emphasizing social welfare. It is intervention and reform justified in terms of individual and social welfare and the "greatest good for the greatest number."

Thanks to Benthamite ideas, economics could henceforth easily incorporate the most laissez-faire individualist as well as the most thoroughgoing social reformer.[5] The analytical apparatus is the same for both. The important differences arise from the assumptions and conclusions that each reach. This is an attribute that economists preserve to the present time.

All was not well in the post-Napoleonic world. The French Revolution did not bring forth "liberty, equality, and fraternity," nor did the rapid economic and technological advance usually called the "Industrial Revolution" abolish poverty. Indeed, the post-Napoleonic reaction and repression and the reestablishment of old political, social, and economic privileges served to increase poverty and arrest democratic advances for the general public. Critics seize upon the observed inequalities to push from theory to practice an alternative vision of society based on the cooperative element in man's nature, rather than the materialistic profit motive of private capitalism, and egalitarianism in place of the unequal distribution of income that prevailed at that time. To these early socialist critics, society is an organic whole composed of classes, rather than independent individuals as held by classical economists. The roots of modern socialism are in the post-Napoleonic Europe nurtured by reaction against economic and political circumstances of the era.

Private property and private ownership of the means of production, argue the socialists, is the root cause of failure of the two great revolutions to abolish poverty and create a political order of full democracy. A few owners of capital benefited from these social and technological revolutions while the majority of people remained mired in poverty. The socialists called for the abolishment of private property and privilege as a first step into a new society of greater opportunity and dignity for all people.

The humanitarian and idealistic roots of early socialism is typified in the work and writings of Robert Owen (1771-1858). His attempts to establish, in England and America, cooperative communities in which land was owned in common, and worker-owned enterprises in which profit was not permitted, were not particularly successful. This is not surprising. Individualism dominated the era.

Unlike the utopian reformers, Karl Marx (1818-1883) coupled scholarship with revolutionary agitation. It is not enough, according to Marx, to theorize; one must build a revolutionary party capable of seizing power when capitalism collapses. He did not suffer lightly other socialists who happened to disagree with his views. In fact, he established the practice of the vitriolic denunciation of opposing views which burdens so much contemporary socialist literature.

Capitalism, in Marx's view, and a term which he invented, is doomed. His demonstration of its demise draws on so-called laws of motion of capitalist society. On one level Marx bases his argument on the inherent injustices of capitalism which lead ultimately to economic and social conditions that cannot be maintained. At another level his argument is sociological in that class conflict between increasingly affluent capitalists and an increasingly miserable working class will break out in social revolution. At still another level the argument is economic in that the accumulation of capital in private hands, while creating increasing abundance, also leads to the inevitable breakdown of capitalism. At all three levels the idea of conflict is underscored: conflict between ideal and reality—the moral issue; conflict between labor and capital—the sociological issue; conflict between growth and stagnation—the economic issue. This conflict generates change, and so capitalism, according to Marx, must eventually give way to another social system in which conflict is replaced by ethical, social, and economic harmony. This change is the "dialectical process" whereby socialism will replace capitalism. Thus Marx created one of the world's most powerful ideologies whose vision of abundance, equality, and freedom stands in challenge to classical-liberal individualism, private property, and private enterprise.

Neoclassical Contributions

Rise of socialism, demand for social justice, and Marx's use of such instruments of the dominant ideology as the labor theory of value and the theory of capital accumulation to attack its legitimacy, prompted a search for a theoretical defense of the existing system. In part, the new defense presented is that of the philosophy of the individual developed and cultivated for the most part by dominant business and economic interests from the mid-nineteenth century up to and beyond World War II. In effect, it is a reinforced version of the laissez-faire argument discussed earlier in this chapter.

Economists for the most part did not take the extreme position of individualism very seriously. For one thing, Benthamite utilitarianism suggested that government intervention may on occasion be justified by the greatest-good argument. For another, economists concerned themselves with pressing social issues for which the philosophy of extreme individualism provided little insight. This did not mean, however, that economists rejected the individual philosophy. On the contrary, they remained within its general framework.

More important, economists intentionally or otherwise developed a new theoretical apparatus that presumably serves to refute the Marxian critique of capitalism. This is the neoclassical economics developed since 1870. In effect, the foundation of economics is reduced to the desires and wants of the individual, and the whole theoretical explanation of production, distribution, and prices is based on the single assumption of rational individual self-interest. Neoclassical economics is a significant scientific advance, since it reduces to the simple but elegant idea of marginalism a complex set of separate theories of value, distribution, and returns to factors of production. The value of a product or service is not the result of the amount of labor embodied in it, but of the usefulness of the last unit purchased. With marginalism a new approach to economics developed.

Carl Menger (1840–1921), William Stanley Jevons (1835–1882), Leon Walras (1837–1910), and Alfred Marshall (1842–1924) shifted the focus of economics from social classes and their economic interests underscored by David Ricardo and Karl Marx to that of the individual. The individual consumer becomes centerpiece to the theoretical apparatus of economics displacing the principle of income distribution envisioned by Ricardo as the mainspring of economic progress and on which Marx bases his theory of the breakdown of capitalism. The system of free markets does maximize individual welfare. Since consumers are assumed to maximize their satisfaction and since production responds to consumer wants, it follows that the result will be welfare maximizing. Moreover, marginalism also shows that the costs of production are pushed to the lowest level possible by competition. If allowed to operate without constraints, the entire economy becomes a pleasure-maximizing machine in which the difference between consumer benefits and production costs are increased to the highest level possible. In short, economics is transformed into a service consistent with the individualist social philosophy of Herbert Spencer and William Summer Graham.

The development served also to reinforce, at least in the United States, the legal theories of United States Supreme Court Justice Stephen Field (1816-1899) and the philosophy of unrestricted individualism in American constitutional law. One result of Field's interpretation was to eliminate much state legislation dealing with economic affairs, including the regulation of hours of work, child labor, factory conditions. Private property is thus viewed as a natural right that no government can interfere with lightly.

Marx's challenge is also taken up in the application of marginal analysis to income distribution, which demonstrates that all factors of production — labor, land and capital — earn a wage exactly equal to their contribution to the value of output. Called the theory of marginal productivity and based on the last marginal unit, its conclusion is that workers would be paid a wage equal to the last unit of output they produced. The same idea is applied to profits earned from capital and to rent from land. In effect, to each factor of production the same law applied. No one could exploit anyone else since everyone received what he deserved. The entire product is exhausted and no surplus value exists. Marx's concerns are simply irrelevant.

This happy state of affairs, critics are quick to point out, depends very much on the assumptions of marginal productivity theory. In the first instance, the theory rests on the assumption of perfect competition. Second, all factors of production must be completely substitutable for one another. Third, there must be no change in costs of production per unit of output as the level of production falls or rises. Not all economists are satisfied by such assumptions. Indeed, some economists have never accepted the theory of marginal productivity, which they view as singularly unreal.

It is the issue of periodic booms and depressions that seem to plague the rapidly industrializing countries which attracted considerable public and government attention. During the first half of the nineteenth century, little concern was shown by most economists, thanks to their acceptance of the general propositions of Say's Law of Markets, according to which there should be no periodic economic breakdowns and the economy should continue to operate at uninterrupted high levels of output and employment. Say's Law states that demand is created by production, and in the aggregate the two can never get out of phase with one another. Economists interested in business cycles typically sought causes outside the framework of production and distribution.

Stanley Jevons (1835–1882), for instance, developed a quantitative relationship between sunspots and business fluctuations, arguing that these fluctuations are connected with "periodic variation of weather affecting all parts of the earth, and probably arising from increased waves of heat received from the sun at average intervals of ten years." This serves simply to reinforce Say's Law, since the "cause" is outside the system of production and distribution. Perhaps the best interpretation within Say's Law is provided by the argument that the monetary system generates instability while the basic system of production and distribution is stable. Stabilize the monetary and financial system, and general economic stability is assured.

Walter Bagehot in 1873 in his by now classic on money and finance, *Lombard Street,* spells out how in his view it is to be done. Limit the expansion of credit to legitimate needs of business through effective action by the "central bank." This will prevent excessive credit issue from overstimulating the economy and thus developing into a crisis. Once the situation gets out of hand, the "central bank" can probably moderate the crisis but the economy will simply have to weather out the storm.

These theoretical advances served, among other things, to firmly entrench capitalism and defend it from its critics. Marginal utility, marginal productivity, and the monetary theory of business cycles supplemented the basic analysis of classical economics. The free-enterprise economy is pictured as operating to produce what consumers want, thus maximizing welfare distributing products justly and normally operating at full utilization of resources. The issue of laissez-faire in neoclassical economics is not a rigidly held doctrine. In fact, the major area of exception is monetary policy, which is "assigned" to the government and its agent the "central bank." It is their responsibility to preserve economic stability by properly managing the money supply so as to serve the "legitimate needs of business." This is interpreted to mean the needs of production and distribution. The Banking School influence here in the form of the "real bills" doctrine is obvious. Even so, such monetary intervention is to be held to a minimum and strictly guided by the free market. In short, "discretionary" monetary policy is to be limited by the requirements of the free market, and within the constraints imposed upon it by the gold standard. As a result, the scope for the exercise of discretionary authority by central banks is very limited indeed.

Arguments raised in support of the mercantile or Banking school tradition are based on two principal ideas. One is that the country's bank money will expand only in proportion to the "needs of trade" if banks restrict themselves to discounting only "real bills of exchange." Converse circumstances will prevail when trade declines. The second presumption, closely associated with the first, is that a country's currency will have a desirable elasticity if only commercial banks will maintain a reasonably liquid reserve position and operate competitively. Before 1860 in the United States and elsewhere, the first idea prevails; that is, the limiting effect of quality on the quantity of loans is stressed. Thereafter, the quest for elasticity and liquidity dominates the banking scene. These two concepts constitute what economists call the "real bills" doctrine.

Although the rationale of the real bills doctrine has been attacked throughout history by economists and others, it has never been completely vanquished. Indeed, the doctrine is firmly lodged in central and commercial banking practices. Supporters of the doctrine argue that it provides an intrinsic, self-regulating limit to the quantity of bank money. It is the chief support for banking reform in the United States before 1913, and the Federal Reserve Board embraced it after 1913. It is to be found in various "qualitative" control measures over bank credit. It also influences the preferences of central banks for interest rates and money market conditions as policy targets over monetary magnitudes. Neoclassical economists also approve other types of government intervention. Such intervention serves to facilitate the operation of free competition and free markets. On this score, concern with monopolies and legislation designed to control their practices tend to be supported by most economists. The fact is that neoclassical economics does not adopt "lock, stock, and barrel" the simple individualism and laissez-faire, as critics assert; neither does it opt for wholesale intervention. It does accommodate to realistic needs of society. It does have strong ideological implications since it serves to rebuild the theory of free private-enterprise on a new basis, thereby making the refutation of Marx unnecessary. Private property and free private enterprise weathered the Marxist storm more or less intact, thanks to the efforts of neoclassical economists.

Philosophy of the Welfare State

These issues, however, are not settled to the satisfaction of all concerned. As we noted above, with the close of the nineteenth century, concern about the complex nature of man and his society is simply not adequately addressed by those who argue that society is the sum of individual units which is brought into an easy equilibrium by market forces and those who argue that the social system is divided into antagonistic classes with social conflict as the source of change. There is a third view, which argues that the chief objective of a society is to promote human welfare. It is, in effect, the philosophy of the welfare state. Its exponents include, among others, such diverse entities as Roman Popes, Fabian socialists, New Dealers, and Great Society advocates.

Papal economics attempts to come to terms with the social problems bubbling up from the European industrialization and nationalism which brought about a new socioeconomic and political order to the continent during the last quarter of the nineteenth century. Pope Leo XIII (1810–1903), in a series of encyclicals issued between 1871 and 1901, opts for the middle ground in the feud between labor and capital. The problem, argues Pope Leo, is not economic but moral. The solution must be based in justice animated by charity. Since these are nonmarket phenomena, they cannot be measured in the marketplace in terms of profit and loss, wages and costs.

The Papal tilt is at first toward capitalism in the condemnation of socialism and in the defense of private property. Subsequently, a compromise of sorts came about in an indictment of laissez-faire policies *(On Conditions of Labor),* condemnation of socialism, support for private property rights and the natural rights of individuals. The Papal appeal harking back to theories of Thomas Aquinas of the thirteenth century, criticized extreme individualism of the market economy and called for return to human and community values.

Government intervention is justified, according to Papal economics, whenever the welfare and preservation of society is threatened. In these matters justice and fairness are to serve as guides. The tradition established by Pope Leo continued to influence later popes, Roman Catholic labor movements, and some political parties. The idea that man and community are one and the emphasis that both individual freedoms and individual welfare are to be reconciled in a society that stresses community values and social justice continues its attraction, in theory if not always in practice.

For instance, Pope John Paul II's encyclical, written during the summer of 1981, is intended to be a kind of sequel to the encyclicals of Pope Leo XIII's "Rerun Novarum" in 1891 and Pope Pius XI's "Quadragesimo Anno" in 1931. Both are powerful social documents, and John Paul's new encyclical is a comprehensive statement on social issues which backs labor unions, urges worker participation in management, and proposes a "just" family wage and subsidies that would free mothers from the necessity of taking jobs. The encyclical condemns both "rigid" capitalism and the "collectivist system" that eliminates all private ownership of the means of production. It suggests a socialist middle round as a model for economic development. The central theme in the 99-page, 22,000-word "Laborem Exercens" ("On Human Work") encyclical is opposition to the "dehumanizing excesses" of modern economic systems.

The encyclical, written in Polish, reflects John Paul's vision of "a just society based on an ideal economic system." John Paul strongly endorses the workers' right to organize unions, to participate to some extent in the management of their companies, and to strike, except for political purposes or in essential public services. Radical and urgent changes are necessary to rescue farmers from the big landowners and "to restore to agriculture their just value as the basis for a healthy economy." Multinational corporations are engaged in the condemnable practice of fixing high prices for their products while trying to keep down prices for raw materials and semi-manufactured goods, widening the gap between the rich and poor nations. "In order to achieve social justice in the various parts of the world, there is a need for ever-new movements of solidarity of the workers and with the workers," according to Pope John Paul. It is sure to be studied carefully in the Soviet Union, in the Pope's native Poland, and in Latin America as well as other countries where the Roman church is influential.

While the Papacy grappled with the seeming social, economic, and political chaos in Europe brought about by an industrial society, Fabian socialists John A. Hobson and Richard H. Tawney in England pushed forward ideas and programs to deal with similar concerns. Essentially interventionist, the idea cast government's role as one that assists man in developing his talents to the utmost. This is to be done by government working to remove barriers in man's path to the "good life".

A cascade of social legislation descended upon England as a result. Legislation dealing with factory safety became law in 1891 and 1895; limiting working hours for women and children in 1891; slum clearance in 1890; increased powers for labor unions 1890–1900; workmen's compensation and child welfare in 1906; old-age pensions in 1908; town planning and redevelopment in 1909; sickness and disability insurance in 1911. In effect, a good deal of welfare legislation — serving as mainstays to contemporary economies — were put into place by the turn of the century.

Even though their vision is behind much English social legislation, such generators and spokesmen of unorthodox ideas as John Hobson received little in the way of gratitude from significant numbers of their contemporaries. In fact, Hobson could not find employment in English universities. Fortunately for Hobson, such of his writings as *Work and Wealth Incentives in the New Industrial Order, Physiology of Industry, Evaluation of Modern Capitalism and Imperialism* did much better. Indeed, V. I. Lenin (1870–1924) incorporated into communist ideology Hobson's *Imperialism,* which attacked the selfish expansion of European states.

Similar to Hobson's ideas, Fabian socialists envisioned "a reorganization of society in accordance with the highest moral possibilities" through a democratic socialist regime designed to promote "the greatest happiness of the greatest number." A small but influential intellectual group included such members as George Bernard Shaw, Sidney and Beatrice Webb, H. G. Wells, and Annie Besant. Named after the Roman general Fabius Maximus, "the delayer," who fought Hannibal with guerilla tactics instead of frontal confrontation, the name signifies the society's philosophy and plan of action. Their vehicle, *Fabian Essays,* established in 1889 under the editorial leadership of Shaw, promoted gradual extension of state intervention in economic affairs to improve working conditions, replace monopoly with government ownership, and promote a more egalitarian distribution of income.

Unlike the Marxists, the Fabians did not view the state as an instrument of class warfare that must be destroyed but rather as a means of social control that, once seized, can be used to promote social welfare. They pushed successfully for the formation of a labor party with a socialist platform in 1906. Their tactics, in effect, involved political action within the framework of democratic, parliamentary government. In short, resort to persuasion rather than revolution is a singular Fabian characteristic. That these efforts bore fruit is indicated by the existence of the British Labor party and much of contemporary social and welfare legislation in Great Britain.

The economic historian Richard Tawney (1880–1963), drawing on past and present world experience, argues for a society reformed along the functional lines of a socialist society. Rewards are to be received by those productive members of society who expend work and effort in the tasks society requires and not to such unproductive elements as the promoter, speculator, and rentier who collect large sums of unearned income. Property rights, according to Tawney in *The Acquisition Society* (1920), should not be maintained for which no service is performed. In *Religion and the Rise of Capitalism* (1926), he debates the issue raised by Werner Sombart and Max Weber over whether the Protestant Reformation created the intellectual atmosphere that made possible the rise of modern capitalism. He argues that the two are related, but also that modern society and its business activities are completely amoral. In *Equality* (1931), Tawney's theme is that egalitarianism can support and sustain a democratic political framework. In effect, it is through socialism that human values can receive the necessary development.

The American approach to these same problems of industrialism is characteristically pragmatic, lacking much of the socialist philosophy prevailing in Great Britain and Europe. Workable solutions to specific problems are sought within the traditional framework of American Society. Much of the necessary work is attributed to a small group of economists investigating such issues as business cycles, labor relations, monopoly, big business, and social welfare. Through their influence on progressive political leaders at the turn of the century and later the New Deal, they promoted the theme that modern industrial society faced serious problems that would not solve themselves. Government intervention is necessary if the destructive forces of the free market are not to have singularly tragic consequences for both society and the individual.

Thorstein Veblen (1857–1929) represents one of the more important economists in terms of his influence on American reform thought. Essentially, his argument is that fundamental forces of change are at work which require adaptations of the social, economic, and political institutions inevitably opposed by the establishment and represented by wealth and influence—the conflict between change and vested interests. His critique of the "pecuniary society" and the "business system" gave both direction and viewpoint to the movement for economic and social reform. Veblen's two books *The Theory of the Leisure Class* (1899) and *The Theory of Business Enterprise* (1904) are considered economics classics.

John R. Commons (1862–1945), along with his followers, formulated specific reform measures and legislation adopted first by some states and later incorporated into the New Deal platform of F. D. Roosevelt. Such programs and policies as utility regulation, collective bargaining, and mediation to settle disputes between labor and management on a voluntary basis; unemployment insurance and worker's compensation; promotion of economic growth, employment, and stability, are cases in point. Clearly a remarkable achievement.

The government, according to Commons, must serve as a mediator between conflicting economic interests and between economic forces and the individual. He does not necessarily reject the view of neoclassical economists that harmony emerges out of the equilibrating forces of the market nor the Marxist view of class conflict. In fact, he goes beyond both of them to argue that the market can reconcile some but not all conflicting interests which arise in a modern economy. Continual conflicts arise in such an economy, and government intervention is necessary if equitable solutions are to be obtained.

The New Deal philosophy in essence owes much to Veblen, Commons, and their followers. Through government intervention the public is protected from presumably the worst consequences of an industrial market-oriented society. It represents a singular shift from the view of a harmonious self-regulation free enterprise market-oriented economy as advocated by the classical and neoclassical economists.

The New Deal administration intervention into the economy followed along three paths. One focuses on the use of the federal budget to promote adequate aggregate spending in the economy and offset short-falls in the private sector of the economy. It recognizes government responsibility for economic stability in the economy. This recognition is now embodied in the Employment Act of 1946 and institutionalized in the Council of Economic Advisors to the President. The second deals with attempts to promote cooperation between businessmen and labor in various industries. The third deals with government intervention into regional land-use planning based on water resources, e.g., Tennessee Valley Authority.

Moreover, the individual, according to liberal reform philosophy of the New Deal and in contrast to classical and neoliberal views, does not necessarily contribute most to society by pursuing his own interest nor is he necessarily responsible for all of his misfortune. Society, accordingly, must accept responsibility for the welfare of each individual so as to enable him to function effectively in society. The passage of such welfare measures as unemployment insurance, workmen's compensation, social security, and federal grants-in-aid in health and education are aimed at providing security for the individual.

In addition, businessmen are to accept social responsibility beyond mere profit making. The pre–New Deal situation whereby, presumably, businessmen ran roughshod over human and social values is no longer tolerated. In short, business must justify itself by something more than a profit. What that "something" is, however, is not specified. All of this does not serve to endear the reform liberals to the business community.

The liberal reform philosophy of the New Deal extended into President Truman's Fair Deal and afterwards into the short-lived administration of President Kennedy to be picked up in the Great Society programs of President Johnson and essentially carried on through the administrations of Presidents Eisenhower, Nixon, Ford and Carter. What appears to be a resurgence of neoliberalism and neoclassical economics in the form of "supply-side" economics in President Reagan's administration we discuss below. The fact is that reform liberalism as manifested in the several past American Presidential administrations managed to restructure much of the country's economic and social framework without gross violations of individualism, private property rights, and the market-oriented private enterprise economy.

Events took a less satisfactory course in Russia and in Eastern European countries during and following the two World Wars. War, revolution, and counterrevolution served to wreck what appeared to be promising liberal reforms which began at the turn of the century and continued, albeit in a halting fashion, into World War I.

At the time, Russia was the most backward country in Europe. It had primitive agriculture and industry staffed, for the most part, by an illiterate population. By professing its allegiance to a Marxist ideology which postulated that socialism would naturally evolve in highly industrialized economies in which the working class comprised the majority of the population, Russia was simply at odds with received socialist doctrine. The country simply did not square with what Karl Marx and his followers had in mind. To complicate matters, the world revolution had failed and the new Soviet state was surrounded by antagonistic capitalist countries who considered it an "illegitimate child of history."

V. I. Lenin (1870–1924) led the Bolshevik revolution to a successful conclusion. He did so after convincing his followers that Russia could bypass the capitalist industrial era and move directly from an agricultural, semi-feudal society into the socialist era. It was Lenin who formulated the basic idea on how to accomplish the goal of a socialist society. In essence, rapid and large-scale industrialization of Russia would serve as a means for building the working-class society in which socialism could flourish. This required an alliance between workers and peasants under a worker's dictatorship, although priority is given to the construction of an urban and industrial society. Lenin died before his strategy was translated into specific programs of action. A debate on goals and means continued in the 1920s and into the 1930s when Stalin ended discussion with the first of the purge trials that were to shake the very foundations of the new Soviet state.

Joseph Stalin (1879–1953) manipulated the great urbanization-industrialization debate to his favor. The moderates led by the leading Marxist theoretician Nikolai Bukharin argued for balanced economic development and the postponement of World revolution until the Soviet state was strong enough domestically to support such a revolution successfully. Although urbanization and industrialization are to be encouraged, it was dangerous for the Soviet state to push the peasants too far and to further threaten their loyalty to the regime. In short, a slower development pace tuned to the realistic possibilities of the Soviet state is prudent. Stalin called this approach the *right deviation*.

Opposing the moderates was the so-called left wing of the Communist party led by Leon Trotsky (1879–1940), who, in fact, was Lenin's key man during the Bolshevik revolution. The idea pushed by the "left-wing" called for mobilizing the country's economy to the utmost, squeezing living standards in order to free resources for industrial development, and using the power of the state to extract the maximum surplus from agriculture for food, raw, materials and export. According to their view, agriculture was to be collectivized and mechanized. In effect, the economy was to be deliberately unbalanced so as to force industrialization. As for the international scene, the Soviet state would never be secure in a capitalist world. As a result, it can best protect itself by exporting world revolution principally by demonstrating the superior productivity of socialism through economic growth.

Stalin, at first, took the position of supporting rapid industrialization and forced draft development advocated by the "left-wing" but ruled against collectivization of agriculture so as not to alienate the peasants. As for world revolution, he sided with the moderates and Bukharin, forming an alliance which drove Trotsky into exile. Whereupon Stalin then sided with the "left" and opted for collectivization of agriculture, a rapid rate for the accumulation of capital beyond anything called for by Trotsky and his faction. It was also enough to gain for Stalin the support necessary to purge Bukharin. In essence, the debate resolved into the establishment of ambitious development goals and a planning apparatus to carry them out, with the Stalin dictatorship the driving force of the system.

This is the Soviet model with more or less appropriate modification imposed in East European countries following World War II. It is also the model and systems dropped by Josef Broz Tito (1892–1980) and Yugoslavia following the Tito-Stalin split in 1948. With the departure of Yugoslavia on its own independent road to socialism in its unique model of "worker-self management," a new chapter in socialism began. The world would not be the same again.

It is with post–World War I Europe and the Bolshevik revolution as background that a useful insight is had into John Maynard Keynes' (1883–1946) efforts to formulate new policies designed to preserve and revitalize the market economies of Europe. To Keynes, the challenge was clear enough. The Marxist-Leninist socialists had engineered a revolution that not only brushed aside everything before it but transformed a backward, rural economy into an industrial giant. European civilization already weakened by war was now threatened with extinction.

Against the apparent socialist success, Britain continued, as it had in the post-Napoleonic years, a deflationary policy designed to achieve international stability at the expense of internal stability. Keynes argued that Britain's return to the gold standard at the British pound's prewar par would diminish British exports and cause domestic wages, prices, employment, and output to fall as they had a hundred years before in the post-Napoleonic period because of similar policies. Keynes argued for a managed monetary system in place of the classic gold standard. His advice disregarded, Britain returned to the gold standard, only to realize Keynes' prophecy. The subsequent economic stagnation in Britain, already crippled by war and dissolution of its empire, joined the rest of Europe in waiting for a miracle. In Keynes' view Europe could not afford to wait.[6]

This is Keynes' vision. He lacked, however, a theoretical apparatus to provide a convincing case to an audience educated in classical and neoclassical economics. To demonstrate the futility of the British government's deflationary monetary policy, he must show the inadequacy of the classical theoretical apparatus which rested on the relationship between the gold standard, the domestic level of employment, and Say's Law of Markets. Keynes realized the need to demonstrate convincingly the relationship between the theory of employment and monetary theory. He devoted more than a decade to the task.

The two-volume *Treatise on Money,* published in 1930, is his first effort to unravel the problem. Essentially, Keynes argues the distinction between investment and savings and their different underlying motivations. Unlike Say's Law, which holds that the two must be equal, Keynes argues that this need not be the case. For instancee, if savings is greater than investment, general economic activity will decline; conversely, Keynes' policy prescription, which he argues in the various *Essays on Persuasion,* is similar in the *Treatise* that the monetary system be so managed as to assist in maintaining equality between savings and investment and thereby promoting economic stability. In addition, a program of public works should be put in place whenever called for to reduce undesirable effects of economic depression on employment.

The collapse of the world economy and the onset of the Great Depression of the 1930s created a political and economic environment receptive to new ideas along the lines advanced by Keynes and others. In fact such contributions to economics as those made by members of the National Bureau of

Research, the University of Stockholm (Swedish School), including such economists as Knut Wicksell (1851–1926), D. H. Robertson, William T. Foster, W. Catchings, and others, paved the way for the acceptance of Keynes' ideas now presented in *General Theory of Employment, Interest, and Money*, published in 1936. The principles essentially are those he put forward in the *Treatise*. The new development which he added in the *General Theory* is the concept of equilibrium at less than full employment. Accordingly, an equilibrium is possible at a depresssion level, and unless a change takes place in the relevant variables, the economy will stagnate indefinitely. These ideas stood in direct opposition to the classical and neoclassical theories that dominated economic thought and practice for more than a hundred years.

For practical politicians in search of theoretical justifications for deficit financing already under way in many industrial countries, the *General Theory* came at the right time.[7] It provides a theoretical foundation to the common-sense view that large government expenditures financed by borrowing are needed to ease the hardships of the depression on the population. It appears to recognize the advantages of self-adjusting market mechanism argued so eloquently by classical and neoclassical economists, although its important assumption that wages and prices are determined external to the system is at odds with received theory. This is important, for it reinforces the theory's basic interventionist position. It called for the government to manage the general level of economic activity in the interests of society in a manner consistent with individual freedom and a stable social order. In effect, Keynesian economics provides and articulates the theoretical framework for reform—liberal policies pushed in the United States, Great Britain, and elsewhere since the beginning of the twentieth century. Keynes thus manages to give coherence to his vision and to socioeconomic and political changes accelerated by the tragedies of World War I and collapse of the world economy in the postwar years.

Correct or not, Keynes offers a politically attractive alternative to received theories and policies which appeared detached from reality. This does not mean that other explanations are not consistent with the evidence. I have discussed elsewhere these explanations and will again call attention to a number of them in later chapters of this study.[8]

Notes

1. In the mountain of literature on the evolution of ideas, see, for example, Ellis T. Powell, *The Evolution of the Money Market, 1385–1915* (London: Frank Cass, 1966); Warren J. Samuels, "Adam Smith and the Economy As a System of Power," *Review of Social Economy*, October 1973, pp. 123–37; L. Rogin, *The Meaning and Validity of Economic Theory* (New York: Harper & Row, 1958); J. J. Spengler and W. R. Allen, *Essays in Economic Thought* (Chicago: Rand McNally, 1960); George Stigler, *Production and Distribution Theories* (New York: Macmillan, 1941); J. Dorfman, *The Economic Mind in American Civilization*, vol. 3 (New York: Viking Press, 1949);

E. K. Hunt, *History of Economic Thought: A Critical Perspective* (Belmont, Calif.: Wadsworth Publishing Co., 1979); Carl Menger, *Problems of Economics and Sociology* (Urbana: University of Illinois Press, 1963); J. A. Schumpeter, *History of Economic Analysis* (New York: Oxford University Press, 1954); Ludwig von Mises, *The Anti-Capitalistic Mentality* (New York: D. Van Nostrand, 1956); E. J. Hamilton, A. Rees, and H. G. Johnson, eds., *Landmarks in Political Economy*, selections from the *Journal of Political Economy* (Chicago: University of Chicago Press, 1962); Frank H. Knight, *The Ethics of Competition* (New York: Augustus M. Kelley, 1950); E. Whittaker, *Schools and Streams of Economic Thought* (Chicago: Rand McNally, 1961); J. Viner, *Studies in the Theory of International Trade* (New York: Harper and Bros., 1937); D. Vickers, *Studies in the Theory of Money* (Philadelphia: Chilton Co., 1959).

2. Indeed, in some of the early writers we see anticipations of theories advanced much later, e.g., Thomas Joplin (1790-1847), Thomas Attwood (1783-1856), Nicholas Barbor (1640-1698), William Lowndes (1652-1724), Bishop George Berkeley (1658-1783). D. Vickers, *Studies in the Theory of Money, 1690-1776* (Philadelphia: Chilton Co., 1959) makes the point that there was more Keynesian-type economics in the early period than often has been recognized.

3. For instance, Anna J. Schwartz, *A Century of British Market Interest Rates 1874-1975* (London: The City University, 1981), p. 1., writes that Henry Thornton (1760-1815), concerned with the British monetary system during the Napoleonic era, understood

the fallacy of the real-bills doctrine; the distinction between the first-round and ultimate effects of monetary change; the lag in effect of monetary change; the problem market participants faced in distinguishing relative from general price changes; the distinction between internal and external gold drains; the factors influencing the foreign exchanges including the role of purchasing power parity; how to bring inflation under control; the relation of the Bank of England to other English banks; types of effects of monetary disturbances on interest rates; the distinction between the market rate and the natural rate of interest and between nominal and real rates of interest.

See also the interesting exchange between Jacob A. Frenkel and Charles Nelson on whether David Hume, *On Money*, believed in a stable long-run Phillips Curve; Charles R. Nelson, "Adjustment Lags Versus Information Lags: A Test of Alternative Explanations of the Phillips Curve Phenomenon," *Journal of Money, Credit, and Banking*, February 1981, pp. 1-11; Jacob A. Frenkel, "Adjustment Lags Versus Information Lags: A 'Comment' and 'Reply' by Charles R. Nelson," *Journal of Money Credit and Banking*, November 1981, pp. 490-96.

4. See, for example, J. J. Spengler, *Origins of Economic Thought and Justice* (Carbondale and Edwardsville: Southern Illinois University, 1980), for a useful review of the early contributions of economic thought as well as bibliography.

5. Indeed, George Tavalas, "Some Initial Formulations of the Monetary Growth-Rate Rule", *History of Political Economy*, Winter 1977, pp. 525-47, writes "even more significantly, early formulations of Friedman's rule span backward to the writings of Jeremy Bentham and Henry Thornton at the start of the nineteenth century, and also to the neglected writings of John Gray, during the 1830s and 1840s." [p. 536]

6. It is useful here to quote at length Keynes, when he writes, in 1925:

On the economic side I cannot perceive that Russian Communism has made any contribution to our economic problems of intellectual interest or scientific value. I do not think that it contains, or is likely to contain, any piece of useful economic technique which we could not apply, if we chose, with equal or greater success in a society which retained all the marks, I will not say of nineteenth-century individualistic capitalism, but of British bourgeois ideals. Theoretically at least, I do not believe that there is any economic improvement for which Revolution is a necessary instrument. On the other hand, we have everything to lose by the methods of violent change.

In Western industrial conditions the tactics of Red Revolution would throw the whole population into a pit of poverty and death.

But as a religion what are its forces? Perhaps they are considerable. The exaltation of the common man is a dogma which has caught the multitude before now. *Any* religion and the bond which unites co-religionists have power against the egotistic atomism of the irreligious.

The modern capitalism is absolutely irreligious, without internal union, without much public spirit, often, though not always, a mere congeries of possessors and pursuers. Such a system has to be immensely, not merely moderately, successful to survive. In the nineteenth century it was in a certain sense idealistic; at any rate it was a united and self-confident system. It was not only immensely successful, but held out hopes of a continuing crescendo of prospective success. Today it is only moderately successful. If irreligious Capitalism is ultimately to defeat religious Communism, it is not enough that it should be economically more efficient — it must be many times as efficient. [J. M. Keynes, "A Short View of Russia," *Essays in Persuasion* (New York: Harcourt, Brace and Company, 1932), pp. 306-7]

According to Keynes, the moral issue of the age

is concerned with the love of money with the habitual appeal to the money motive in nineteenths of the activities of life, with the universal striving after individual economic security as the prime object of endeavour, with the social approbation of money as the measure of constructive success, and with the social appeal to the hoarding instinct as the formation of the necessary provision for the family and for the future. The decaying religions around us, which have less and less interest for most people unless it be as agreeable form of magical ceremonial or social observance, have lost their moral significance just because — unlike some of their earlier versions — they do not touch in the least degree on these essential matters. A revolution in our ways of thinking and feeling about money may become the growing purpose of contemporary embodiments of the ideal. Perhaps, therefore, Russian Communism does represent the first confused stirrings of a great religion. [Ibid., pp. 308-9]

7. See also the interesting discussion in W. R. Allen, "Irving Fisher, FDR, and the Great Depression," *History of Political Economy,* Winter 1977, pp. 560-87. Indeed, John Kenneth Galbraith writes

By common, if not yet quite universal agreement, the Keynesian revolution was one of the great modern accomplishments in social design. It brought Marxism in the advanced countries to a halt. It led to a level of economic performance that now inspires bitter-end conservationists to panagyrics of unexampled banality. For a long while, to be known as an active Keynesian was to invite wrath of those who equate social advance with subversion. Those concerned developed a habit of reticence. As a furtive consequence, the history of the revolution is, perhaps, the worst-told story of our era. [John K. Galbraith's "Came the Revolution" (Review of Keynes' General Theory), *New York Times Book Review,* 16 May 1965.]

Useful on this score are sections of the four essays published by *The Economist* to commemorate the century of J. M. Keynes' birth: Milton Friedman, "A Monetarist Reflects," *The Economist,* 4 June 1983, pp. 17-19; F. A. Hayek, "The Austrian Critique," *The Economist,* 11 June 1983, pp. 39-41; Paul Samuelson, "Sympathy from the Other Cambridge," *The Economist,* 25 June 1983, pp. 19-21; John Hicks, "A Sceptical Follower," *The Economist,* 18 June 1983, pp. 17-19.

8. See George Macesich, *The International Monetary Economy and the Third World* (New York: Praeger Publishers, 1981), especially chap. 2.

3

The U.S. Congress and Two Views
of Inflation

The Joint Economic Committee of the U.S. Congress and Two Views of Inflation

By the mid 1960s, and probably earlier, the general public became increasingly aware of the country's changed monetary environment. They came to regard the price level and the level of economic activity as largely affected by government authorities and not by a specielike monetary system operating within given constraints.[1] The uncertainty so generated increasingly cast doubt not only on money but on the monetary system itself.

Even earlier similar anxieties prompted the Joint Economic Committee of Congress to request a "broad-gauged, factual, and analytical examination of the problems and possibilities of reconciling the national objectives of providing substantially full employment and achieving an adequate rate of economic growth while maintaining substantial stability of the price level."

It is useful now to examine two principal views presented before the Joint Economic Committee over the cause and control of inflation. The two views are those of the traditionalist/Monetarists who stress monetary factors and antitraditionalist/Keynesian or reform-liberal view which emphasizes nonmonetary phenomena as explanations of inflation. The various positions taken are also instructive in the manner in which money is pushed into the political arena.

Thus the fact that the Keynesian view takes the position that prices and wages are determined outside the system through sociopolitical processes has important implications for discretionary policy and growth of government intervention. These processes constitute for the most part arbitrary exercise of power by unions and large corporations. The power is arbitrary in the sense that its exercise is not tempered by competitive market forces, nor answerable to society as a whole.

There is little to assure that these unions and corporations will respond appropriately to government manipulation of aggregate demand by monetary and fiscal policies. As a result government must of necessity participate in the formation of these prices and wages to assure a desired outcome. This will typically lead to price and wage control. Since controls inevitably fail, the system is increasingly driven into collective participatory planning where wages and prices are determined. Such an arrangement offers little chance that money and the monetary systems will be allowed to play a nondiscretionary and autonomous role within the constraints of a rules based policy system.

In sum, these differences over the cause of inflation are manifested in the manner in which the two theories provide a solution to the problem of the missing price-level equation. The Keynesian solution reaches out to sociopolitical and institutional factors. Monetarists turn to the quantity theory of money.

In the quantity theory tradition, Monetarists argue that the direction of causation is from monetary expansion to increases in the general level of prices. Others in the Keynesian tradition argue that monetary expansion per se is simply in response to inflationary "cost-push" pressures caused for the most part by nonmonetary sociopolitical factors.[2]

Traditionalist/Monetarist View

The traditionalist view attributes inflation to the increasingly favorable state of demand which is permissive to a rise in the general level of prices. According to this view, inflation occurs whenever the general level of demand for goods and services exceeds available supply at existing prices. The emphasis is based on the assumption of reasonable price flexibility and a competitive nature of the economy as a whole. Thus a change in the composition of demand with no change in its level means that the prices of goods and services which benefit from an increase in demand will rise while prices of goods and services which suffer from a decline in demand will fall, so that on balance there will tend to be no change in the general level of prices.

Favorable demand-supply situation may appear from the demand side and supply side. Its source will depend on the nature of the changes in the given conditions underlying demand and supply. For instance, a favorable state of demand may be generated from the supply side owing to catastrophes, manmade or natural, and changes in production functions. A decline in the supply of goods and services owing to catastrophes may result in a higher price level until such time as conditions return to normal and prices decline. If we assume catastrophes aside on the basis of their random occurrence, changes in production functions may present sources of favorable state of demand so that price rises are permissive. However, changes in production functions over the years have tended to increase and not to decrease supply. The notable exceptions are the supply-rendering effects of OPEC price increases in the 1970s.

We are thus left with increases in the level of demand as the most likely source for generation of a favorable demand-supply situation, and hence inflation. An increase in the level of demand may appear owing to an increase in the supply of money or to changes in the given conditions underlying the demand for money, e.g., increase in the cost of holding money such as an increase in interest rates and expectations of a future price increase. Of these two sources, the traditionalist view is that the most likely source is an increase in the supply of money. The reasons for this view are mainly two. First, it is the money-supply variable which is the most easily manipulated. Second, the historical record tends to support the view that countries that pursue easy money policies also experience rises in the general level of prices.

This relationship between movements of prices and money supply when the competing views of inflation gained currency during the decade of the 1950s is suggested by the evidence presented in Tables 3.1, 3.2 and 3.3. The relationship has varied among countries, and within any particular country from time to time. This may be attributed to growth in physical output and trade such as in the case of Germany, Italy, and Venezuela; to the volume of liquid assets existing at the beginning of the period (e.g., Belgium and Germany, following currency reform that reduced very sharply the public's holdings of liquid assets, permitting an expansion in the money supply to reconstitute the public's holdings with a large rise in prices); and to variations in computed velocity. The broad groupings of countries in Tables 3.1, 3.2, and 3.3 indicate, however, a rough correspondence between increases in the money supply and prices. William Martin, former chairman of the Board of Governors, has observed in reference to these tables:

> The six countries where the money supply more than quadrupled during the decade (group I) where, with one exception (Colombia), the countries experiencing the largest increases in the cost of living — in no case less than 120 percent. In all but 3 (Germany, Venezuela, Italy) of the 10 other countries where the money supply at least doubled (group II), there occurred increases in the cost of living of at least 75 percent. In only one (Austria) of the remaining countries (Group III) did the money supply increase more than two thirds, and this country was the only one in which the cost of living is also two thirds."[3]

Table 3.4 provides a cross-country comparison of the rate of money growth and inflation over the 20-quarter period from IV/1975 to IV/1980 for the major industrial nations. The countries are ranked in descending order according to the rate of money growth experienced during the period. If the demand for money is relatively stable across countries, the analysis above predicts a positive relationship between money growth and inflation. This relationship can be clearly identified in the table. In particular, Italy had the highest rate of inflation; the United Kingdom experienced the second-highest growth rates of money and prices, and so forth. In fact, if this comparison is continued, only West Germany violates the ordering of inflation with the rate of money growth. These results are extremely robust when one considers the heterogeneity of this group of countries.

Table 3.1 Index Numbers of Money Supply and Prices (1948 = 100)

Group 1. Countries Where Money Supply More than Quadrupled, 1948-58

		1948	1949	1950	1951	1952	1953	1954	1955	1956	1957	1958
Bolivia	Money	100	115	155	185	275	500	840	1,650	5,985	9,030	9,075
	Prices	100	104	130	174	217	435	970	1,748	4,870	10,435	10,870
Chile	Money	100	119	137	178	244	370	544	885	1,226	1,533	2,100
	Prices	100	121	138	169	205	256	444	774	1,208	1,608	1,928
Brazil	Money	100	119	137	178	224	370	544	885	1,226	1,533	2,100
	Prices	100	97	103	108	132	161	190	234	277	332	384
Israel	Money	100	128	167	210	228	256	308	372	456	510	582
	Prices	100	104	96	104	163	208	233	248	263	281	290
Argentina[a]	Money	n.a.	n.a.	100	122	140	172	200	236	276	309	452
	Prices	n.a.	n.a.	100	135	188	196	204	229	259	324	425
Colombia	Money	100	120	127	147	173	204	243	251	312	355	431
	Prices	100	107	129	140	144	147	160	159	169	194	222

[a] 1950 = 100.

Note: Money = end-of-year data; Prices = cost of living

Source: International Monetary Fund, International Financial Statistics: 1948–49, January 1956; 1950–58, September 1959. *Employment, Growth, and Price Levels*, Washington: (U.S. Government Printing Office, 1960), p. 3354.

Table 3.2 Index Numbers of Money Supply and Prices (1948 = 100)

Group II. Countries Where Money Supply More than Doubled, 1948–1958

		1948	1949	1950	1951	1952	1953	1954	1955	1956	1957	1958
Japan	Money	100	109	95	125	151	233	242	279	326	340	381
	Prices	100	132	124	144	150	161	171	168	169	174	176
France	Money	100	123	143	168	191	213	243	272	300	328	347
	Prices	100	115	128	150	168	167	167	168	172	177	202
Germany	Money	100	120	145	167	186	204	231	304	271	306	347
	Prices	100	106	100	108	110	108	108	110	113	114	118
Mexico	Money	100	112	154	174	180	200	224	268	298	318	342
	Prices	100	104	111	125	144	141	148	172	180	190	211
Peru	Money	100	108	128	156	176	200	212	224	272	282	302
	Prices	100	113	128	141	151	164	172	180	190	205	221
Venezuela	Money	100	112	114	120	140	152	158	176	200	265	292
	Prices	100	108	109	118	119	118	118	116	119	115	121
Austria[a]	Money	n.a.	100	111	134	146	179	225	229	238	257	284
	Prices	n.a.	100	117	148	168	167	172	175	180	187	190
Italy	Money	100	115	126	147	169	187	202	226	244	260	277
	Prices	100	101	100	110	114	117	120	123	128	129	132
Uruguay	Money	100	106	130	128	139	156	169	177	198	211	275
	Prices	100	106	101	115	132	141	158	172	183	210	246
Finland	Money	100	110	128	182	160	167	183	195	208	215	235
	Prices	100	108	122	147	153	156	156	152	169	188	198

[a]1949 = 100

Note: Money = end-of-year data; Prices = cost of living index, annual average.

Source: International Monetary Fund, International Financial Statistics: 1948–49, January 1956; 1950–59, September 1959. *Employment, Growth, and Price Levels,* Washington: (U.S. Government Printing Office, 1960), p. 108.

Table 3.3   Index Numbers of Money Supply and Prices (1948 = 100)

Group III. Other Countries

		1948	1949	1950	1951	1952	1953	1954	1955	1956	1957	1958
Australia	Money	100	118	149	167	162	182	187	191	189	198	193
	Prices	100	111	121	146	171	179	180	184	193	202	205
Switzerland	Money	100	108	111	115	119	125	129	132	142	146	163
	Prices	100	99	98	102	105	104	1055	106	107	109	111
Sweden	Money	100	103	107	101	135	141	144	145	155	158	161
	Prices	100	101	103	118	127	130	131	135	142	147	155
Canada	Money	100	113	113	114	121	119	129	137	136	140	158
	Prices	100	104	106	117	120	119	120	120	121	126	129
New Zealand	Money	100	110	125	128	127	149	163	163	163	163	154
	Prices	100	101	108	119	128	133	140	144	149	152	159
Ireland	Money	100	107	111	120	125	132	138	141	14	150	149
	Prices	100	101	103	110	120	127	127	130	135	142	148
Norway	Money	100	101	101	118	126	132	137	141	145	145	147
	Prices	100	100	105	122	132	135	141	142	147	151	158
Netherlands	Money	100	102	97	99	109	116	124	135	130	127	142
	Prices	100	105	115	128	128	128	133	136	138	147	150

Belgium	Money	100	105	104	112	117	120	123	129	133	133	140
	Prices	100	98	97	106	106	106	107	107	111	114	115
Denmark	Money	100	96	94	97	102	106	103	105	107	111	133
	Prices	100	101	107	119	123	123	123	129	135	140	144
United States	Money	100	100	106	112	116	118	121	124	126	125	129
	Prices	100	99	100	108	110	111	111	111	113	117	120
United Kingdom	Money	100	100	102	104	104	108	111	111	112	111	114
	Prices	100	103	105	116	126	130	132	138	145	149	155

Note: Money = end-of-year data; Prices = cost of living index, annual average.

Source: International Monetary Fund, International Financial Statistics: 1948–49, January 1956; 1950–58, September 1959.

Employment, Growth, and Price Levels, Washington: (U.S. Government Printing Office, 1960), p.3354.

Table 3.4   **Money Growth and Inflation in the Major**
             Industrial Nations (IV/1975–IV/1980)

Country	Annual rates of money growth[a]	Annual rates of Inflation[b]
Italy	20.5%	17.1%
United Kingdom	12.3	13.7
France	10.0	10.7
West Germany	7.8	4.1
United States	7.5	9.1
Canada	7.5	9.0
Japan	7.2	6.3
Netherlands	6.6	5.8
Switzerland	5.3	2.5

[a]M1 for all countries except the United States, for which M1B is used.

[b]Consumer price index used as a measure of inflation.

Source: D.S. Batten, "Inflation: The Cost-Push Myth," *Review* (Federal Reserve Bank of St. Louis, June/July 1981), p. 23.

Anti-Traditionalist / Reform-Liberal / Keynesian View

The reasoning underlying many of the inflation theories based in the Keynesian tradition may be summarized by the now familiar term *cost-price spiral inflation*. Although there are many variations on the theme, their common thread is the assertion that the pricing mechanism is becoming progressively less sensitive. Whatever the alleged "cause" of inflation, the monetary preconditions must be satisfied so that the distinction among theories in the Keynesian tradition is between different mechanisms of inflation. Three variations on the theme, however, appear sufficiently important from a public policy viewpoint to warrant consideration. One is that union pressures for wage increases are the causal element in inflation. The second is that oligopolistic sectors administer prices and so are the causal element in inflation. The third incorporates elements of the first two and tangentially places the blame for inflation on the existence of both unions and oligopolistic industries.

The first variation argues that unions are responsible for inflation in that they fail to recognize that wage increases that go beyond overall productivity gains are inconsistent with stable prices. Thus the argument is that unions push up wages, which raises costs and prices. In order to avoid a logical fallacy, the more sophisticated argue that since the monetary authorities are committed to a policy of full employment they will expand the money supply so as to make possible the sale of the old output at the new price level.

The second variation argues that prices are set in a different way in those sectors of the economy composed of many firms than in industries where there are a few major producers.[4] According to this argument, prices set by oligopolistic industries are "administered" so that they are excellent conductors of inflationary pressure. They are relatively immune from traditional anti-inflationary policies in that their prices, having once reached a high level, are stickier in declining than those of competitive industries when demand declines.

The third variation argues both unions and oligopolistic industries are primarily responsible for inflation. Unions, so the argument goes, lodge themselves in oligopolistic industries and share in the "spoils" derived from the product side.[5] Thus unions in such industries may take advantage of the inelastic or expanding demand conditions on the product market to obtain higher wages without fear that the entry of new firms will reduce union wage gains. According to this variation, the product market permitting, the oligopolist will grant a higher wage rate as a means of avoiding a more costly strike. Moreover, in contradistinction to more traditional views, such unions need not be old craft unions; they may be the new industrial unions that economists have tended to treat as relatively powerless in setting excessive wages. It is for this reason, presumably, that the advent of new industrial unions, coupled with oligopolistic industries, has changed our economic system so greatly as to largely frustrate attempts to control inflation along traditional lines. In effect, the argument implicitly assumes that the pricing mechanism is becoming progressively less fluid or "automatic."

In place of traditional methods for coping with inflation, which some Keynesians consider largely ineffective or inappropriate, they advocate a "direct" assault on the problem of inflation.[6] Although such an assault may take many forms, three seem to be dominant. First, government should resort to "moral suasion" so as to induce business and labor to exercise their power in a socially desirable (noninflationary) way. Second, government could increase the degree of competition in the marketplace by a more vigorous enforcement of antitrust legislation. Some people argue that since labor unions are monopolies they should also be subject to antitrust legislation. Third, government can participate more actively in, or control, the price and wage setting process. Needless to say, these forms of control are not mutually exclusive.

Eclectics view the discussion of whether inflation is "demand-pulled" or "cost-pushed" as analogous to the discussion "which comes first, the chicken or the egg." They attempt rather to synthesize in varying degrees of sophistication the two views of inflation.

Of the several syntheses available we shall present and consider only two. One synthesis, which draws heavily from the Keynesian tradition, turns on the assertion that we can not empirically isolate inflation by types.[7] And the other, which draws heavily from the Monetarist tradition view, asserts that we cannot conceptually isolate inflation by types.[8]

The synthesis that draws from the Keynesian tradition asserts that it is impossible empirically to test for the existence of leads or lags from the cost or demand side, which is necessary if we are to classify inflation by types. For such a purpose we need minute data on the cost and demand sides. And since such data presumably are not available, we cannot meaningfully classify inflation by types.

Even if such data were available, however, they would shed little light on the "causes" of inflation. Prices and wages, according to this view, are not set in the traditional manner. They are set rather with reference to some "mark-up" over the cost of living. Accordingly, inflation is generated whenever labor and management attempt to get more than 100 percent of the selling price. This is an impossible situation. Yet it is on the very impossibility of the situation that the continuing process of inflation depends. Thus each party increases the part it tries to take by increasing wages or by increasing prices. Since together they cannot succeed in getting more than 100 percent of the selling price, wages and prices are continually raised, thereby generating a continuing process of inflation.

The process of inflation, though it may originate in the noncompetitive sector where market power is sufficient to raise prices and wages, will "spill over" into the competitive sectors, thereby gaining momentum.[9]

This may occur, it is argued, from either the demand side or the cost side, or both. Since the prices of the products and services of the noncompetitive sector rise, there will be a change in the composition of demand. Consumers will switch their demand to the products and services produced by the competitive sector so that prices rise in this sector. There is excess demand in the competitive sector and a deficiency of demand in the noncompetitive sector. The deficiency of demand will result in some unemployment in the noncompetitive sector. Owing to factor immobility, however, unemployment in this sector will not cause wages or prices to fall, so that unemployment persists.

Attempts by the government to remove excess demand along traditional lines so as to check the overall price rise, while removing excess demand in the competitive sector, increases still further the unemployment in the noncompetitive sector.

The same situation will prevail even if the "spillover" occurs from the cost side. Thus the "spillover" will occur because wage or price rises in the noncompetitive sector are signals for labor and employers in the competitive sector to do the same in order to protect if not increase their relative income shares. Accordingly, the government is confronted with the dilemma of either inflation or unemployment.

The other view, borrowing heavily from the traditional position, argues that we cannot even conceptually identify inflation by types, much less classify them empirically. In essence this view turns on the proposition that one cannot isolate the portion of the cost increases that are attributable to increased demand. Traditional Monetarists and Keynesians accordingly have erred in attempting to establish rigid links between types of inflation and public policy.

The eclectic views essentially do not consider as practical the argument that the monetary authority, by refusing to expand the money supply, could "nip in the bud" an inflationary spiral.[10] The bases for such an assertion are, first, that velocity would increase, thereby frustrating the efforts of the monetary authority; second, that even if velocity could no longer increase, the monetary authority could perhaps overcome the strong institutional forces making for rigidity in the pricing system, only at the expense of possibly a serious depression.

In order to control inflation, therefore, steps should be taken to remove institutional and other rigidities from within our economic system. It is only then, presumably, that the control of inflation along more traditional lines would have effect.

Notes

1. Milton Friedman and Anna J. Schwartz, *Monetary Trends in the United States and the United Kingdom: Their Relation to Income, Prices, and Interest Rates, 1867-1975* (Chicago: University of Chicago Press, 1982), p. 571.

2. These views are also highlighted in the papers submitted by economists, and others in U.S. Congress, Joint Economic Committee, *The Relationship of Prices to Economic Stability and Growth, Compendium,* March 1958 (hereafter called *Compendium*) and U.S. Congress, Joint Economic Committee, *Staff Report on Employment, Growth, and Price Levels,* 24 December 1959 (hereafter called *Staff Report*).

For various emphases on these views, see, for example, Yossef A. Attiyeh, "Wage-Price Spiral Versus Demand Inflation: United States, 1949-1955" (Ph.D. dissertation, University of Chicago, 1959); Albert Rees, "Do Unions Cause Inflation?" *Journal of Law and Economics,* 2 October 1959, pp. 84-94, and "Price Level Stability and Economic Policy," *Compendium;* Milton Friedman, "Current Critical Issues in Wage Theory and Price," (Industrial Relations Research Association, Proceedings of the Eleventh Annual Meeting, Chicago, 1959), and "The Supply of Money and Changes in Prices and Output," *Compendium;* Martin J. Bailey, "Administered Prices in the American Economy," *Compendium;* Walter Morton, "Trade Unionism Full Employment, and Inflation," *American Economic Review,* March 1950, pp. 13-40. This list is by no means complete, but it does give the flavor of the debate in the late 1950s and 1960s. See also J. R. Barth and J. R. Bennett, "Cost-Push Versus Demand-Pull Inflation: Some Empirical Evidence, *Journal of Money, Credit and Banking,* August 1975; S. Lustgarten, *Industrial Concentration and Inflation* (Washington, D.C.: A.E.I., 1975); D. S. Batten, "Inflation: The Cost-Push Myth," *Review,* (Federal Reserve Bank of St. Louis, June/July, 1981), pp. 20-26; George Macesich, *Monetarism: Theory and Policy* (New York: Praeger Publishers, 1983); Arthur Okun, *Prices and Quantities* (Washington, D.C.: Brookings Institution, 1981).

3. William Mac. Martin, Hearings before Joint Economic Committee, 86th Congress, 1st Session in Part 10, "Additional Materials Submitted for the Record," pp. 3352-53. Tables 3.1, 3.2, and 3.3 presented in this chapter are contained in Mr. Martin's testimony on p. 3354.

4. Martin J. Bailey's discussion on this view in *Compendium* and William J. Baumol's discussion in *Compendium* of J. K. Galbraith's "Market Structure and Stabilization."

5. See, for example, James R. Schlesinger, "Market Structure, Union Power, and Inflation," *Southern Economic Journal,* January 1959, pp. 269–312.

6. Emmette S. Redford, "Potential Public Policies to Deal with Inflation Caused by Market Power," Study Paper No. 10 for *Staff Report.*.

7. Gardner Ackley, "A Third Approach to the Analysis and Control of Inflation," *Compendium;* Abba P. Lerner, "Inflationary Depression and the Regulation of Administered Prices," *Compendium.*

8. William G. Bowen, "Cost Inflation Versus Demand Inflation: A Useful Distinction?" *Southern Economic Journal,* January 1960, pp. 199–206.

9. Economic Research Department, *The Mechanics of Inflation* (Washington: Chamber of Commerce of the United States, 1958), pp. 32, 37.

10. Ackley, "A Third Approach"; Lerner, "Inflationary Depression"; and Bowen, "Cost Inflation."

4

An Appraisal of Inflationary Views

An Overview

Our discussion elsewhere underscored the importance of the differences in the manner in which Monetarists and Keynesians solve the price equation. In effect, the antitraditionalist views discussed above are in keeping with the Keynesian approach. Prices do not automatically equilibrate supply and demand. They do not register the index of real scarcities. Instead, these prices are administered and controlled by large corporations and unions and not by free and open competition in the marketplace, as argued by neoclassical theory. Prices and wages, in effect, are a function of an autonomous and arbitrary power not answerable for their effects nor responsible for their consequences on the economy and society.

Moreover, government manipulation of money and fiscal policy so as to influence aggregate demand may not be successful. If government reduces aggregate demand by monetary policy and fiscal policy so as to reduce inflationary pressures, unemployment may well be the result without a decline in prices. On the other hand, if government increases aggregate demand so as to reduce unemployment, the increases in aggregate spending will be absorbed by high wages and prices administered by unions and corporations on their own behalf. The simultaneous occurrence of inflation and unemployment is the result. This phenomenon is now called *stagflation*. It is a manifestation of the arbitrary use of power by large unions and corporations — arbitrary in the sense that is not tempered by competitive market forces. It can be controlled only by the intervention and exercise of government power, since nothing else is available. As a result, the power of the state and its bureaucracy is enhanced.

Fortunately there is reason to believe that the antitraditionalist case is overdrawn. We may turn now to an appraisal of the above views of inflation by drawing both on economic theory and on recent experience. I shall argue the position that the evidence both theoretical and empirical, though not completely inconsistent with alternative views, tends to support traditional Monetarist views of inflation.

The fundamental discovery of those de-emphasizing the traditional view of inflation is that prices and wages go up when somebody raises them.[1] There is general agreement as to the facts. We take it to be true that most sellers would always like to raise their prices. We also take it to be true that sellers will never raise their prices without limit in all circumstances. What are the limits and circumstances under which sellers will raise their prices? It is precisely to the answering of this question that economists have directed their labors.

The fruits of these labors have produced the consensus that the state of demand will set the limit and the circumstances under which the sellers can "raise" or "lower" their prices. The state of demand permitting, sellers can raise their prices without being penalized by a loss of sales and income, and so they decide to "raise" prices. If, on the other hand, the state of demand permits a rise in prices only at the expense of losing net income, sellers will decide not to "raise" prices. There is thus no conflict between the view that prices rise because somebody raises them and the view that somebody decides to raise them because of the state of demand.

The views discussed in the last chapter which de-emphasize the traditional approach to inflation do not provide an alternate theory of inflation that is independent of the state of demand. Although not new, these views gained currency in the postwar period when a favorable state of demand was assured by the existence of large liquid asset holdings by individuals and firms.[4] The assurance of a favorable state of demand permitted price increases without the loss of incomes, and so sellers decided to "raise" prices. In effect, the decision of sellers to "raise" prices is simply the form whereby a disequilibrium situation was brought into balance. In the absence of a favorable state of demand, however, such a decision may result in "distortions" in the relative price structure, or a one-time increase in the general level of prices coupled with a loss of sales and increased unemployment.[5] There is nothing in the process whereby sellers decide to "raise" prices which will thus assure a favorable state of demand.[6] It is for this reason, essentially, that these views have descriptive but not analytical validity.

Consider the view that unions are responsible for inflation in that they push up wages. In support of this view, evidence is presented that unit labor costs (in money forms) have risen faster than average productivity. Needless to say, in a period of inflation this observation is a truism. It does not help us to tell whether wages pushed up prices or demand pulled up wages.[7]

It has been pointed out by Rees, and quite correctly, that in the absence of a favorable state of demand, "unions" can cause either shifts in the relative wage structure or a one-time increase in the general level of wages, together with increased unemployment. The flexibility of nonunion wages determines which of the last two possibilities will actually occur.[8] On the other hand, if the state of demand is favorable, union wage increases can be followed by inflation and continued full employment.

An important but unfortunately neglected point is that a necessary but not sufficient condition for unions to set off a "wage-price spiral" is that they need not simply power to raise wages, but increasing power to do so. As Milton Friedman has noted:

> The existence of a strong union in one area simply means that wage rates in that area will be higher relative to wage rates elsewhere, and employment elsewhere than wages and employment would have been in the absence of a union. . . . Increasingly strong unions not simply strong unions are a necessary (though not sufficient) condition for setting the wage-price spiral in motion.[9]

There is very little serious scholarly evidence to substantiate the view that unions are becoming increasingly strong. Indeed, to judge from the size of union membership rolls and recent unfavorable legislation, that power may actually be decreasing.

The above limitations restrict similarly the usefulness of the eclectic view that inflation is triggered and generated whenever labor and management attempt to get more than 100 percent of the selling price. It too depends on the existence or assurance of a favorable state of demand. At the same time, each party must increase its power as a ncessary condition for setting off the "wage-price spiral."

The positions arguing that union demands "spillover" into competitive sectors and so cause wages and prices to rise in this sector also depend, contrary to many of their adherents, on the existence of a favorable state of demand.[10]

The state of demand permitting the "spillover," contrary to adherents adding this view adherents,[11] will occur when union employers bid away more and better workers from other employers and so lead these employers to raise wages in order to hold their employees. Again, there is no conflict between the view that wages and prices rise because somebody raises them and the view that somebody raises them because a favorable state of demand for such a rise exists.

If the state of demand is not favorable to such a rise, a very different story will unfold, and we might just as well talk in terms of a "spill-in" (movement of labor from union to nonunion activities) effect. If, owing to higher wages, union employers curtail employment, the movement of general wages will depend upon two conditions. First, if wages elsewhere are flexible downward, the union workers will "spill into" nonunion activities, and so nonunion wages will tend to fall. The movement in the general level of wages, if any, will depend, as Rees notes, "on the precise shapes of demand schedules of union and nonunion employers."[12] Second, if wages elsewhere, on the other hand, are not flexible downward, the general wage level will rise but the resulting unemployment will check any further rise. Under these circumstances the nonunion employers are very unlikely indeed to repeat the wage rise experiment of union employers.

Consider now the view that oligopolies and monopolies, by "administering prices," cause inflation. As noted elsewhere in this chapter, the assertion is that "administered prices" are more rigid than competitive prices and so are excellent conductors of inflationary pressures.

Many economists, however, and most notably Martin Bailey, argue that administered prices are not as rigid as they seem.[13] And insofar as these prices are rigid, they argue, their role in inflation is misunderstood. On this interpretation, administered prices during periods when the state of demand is favorable do not rise as rapidly as competitive prices, so that in effect they may well be below levels that would clear the market, thereby creating waiting lists and grey markets. When administered prices do rise, however, they are apt to do so in large jumps, thereby attracting widespread attention and charges that they are "responsible" for inflation.

The converse argument is that administered prices are rigid on the downward side and so respond more slowly to an unfavorable state of demand that competitive prices also leaves much to be desired. In the first instance the evidence used to support this assertion is far from conclusive. Thus the usual evidence cited is that during the postwar periods (particularly 1957–58), when the state of demand was unfavorable, output and employment declined but prices, as judged by price indexes, did not. An examination of the past record, however, suggests that this is not a unique experience. Other than that of 1957–58, of the seven recessions since 1920, in four of them the consumer price index rose in the early months.[14] Furthermore, these price indexes among other limitations do not pick up price changes that take the form of special discounts or other informal price concessions, such as freight absorption or advertising allowances. The effect is an understatement of actual price changes, and so overstates the actual degree of rigidity.[15] In the second instance, it should be noted that insofar as the administered price argument throws the blame for inflation on large corporations, et al., available studies suggest little if any relation between concentration ratios and price rigidity.[16]

The source of price rigidity is not, in the view of many economists, the market sector of the economy but, ironically, the government sector.[17] It is this sector that administers rigid prices through the medium of various regulatory agencies, price support programs, minimum wages, agricultural marketing programs, support of "fair trade," and restriction on both domestic and foreign trade. Such policies are largely inconsistent with attempts to remove monopoly elements from the economy.

According to the view that incorporates unions on the factor side and oligopolies on the product market side, "large wage increases won by strategically placed unions may lead either to (1) distortion of the wage structure if other wages lag or (2) rising costs and upward pressure on prices if other wages rise equivalently" or a combination of the two. The net effect will be that the "economy will move between episodes of price plateaus (accompanied by a stretching of the wage structure) succeeded by periods of rising prices.[18]

But this view, as with others that de-emphasize the traditional approach to inflation, contributes nothing essentially new to our understanding of inflation. The traditional view does not deny that unions may "distort" wages or that unions may share in monopoly spoils. As noted elsewhere in this chapter, in the absence of a favorable state of demand this may be one of the effects of a union wage rise. And as the above view claims, "the precise proportion between wage-distorting and cost-inflationary forces depends upon the economic climate — in particular upon the level of national income." It simply reasserts the traditional view with its emphasis on the favorable state of demand.[19]

The interesting point about the view is, as noted elsewhere, the implicit assertion that new industrial unions and oligopolies have, apparently, sufficiently changed the economic structure so that the pricing system lacks fluidity. Little evidence other than casual empiricism is offered in support of the above view.[20]. Indeed, such evidence as we do have supports precisely the opposite view along traditional lines that the pricing mechanism is not becoming progressively less sensitive.[21]

Let us turn now and examine the views that consider the distinction between "demand-pull" and "cost-push" inflation as useless.

One view asserts that we cannot empirically identify inflation by types.[22] This view turns apparently on the question of the timing of demand-pull and cost-push types of inflation; that is, on the identification of the lead and lag series. If the inflation is the demand-pull type, then presumably demand should lead the increase in costs. If it is cost-push, then costs should lead demand.

To put the distinction between the two types of inflation in this manner is to hopelessly confuse the issue. One would be hard put indeed to identify the existence of leads and lags in the various relevent series. The consensus, however, seems to be that the essential difference between the two types of inflation is to be found not in the timing of the various series but rather in their sensitivity to changes in demand.[23]

Thus, if the struggle to obtain more than 100 percent of the selling price is sensitive to sales losses and unemployment, then it is very likely indeed that the struggle will continue in the absence of a favorable state of demand. On the other hand, if in the face of an unfavorable state of demand the struggle is such that substantial losses in sales and unemployment are the consequence, it does make sense to talk in terms of types of inflation.

Another view is that we cannot even conceptually classify inflation by type.[24] This view is interesting in that at times its argument is that which raged in the latter part of the nineteenth century over the determination of value. The view is that we cannot identify that part of the price rise attributed to a cost increase and that part attributed to an increase in demand — and so the similarity to the controversy in the latter half of the nineteenth century over the Austrian theory of value as to whether demand or cost determines price. The argument was settled, of course, when it occurred to economists that "each blade in a pair of scissors cuts."

The analogy between the controversies, however, breaks down because the above view claims too much. Economists have long held that although "each blade in a pair of scissors cuts," it does make sense to distinguish between the blades. Changes in the price level may occur with shifts in either the supply schedules or the demand schedules or both. To argue that we cannot conceptually identify the part of a price rise which is attributed to costs and that which is attributed to demand is to assert that we are always in a position whereby both schedules shift simultaneously and by about the same amount. It would not be difficult to conjure up cases in which either demand or supply is the dominant element in price rises.

Although arguments against traditional methods of controlling inflation take many forms, they do possess a common thread — that we cannot expect high levels of employment and output and at the same time maintain stability in the general level of prices.

This is the now familiar "unemployment" versus "inflation" dilemma. Owing to the lack of fluidity in our pricing system we cannot, so the argument goes, attempt seriously to use traditional methods against inflation because their use would simply add to unemployment. Inflation, accordingly, is the necessary price we must pay for avoiding unemployment and, presumably, maintaining high levels of output.

This represents another aspect of inflation views drawing on the Keynesian tradition. It attempts to rationalize the relation of wage and price movements to aggregate demand and supply through the Phillips curve, which argues a link between variations in employment (capacity utilization) and price changes. A critical question for this analysis is whether adjustments are made in money or in real terms.

Phillips Curve, Adaptive Expectations, and Rational Expectations: Is There a Choice?

The trade-off between inflation and unemployment attracted considerable attention in the 1950s and 1960s. An article by A. W. Phillips appears to establish an empirical relation linking unemployment and the rate of change of money wage rates over almost a century in the United Kingdom.[25] Phillips fitted a curve to observations of the percent of unemployment and the percentage rate of change of money wage rates per year in the United Kingdom. Separate curves are also fitted for different subperiods 1861 to 1957. This has

Figure 4.1 Phillips Curves

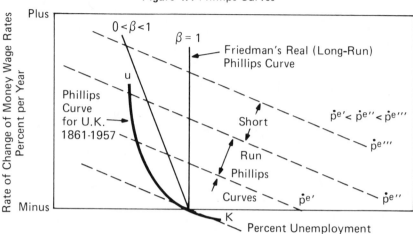

become known as the Phillips Curve. Its general appearance is presented in Figure 4.1. The interpretation of the "Phillips Curve" suggests that at low levels of unemployment, money wage rates increased more rapidly than at high levels of unemployment.

For the most part, Phillips Curve contributions are in the Keynesian tradition and represent attempts to link real magnitudes and the rate of change in prices from their historically determined level. Subsequent studies, in effect, substituted the rate of change of the price level for the rate of change of money wage rates. They purported to show that price stability had a calculable cost in unemployment and that a low level of unemployment had a similar cost in inflation. Indeed, the issue spilled over into policymaking with the status of a near law. Paul Samuelson and Robert Solow argued, shortly after the publication of Phillips study:

> In order to have wages increase at no more than the 2½ percent per annum characteristic of our productivity growth, the American economy would seem, on the basis of twentieth-century and postwar experience to have to undergo something like 5 and 6 percent of the civilian labor force's being unemployed. That much unemployment would appear to be the cost of price stability in the years immediately ahead. . . . In order to achieve the nonperfectionist's goal of high enough output to give us no more than 3 percent unemployment, the price index might have to rise by as much as 4 or 5 percent per year. That much price rise would seem to be the necessary cost of high employment and production in the years immediately ahead. . . .[26]

Subsequent events, however, cast doubt on the relationship uncovered by the Phillips Curve. By the end of the 1960s, it became clear that ever higher rates of inflation are required to keep employment high. Albert Rees and

Mary T. Hamilton report in their study of American experience over the
period 1900 to 1957 and describe the usefulness of Phillips Curves in the
following:

> The construction of plausible Phillips Curves from annual data for a long
> period is a *tour de force* somewhat comparable to writing the Lord's Prayer on the
> head of a pin, rather than as a guide to policy. This is because it is highly prob-
> able that the relationship is changed during the period, because the data are of
> poor quality for much of the early part of the period, and because of the large
> changes in some of the variables that take place during the course of a calendar
> year and are blurred in annual data. If we are making policy recommendations,
> we should prefer to test them on an analysis of monthly or quarterly data for the
> post War period . . . the authors of Phillips Curves would do well to label them
> conspiciously "Unstable — Apply with Extreme Care."[27]

These doubts are underscored by other studies as well as most notably by
Milton Friedman.[28] Esssentially, if workers can correctly forecast current
and future prices there should be no relationship between the ratio of wages
to prices and the rate of inflation. For instance, an increase in all prices and
wages which leaves the ratio of wages to prices unchanged does not alter anyone's decision to employ more or less labor. In effect, when everyone's expectations about current and future prices are correct, unemployment will come
to rest at a "natural rate." Fluctuations around the "natural rate" are the consequence of incorrect expectations about current and future events. Moreover, the "natural rate"of unemployment may itself change over a longer
period. Thus, in the 1950s and early 1960s it may have been about 4 percent.
It is likely that various institutional changes occurring since then may have
pushed up the natural rate. Energy and raw material price increases during
the 1970s may well have served to reinforce the movement.

Friedman and others underscore that the relationship between
unemployment and inflation depends on how individuals form these expectations about future inflation. If people believe that prices will rise at, say, 3
percent per year, any inflation above that level will be underestimated and
this will push the unemployment rate below its "normal" or "natural" rate.
Conversely, any rate of inflation below 3 percent per year would push the
unemployment rate above its "natural rate." So long as the expected rate of
inflation remains rigidly at 3 percent per year, there will appear to be a stable
trade-off between inflation and unemployment.

For the 1950s and up to the mid-1960s a 3 percent inflation rate is probably
a reasonable expectation that would not have led to large forecasting errors.
Since the mid-1960s the average rate of inflation is closer to 7 plus percent. A
rigidly held 3 percent expectation of inflation will lead to very large forecasting errors. Moreover, deviations from the average rate of inflation are no
longer random as in the earlier period. Their pattern is very different. Deviations from the average rate are now highly correlated. If one year's rate of

inflation is over 7 percent, the following year's rate of inflation will probably be over 7 percent as well. In effect, when inflation rates are correlated, past rates of inflation contain a lot of information about future inflation rates. One consequence of this change in the pattern of inflation rates is that people now appear to use a weighted average of past rates to forecast future inflation. In effect, people no longer hold to rigidly fixed expectations regarding future inflation rates. To do otherwise is no longer rational.

This change in the way people form expectations undermines the long-run trade-off between inflation and unemployment. Thus, an increase in the rate of inflation will not permanently reduce the unemployment rate, since people will revise their forecasts of inflation upwards on the basis of past inflationary experience. As expectations of inflation adjust to the new situation, the unemployment rises back to its normal or "natural" rate. If the unemployment rate is to be kept below the "natural rate," the actual rate of inflation must exceed the expected rate of inflation. Since expectations eventually adjust upwards as a result of past inflation, an accelerating rate of inflation is required to maintain the gap between actual and expected inflation. To take account of the problem, the Phillips Curve incorporates inflationary expectations and it is now called "expectations-augmented Phillips Curve analyses."

The requirement that prices rise faster and faster so as to maintain unemployment below the natural rate has come to be known as the *accelerationist hypothesis*. It represents a significant change in emphasis from earlier formulations of Phillips Curve analyses. Earlier studies focus on the rate of change or prices as a function of the level of unemployment as well as other variables. The expectations-augmented Phillips Curve analysis makes unemployment a function of changes in the rate of changes or prices and price expectations. [29]

We may present the above analysis more formally. Figure 4.1 presents short-run and long-run Phillips Curves. Two assumptions underline the explanations offered by the Phillips Curve. One is that even though workers and employers adjust to inflation equally rapidly, they have different pieces of information upon which to react. Employers are able to react more rapidly since they have fewer prices upon which to react in determining whether or not it is profitable to take on additional workers. Typically, employers are concerned with a relatively limited range of prices of goods and services with which their individual enterprises are associated. Workers, on the other hand, typically take into account the general level of prices in determining their real wage and thus their reaction to price changes. The second assumption is that the "natural rate" of employment is basically stable and predictable, though it may change owing to changes in its basic determinants. These determinants include the structural characteristics of the commodity markets. Including market imperfections, stochastic variability in demands and

supplies, the cost of gathering information about job vacancies and job avail-
abilities, the costs of unemployment and mobility, and perhaps also upon the
regional dispersion of employment. Indeed, the "natural rate" itself may be
influenced by inflation by impairing the economy's resource allocative mechanism. Estimates of the "natural rate" of unemployment are between 5 and 6
percent for the United States according to James Tobin.[30] These estimates for
other countries appear to be lower owing in part to differences in measuring
unemployment and in the structure of the respective labor markets.[31]

Mathematically, the "expectations-augmented Phillips Curve" can be
stated as

(1) $W = f(U) = \beta p^e$
     where: W = rate of wage change
             U = unemployment
             p^e = expected rate of inflation

Monetarists argue that $\beta = 1$ so that the expected rate of wage increase is
equal to a component of excess demand plus the expected rate of inflation.
The Phillips Curve is vertical. The rate of increase in money wages is equal
to the expected rate of inflation, if we have no excess demand. In the special
case where the expected rate of inflation is zero, wage inflation would also be
zero. Inflation in the Monetarist view is the result of excess demand
propelled by excessive monetary expansion and expectations regarding future
price increases.

According to the Monetarists, there is no long-run trade-off between
unemployment and inflation. A short-run trade-off may be had but only at
the expense of faster inflation as postulated by the "accelerationist hypothesis." This assumes, of course, that inflation is fully anticipated. If it is not,
the coefficient β in equation (1) would be less than 1. In this case the slope of
the long-run Phillips Curve is less than vertical, but steeper than in the short-
run. There is thus some permanent trade-off between unemployment and
inflation in the long run but less so than in the short-run. If $B = 0$ the short-
run and long-run will be the same.

To judge from recent studies the empirical evidence offers support to the
Monetarist view that $\beta = 1$. There appears to be no trade-off between
unemployment and inflation in the long run. Not everyone is convinced by
the evidence, however. Indeed, Robert Solow (1969) produces results for the
United Kingdom for $\beta = 0.4$; S. J. Turnovsky (1972) presents results for
Canada for β not significantly different from 1; R. B. Cross and D. Laidler
(1975) report on results for twenty individual countries and find no evidence
of a long-run trade-off for any country.[32]

The Monetarist view of interest rates also distinguishes between the nominal and real interest rates which are determined by a multiplicity of factors
traditionally summarized in productivity and thrift. The importance of price

expectations is emphasized as in the expectations-augmented Phillips Curve. Mathematically the relationship can be expressed as

(2) $r = i + p^e$

where r = market or nominal rate of interest

i = real rate of interest

p^e = expected rate of inflation

In equilibrium, the real rate of interest is determined by real factors largely independent of monetary changes. During transitional periods, which can be quite long, changes in the money supply cause real rates of interest to change owing to slow adjustment of actual and expected rates of inflation to monetary changes. Recent studies support the relationship that inflation expectations play in the determination of interest rates.[33] It is in fact a relationship underscored by Irving Fisher more than half a century ago.[34]

Explanations of the Phillips Curve that focus on peoples' expectations of inflation owe much to Milton Friedman, Edmund S. Phelps, and to an earlier article by John F. Muth, and indeed even earlier contributions of Frank H. Knight and Irving Fisher.[35] The *rational-expectations hypothesis* is perhaps best understood in the context of our discussion of the expectations-augmented Phillips Curve. We noted that workers appear to adjust their expectations to inflation at a somewhat slower rate than employers. This delay on the part of workers produces a change in the unemployment rate from the natural rate and thus produces the real effects.

Now suppose that workers adjust their expectations without delay. Under these circumstances there will be no real effects. Wages and prices will increase simultaneously as a result of the new expectation. The real wage rate will remain constant, and the unemployment rate will remain at the natural rate. There is, in effect, no trade-off. The "rational-expectations hypothesis" argues that this rapid adjustment in expectations may well be the case most of the time.

Monetarists have an affinity for the "rational-expectations hypothesis." Instead of basing the formation of expectations of price level changes on past changes alone, Monetarists focus on the rate of change of the money supply as the most important element in the "rational-expectations hypothesis." Accordingly, money supply changes that are not part of the trend in money supply growth and not predictable lead to unexpected changes in the money supply. Such unexpected changes in the money supply lead to changes in such real variables as unemployment and output, among others. The argument is similar to the expectations-augmented Phillips Curve.

A major problem in assessing the credibility of the idea of "rational expectations," according to some economists, is the apparent lack of details on how one goes about quantifying the crucial learning curve for economic decision makers which takes into account their expectations of future prices rather than simply relying on extrapolation of past experience. In fact, Robert E. Lucas, Jr., one of its founders, doubts that "rational expectations" can ever be used to develop mathematically quantitative forecasts.

The restrictive monetary policy aspects of "rational expectations" has not been fully explored, possibly because the symmetrical aspect is not taken seriously by either the public or the government. Nonetheless, the idea of rational expectations is consistent with Monetarist ideas. Both of these views argue against discretionary monetary policy—the Monetarists because the stimulative effects are found to be lagging too far behind any action taken, and the rational expectationists because stimulative actions are believed to be self-defeating.

In any case, the impact of these ideas on central bankers and the public generally may mean that the magnitude of change in monetary policy in the future will be less than in the past. In effect, monetary policy may not be as manipulative as some people in the Keynesian tradition believe.[36]

Notes

1. That this idea as well as the reasoning underlying the "cost-push" theme was familiar as far back as at least the sixteenth century is indicated in the following quotation:

> During the sixteenth century, when prices were consistently rising because of an influx of gold from America, Bishop Lotimer (1548) put the blame on "land lordes and rent raisers, step-lordes, unnatural lordes," when it was the landowners who were being expropriated by the rise in prices because of long term leases." [Morton, "Trade Unionism, Full Employment, and Inflation," p. 24]

2. See, for example, the following papers in the *Compendium:* Herbert Stein, "A General View of Inflation"; Martin Bailey, "Administered Prices in the American Economy;" George L. Bach, "How Important Is Price Stability in Stable Economic Growth?"; William J. Baumol, "Price Behavior Stability and Growth"; Abba P. Lerner, "Inflationary Depression and the Regulation of Administered Prices."

3. Stein, "A General View," p. 667.

4. According to John G. Gurley:

> There was a tremendous growth of liquid assets during World War II . . . they rose from $95 billion in 1939 to almost $260 billion in 1946. U.S. Government savings bonds easily had the highest rate of growth during this period, followed by the money supply (demand deposits adjusted and currency outside banks), which tripled. There were roughly a doubling of time deposits, savings, and loan shares. Smaller percentage gains were recorded for policy reserves and mutual savings deposits. . . . From this very high level, liquid assets continued to grow during the postwar period, reaching $430 billion in 1958. However, their annual rate of growth was lower in the postwar period than in the war period. [Gurley, "Liquidity and Financial Institutions in the Postwar Period," Study Paper No. 14 for *Staff Report,* p. 4]

5. Rees, "Do Unions Cause Inflation?" *Journal of Law and Economics,* 2 October 1959, p. 68.

6. Ibid., p. 89.

7. Indeed, on the basis of existing evidence, the *Staff Report,* p. 141, concludes that demand forces were the dominant explanation of the upward thrust of wages in the period before 1946–58.

8. Rees, "Do Unions Cause Inflation?" p. 88. The *Staff Report,* with regard to unionization and wage changes, finds no generally applicable relationship (p. 149). See especially Table 5-13, p. 148.

9. Milton Friedman, "Current Critical Issues in Wage Theory and Practice," in *Proceedings of the Eleventh Annual Meeting of the Industrial Relations Research Association 1959*, p. 213. See also Yossef A. Attiyeh, "Wage-Price Spiral Versus Demand Inflation: United States, 1949-1955 (Ph.D. dissertation, University of Chicago, 1959), especially chap. 4.

10. *Mechanics of Inflation* (Washington, D.C.: Chamber of Commerce of the United States, 1958).

11. Ibid., pp. 32, 37.

12. Rees, "Do Unions Cause Inflation?" p. 90.

13. Martin J. Bailey, "Administered Prices and Inflation," *Compendium*.

14. Rees, "Do Unions Cause Inflation?" p. 91.

15. Bailey, "Administered Prices and Inflation"; "Inflation and the Price Mechanism," *The Journal of Political Economy*, October 1959, pp. 463-75.

16. Bailey, "Administered Prices and Inflation."

17. Ibid.

18. Schlesinger, "Market Structure, Union Power, and Inflation," pp. 309-10. Schlesinger uses as his case in point the steel industry.

19. Ibid., p. 310. See also *Staff Report*, pp. 141, 158-60.

20. See, for example, Milton Friedman, "The Role of Monetary Policy," *The American Economic Review*, March 1968, and Milton Friedman, "Inflation and Unemployment," Nobel Lecture, *Journal of Political Economy*, June 1977; Milton Friedman, *Unemployment Versus Inflation? An Evolution of the Phillips Curve* (London: Institute of Economic Affairs, 1975). See also the essays and comments in Robert E. Hall, eds., *Inflation: Causes and Effects* (Chicago: University of Chicago Press, 1982).

21. Wolozin, "Inflation and the Price Mechanism," pp. 474-75.

22. The clearest statement emphasizing this view is contained in Ackley, "A Third Approach to the Analysis and Control of Inflation," *Compendium*.

23. Charles L. Schultz, "Recent Inflation in the United States," Study Paper No. 1 for the *Staff Report*.

24. The best statement perhaps is contained in Bowen, "Cost Inflation versus Demand Inflation: A Useful Distinction?" *The Southern Economic Journal*, January 1960, pp. 199-206.

25. A. W. Phillips,"The Relationship Between Unemployment and the Rate of Change of Money Wage Rates in the United Kingdom, 1861-1957," *Economica*, November 1958, pp. 283-99; R. G. Lipsey, "The Relation Between Unemployment and the Rate of Change of Money Wage Rates in the United Kingdom, 1861-1957; A Further Analysis," *Economica*, February 1960, pp.1-31.

26. Paul A. Samuelson and Robert M. Solow, "Analytical Aspects of Anti-Inflation Policy," *The American Economic Review*, May 1960, p. 192. Samuelson and Solow also add

A final disclaimer is in order. We have not entered upon the important question of what feasible institutional reforms might be introduced to lessen the degree of disharmony between full employment and price stability. These could of course involve such wide-ranging issues as direct price and wage controls, anti-union and antitrust legislation, and a host of other measures hopefully designed to move American Phillips Curve downward and to the left. [Ibid., pp. 193-94]

27. Albert R. Rees and Mary T. Hamilton, "The Wage-Price Productivity Perplex," *Journal of Political Economy*, February 1967, p. 70.

28. See footnote 20.

29. See, for example, Harry G. Johnson, *Macroeconomics and Monetary Theory* (Chicago: Aldine, 1967); Robert D. Auerbach and Ronald Moses, "The Phillips Curve and All That: A Comment," *Scottish Journal of Political Economy* November 1974, pp. 124-66; Thomas Sargent, "A Note on the 'Accelerationist' Controversy," *Journal of Money, Credit, and Banking*, August, 1971, pp. 721-24.

30. James Tobin, "Inflation and Unemployment," *The American Economic Review*, March 1972.

31. George Macesich, *Comparative Economic Stability* (Belgrade: Beogradski Graficki Zavod, 1973).

32. For a discussion of a number of these empirical results, see H. R. Vance and J. L. Thompson, *Monetarism: Theory, Evidence, and Policy* (New York: John Wiley & Sons, 1979),

pp. 86–90; George Macesich, *Monetarism: Theory, and Policy*, (New York: Praeger Publishers, 1983), chap. 7.

33. See, for example, David Meiselman, *The Term Structure of Interest* (Englewood Cliffs: Prentice-Hall, 1962); N. Gibson, "Price Expectations Effects on Interest Rates," *Journal of Finance*, March 1970; J. Foster, "Tests of the Simple Fisher Hypothesis Utilizing Observed Inflationary Expectations: Some Further Evidence," *Scottish Journal of Political Economy*, November 1977.

34. Irving Fisher, "A Statistical Relation Between Unemployment and Price Changes," *International Labour Review* (June 1926), pp. 785–92; ibid., *The Theory of Interest* (New York: Kelley, 1961) (a revision of the *Rate of Interest* (1907); George Macesich, "Irving Fisher," *Dictionary of the History of American Banking*, ed. G. T. Mills and D. A. Martin (Westport, Conn: Greenwood Press, forthcoming). Fisher's specification of the formulation of expectations made the expected rate of inflation a distributed lag formation of past rates of inflation with the most recent observation of inflation most heavily weighted. Fisher's expectations model leads to the conclusion that individuals will underestimate the current rate of inflation if inflation is accelerating. He also recognized the implications of this forecasting bias for the trade-off between inflation and unemployment as early as 1926.

35. John F. Muth, "Rational Expectations and the Theory of Price Movements," *Econometrica*, July 1961. Edmond S. Phelps, "Phillips Curves, Expectations of Inflation and Optimum Unemployment Over There," *Economica*, August 1967, pp. 254–81; Thomas J. Sargent and Neil Wallace, "Rational Expectations and the Theory of Economic Policy," *Studies in Monetary Policy* 2 (Federal Reserve Bank of Minneapolis, 1975). R. E. Lucas, Jr., "Expectations and the Theory of Economic Policy," *Journal of Monetary Economics*, January 1976; ibid., "Rational Expectations," *Journal of Money, Credit, and Banking*, November 1980; Macesich, *Monetarism: Theory and Policy*.

36. See, for example, Robert F. Lucas, Jr., "Tobin and Monetarism: A Review Article," *Journal of Economic Literature*, June 1981, pp. 558–67; L. Weiss, "The Role of Active Monetary Policy in a Rational Expectations Model," *Journal of Political Economy*, April 1980, pp. 221–33. Franco Modigliani, on the other hand, argues that the rational expectations case against discretionary stabilization policies is incorrect. The goal, according to Modigliani, is to make stabilization policies even more effective in the future than they have been in the past. See Franco Modigliani, "The Monetarist Controversy, or Should We Forsake Stabilization Policies?" *The American Economic Review*, March 1977, pp. 1–18.

5

Maintaining Stability: Three Tools

Importance of Maintaining Stability and Disagreement over Tools

Though there is disagreement among participants in the debate on inflation, few will argue with the importance of identifying its causes so that they can be eliminated. That they should be eliminated becomes clear once we consider the consequences of inflation.

One of the consequences of inflation is that it creates monetary policies which serve to reinforce inflationary pressures. Increased government borrowing exerts an upward pressure on interest rates. If the central bank is then called upon to monetize a part of the debt in order to counteract that pressure, inflation is encouraged. The evidence suggests that each time this option has been exercised, interest rates have not stayed down for long. As people become aware of inflation and the increased money supply, they expect prices to rise further. Interest rates rise as inflationary premiums are incorporated into them. The central bank again attempts to resist the rise by increasing the money supply and the whole cycle is renewed.

Problems are then compounded when concern for inflation becomes greater than for interest rates, resulting in attempts to reduce the rate of inflation by sharp reductions in the rate of money growth. The net effect has been that most of the postwar recessions and increases in unemployment in the United States can be attributed to "stop and go" monetary manipulation.

Another consequence of inflation is the arbitrary transfers it creates. Unanticipated inflation brings about a redistribution of wealth from creditors to debtors. People are encouraged to protect themselves by all sorts of methods, including holding smaller cash balances. The result is to push the economy into inefficiencies of bilateral barter transactions. Any decrease in the specialization that the use of money encourages necessarily leads to a reduction in output.

An equally important consequence of inflation is that it increases uncertainty. In the first instance, long-term contracts are jeopardized, thereby adversely affecting the creation of productive capacity and so future consumption possibilities. Secondly, it encourages government to combat inflation at times with such techniques as wage and price controls. The reaction to these techniques can produce serious distortions in the economic process.

Moreover, disagreement exists on how inflation is to be brought under control—more specifically, what instruments available to government should be employed for the task at hand. On the one hand, Monetarists push for money and monetary policy. On the other hand, Keynesians prefer fiscal policy. Others prefer wage and price controls. Needless to say, still others prefer some combination of all three. The extent to which one tool is favored over another is closely associated with preferences for a nondiscretionary policy-based system of rules as against one of discretionary authority. It is thus useful to consider the merits of these three tools of stabilization policy.

Monetary Policy for Stability and Growth

Control of the stock of money and so inflation prompts Monetarists and others to support the use of monetary policy. Monetarists also tend to favor greater reliance on monetary rather than fiscal policy because of the less discriminatory consequences of monetary restraint. Objections to monetary policy come mainly from reform liberals, who tend to opt for fiscal policy as a means of stabilizing the economy.[1] Other critics of monetary policy are also found in groups who believe themselves injured by its operation.

The usefulness of the tool of monetary policy, as with other tools, depends very much on the skill with which it is applied, as well as its effectiveness. Monetary policy as a tool could be highly effective but poorly administered. Alternatively, it could have only limited effectiveness but be well operated.

GOALS, OBJECTIVES AND CRITICISM OF MONETARY POLICY

Discussions of monetary policy as a tool of general economic stability often focus on its speed and effectiveness of action. Its great virtue, argue some of its supporters, is that monetary policy can be altered quickly and adjusted finely to changing circumstances. Critics contend that monetary policy as conducted in practice is slow to adjust to changes in the economic environment, and may therefore aggravate the economic instability it seeks to mitigate.

The management of money, as noted, has had a long history. Monetary policy has varied in instruments used, in stated objectives, and in the economic philosophy of policymakers. Central bankers and others often cite Bagehot's nineteenth-century dictum, "Money will not manage itself," as justification for central bank intervention into the economy. Collapse of the international monetary and financial structure in the Great Depression cast doubt on the ability of central banks to manage money effectively. Indeed, by the late 1930s fiscal policy—the planned balance of Treasury receipts and expenditures—became a more powerful economic factor than monetary policy. In fact, during World War II, the Federal Reserve played the role mainly of interest-rate stabilizer and guarantor of Treasury financing.

Keynesian ideas and influences, as well as the example of World War II, underscored the effectiveness of fiscal policy. Large government spending financed by large deficits shifted the balance in the American economy from unemployment to a labor shortage. Moreover, the standard of living of the civilian population was preserved, while at the same time the country fought a world war. Little wonder, then, that the Employment Act of 1946 put almost sole stress on the use of fiscal policy. Monetary policy in the postwar era served to stabilize interest rates, until it broke free in March 1951. Even after the break, however, monetary policy was expected primarily to support interest rates. Essentially, an increased supply of bank reserves was expected to lower the cost and increase the availability of credit. The cost and availability of credit was then expected to stimulate business and consumers to larger investment spending. It was soon realized that this stimulative action would have some inflationary impact. The matter was presented in terms of a "tradeoff": How much inflation should be tolerated in return for an increase in employment and economic activity? The evidence suggests that the "tradeoff" is largely illusory.

For almost two decades matters seemed to be going well as monetary and fiscal policy management stabilized the economy. To be sure, recession and economic dislocations occurred, but were considered minor departures from an otherwise successsful performance of the economy. Nevertheless, criticism of monetary and fiscal policy, and especially the execution of such policies, long a source of academic criticism, entered the policymaking arena.

Monetarism, as noted, is in the forefront of such criticism. Its central idea that money is the central causative economic factor with respect to prices and economic activity, while not new, received significant theoretical, empirical, and historical support in the studies by Professor Milton Friedman and those of his followers. Among other important results obtained in these studies is that there is a significant and variable lag between stimulative monetary policy and its economic benefits. The length of this lag is estimated at anywhere from six months to more than two years. These results, moreover, are confirmed for other countries as well. Given the length and variability of the lag, the effects of monetary policy appear long after they are no longer appropriate. As a result, discretionary monetary policy may in fact have a destabilizing effect on the economy.

The Monetarist recommendation, with which we deal elsewhere, is to adjust the money supply so as to grow at the same rate as, say, the potential for real economic output. There is thus no need for discretionary monetary policy and management.

These ideas are not new. What is new is that Monetarist ideas have reached policy levels hitherto unattainable by earlier proponents of similar ideas. There are indications that various central banks appear to shape their policies now more in terms of monetary magnitudes than earlier, even though discretionary monetary policy is retained.

Attack on discretionary monetary policy is also closely supported by people promoting the idea of "rational expectations." Essentially the idea, discussed in Chapter 4, is that labor groups and investors will correctly anticipate the inflationary impact of stimulative government policies (monetary and fiscal) and take self-protective measures that will thwart the stimulative policies. Labor will seek higher wages to offset expected inflation. Investors will seek higher interest rates for the same reason. Higher wages and higher interest rates will make investment unattractive, and so stimulative action will not produce the desired results. We shall have inflation but not the trade-off in increased output. In effect, the trade-off between unemployment and inflation is inoperative. Only inflation is in fact realized.

Given the logic of these ideas and that they are well known within the central banking establishment, does discretionary monetary policy have a future? Apart from technological unemployment among central bankers and their understandable hesitancy to be so displaced, there are other reasons that discretionary policy may continue to have a future unless explicitly constrained by rules within a policy-based system. First, the very mechanics of central banking will encourage it. For instance, the reserve supply mechanism is subject to sharp impacts from such sources as Treasury cash management and currency demands, which could be theoretically separated from discretionary monetary management, but in practice it is less likely to be the case.

Second, Treasury financing in practice encourages discretionary monetary policy. Although it is possible to separate Treasury financing from dependence on central bank support as, indeed, it was in the United States before World War I, it is not likely that Ministers of Finance or Secretaries of the Treasury would venture into contemporary financial markets to meet vast government fund requirements without central bank support.

Third, public perception of monetary affairs cultivates the belief that central banks do, in fact, control interest rates. Finally, central banks as bureaucracies of the national state prefer discretionary authority over nondiscretionary policy-based constraints on their operations and accountability as a matter of survival.

Still, new ideas are having an important impact, which is taking the form of a monetary policy that is less variable in its nature. The amplitude of changes in the character of monetary policy is likely to be less than in the past. As we discussed elsewhere, for instance, on October 6, 1979, the Federal Reserve announced the beginning of a new approach to the implementation of monetary policy: it would attempt to achieve better control of the growth of monetary aggregates by "placing greater emphasis in day-to-day operations on the supply of bank reserves and less emphasis on confining short-term fluctuations in the federal funds rate."[2] Nevertheless, during 1980 the Federal Reserve did not achieve the degree of declaration in M1B and M2 money growth rates that it announced as its objective for the year.[3] The experience with reserve targeting procedure, however, does not, according to observers, support the view that fluctuations of the money supply in 1980 reflect problems with monetary control which are basic to the operating procedure. Indeed, under the reserve targeting procedure, short-term monetary control may be improved in future years. We have discussed this issue elsewhere.

Much the same is true in other industrial countries. In Great Britain, for example, the Thatcher government has stuck closely to several principles of monetary policy initiated under the Labor government.[4] These include: (1) Formal targets for monetary growth, which were first adopted in 1976. They are expressed as a range rather than as a single number, recognizing that precise control is impossible; (2) the target has been defined in terms of a single measure of this (sterling M^3) money supply; (3) since 1978 a "rolling target" has been employed: though it applies to the next twelve months, it is reviewed every six months. In practice monetary control by central banks in Great Britain, as elsewhere, has been hard to achieve. Indeed, overshooting of targets has become the norm. The reasons targets are missed vary from year to year. This appears consistent with *Goodhart's Law,* (coined by C. Goodhart, chief monetary advisor to the Bank of England), which states that any measure of the money supply that is officially controlled promptly loses its meaning. It may also be true that central banks, after all, do not take seriously control over monetary aggregates. Their preference may still be interest rates and for monetary policy as an "art" unencumbered by constraints.

INSTRUMENTS OF MONETARY POLICY

In the United States, the Federal Reserve authorities (Fed) are charged with the responsibility of executing monetary policy. This is particularly true since 1951 and the now famous "accord" reached by the United States Treasury and the Federal Reserve Board; it provided, at least tacitly as a matter of public policy, that in case any open differences should arise between them, the Treasury would be expected to accommodate its policies so far as possible to those of the monetary authorities.

In discharging its responsiblities, the Fed has relied almost exclusively on three policy techniques: (1) open market operations; (2) changes in the rediscount rate; and (3) changes in the minimum reserve requirements of the member banks. All three instruments operate on the same basic principle of managing total spending by regulating the availability and cost of credit, and the growth of the country's money stock. The chief instrument for carrying out monetary policy in the United States however, is the Fed's open market operations whereby it buys and sells U.S. Government securities.

In addition, the Fed has at its disposal selective controls. A case in point is that of the securities markets. As a result of the financial reforms of the 1930s, responsibility for regulating margin requirements in connection with trading in and carrying securities was delegated to the Reserve Board.

Selective controls are considered by some as enjoying special merits because they are brought to bear on a particular sector of the economy, presumably without prejudice to the economy as a whole, including, quite conceivably, other "particular" areas where the situation might have called for exactly the opposite treatment. Others consider such controls as needless meddling into economic affairs. They are, so the argument runs, discriminatory, personal and contrary to the principles of the "free market."[5]

Experiences in other economically advanced countries suggest that the several instruments of monetary policy have received different degrees of emphasis.[6] A brief summary of these experiences is useful in illustrating the wide range of instruments deployed in central banking.

The National Bank of Belgium employs as its principal instrument of monetary policy changes in the discount rate and moral suasion. Open market operations in Belgium are carried out by the Securities Stabilization Fund. Resources for these operations are obtained in part by advances from the National Bank. In 1957 the scope and activities of the Fund were greatly enlarged when it was permitted to issue its own certificates and to deal in short- and long-term Government securities. Reserve requirements for the country's banks are established by the Banking Commission. Since 1962 the Commission has been empowered to impose compulsory cash reserve requirements for banks upon proposal of the National Bank.

In Canada, on the other hand, reserve requirements imposed upon commercial banks are very important for the exercise of monetary policy. The law requires chartered banks to maintain cash reserves equal to 8 to 12 percent of a bank's Canadian dollar obligations. Since 1956, and by agreement with the Bank of Canada, the chartered banks also maintain liquid assets at a ratio of 15 percent to their deposit liabilities. Prior to 1962 the discount rate instrument of monetary policy operated uniquely. The rate floated at one fourth of 1 percent above the latest weekly average tender rate of 91-day Treasury bills. Since June 24, 1962, however, the Treasury bill yield rate has ceased to be linked with the discount rate, and the latter has assumed an independent role in monetary policy.

Principal monetary instruments in France are the minimum liquidity coefficient of the banks. Ceilings are imposed by the Bank of France on rediscounts of short-term commercial paper. A penalty rate higher than the basic discount rate is applied to rediscounts in excess of the ceilings. Frequent changes occur in both the rates and the ceilings. The liquidity coefficients, first introduced in 1961, is the relationship between deposit liabilities and such selected assets as cash, Treasury bills, medium-term paper, and export paper. Since 1948, moreover, banks are required to maintain a minimum ratio of deposit holdings to holdings of Treasury bills alone.

Open market operations of the Bank of France are of very limited importance and completely different in character from those in the United States. Thus, for example, the Bank of France stands ready to buy from banks—up to given limits—Treasury bills, bankers acceptance as well as other types of paper in the money market.

By way of contrast in neighboring Germany, the Bundesbank conducts open market operations in such securities as Treasury bills and Government bonds as well as in other bonds admitted to the official stock exchange. It may establish minimum reserve requirements on credit institutions at any level up to a maximum of 30 percent for demand deposits, 20 percent for time deposits, and 10 percent for savings deposits. The Bundesbank may also change the discount rate and the rate it charges for advance on eligible paper.

In addition to these conventional instruments of monetary policy the Bundesbank has developed a technique for influencing the supply of funds on the domestic money market. The technique involves influencing the attractiveness of incentives to German commercial banks in making covered investments on the foreign exchange markets. By making it more expensive for banks to make such covered investments, the supply of funds available to the domestic market is increased, and conversely.

In Italy, owing to the lack of a developed money market, open market operations are not used to govern bank liquidity. Compulsory reserve requirements were established in 1947, and their level remained unchanged until 1962. Changes in the Bank of Italy's rates on advances and rediscounts have been very infrequent.

The Bank of Italy's principal monetary instruments appear to be moral suasion and the determination every four months on the size of banks' lines of credit. Internal credit expansion is also influenced by actions affecting the foreign borrowing and lending power of the country's banks. This is accomplished by (1) regulations concerning the amount of net foreign borrowing that banks are allowed to engage in, and (2) short-term swaps of Italian lire for dollars between the Bank of Italy and commercial banks.

A similar currency swap technique is also used by the Swiss National Bank in influencing the liquidity of Switzerland's banking system. The technique has been used on several occasions since 1961. Its effectiveness, however, depends very much on the traditional susceptibility of the country's commercial banking system to moral suasion.

The use of more traditional instruments of monetary policy is severely restricted. Thus the Swiss National Bank is empowered to change the rates of discounts and advances. It has, however, seldom done so. There are several reasons for this. First, banks rarely go to the National Bank to improve their liquidity positions, because of the substantial volume of funds available to them from foreign depositors and other interests. Second, the National Bank has no authority to adjust reserve ratios of commercial banks, which is considered unconstitutional. Moreover, lack of a portfolio of appropriate securities prevents the National Bank from carrying out open market operations.

In the Netherlands, on the other hand, the Governing Board of the Netherlands Bank has authority to set discount rates and conduct open market. In fact, since 1952, when open market operations were first begun, the Netherlands Bank has made extensive use of this instrument of monetary policy. The maturities have been from one to five years and have consisted of Government securities and bonds quoted on the Amsterdam Stock Exchange.

Reserve requirements are also an important instrument for implementing the country's monetary policy. Under the terms of the "gentlemen's agreement" of March 1954, the Bank is empowered to raise the cash reserve requirements of commercial banks to 15 percent of total deposits. In the 1950s this ratio was as high as 10 percent and as low as 4 percent.

The imposition in Sweden in 1952 of effective liquidity ratios on the commercial banks signalled a more active role for monetary policy in the country. Such a role has also brought about ingenious combinations of tax and fiscal policy measures and labor measures (including relocation measures) capable of rapid implementation in changing economic conditions. A case in point is the Swedish system of investment reserves. The idea is to spread private investment activity more evenly over the business cycle. Thus during expansionary phases business is encouraged by tax incentives to deposit portions of its gross profits with the Bank of Sweden. If the economy should require stimulus, these deposits may be released to finance given types of investment.

The use of more traditional monetary instruments such as open market operations has suffered owing to the pegging by the Bank of the Government bond market. This was considered necessary in order to permit flotation of the large volume of bond issues necessary to finance the budget deficits and housing program. This practice continued until 1955.

British monetary policy is implemented by a combination of discount policy and open market operations. Unlike the situation in the United States, for example, the Bank of England does not lend directly to commercial banks but only to discount houses whose main operations are to underwrite the weekly Treasury bill issue with call loans secured mostly in the London clearing banks. The Bank of England restricts credit by selling Treasury bills or Government bonds through its "special buyer" (a discount house) or the "Government broker" (a securities dealer), thus absorbing cash from the banking system. To restore their cash and liquidity positions, the banks can withdraw their call loans from the discount houses; the discount houses in turn may be forced to borrow from the Bank of England at the bank rate which, in contrast to the Fed's discount rate, is a penalty rate.

The influence of money in the economies of the socialist countries of Europe has increased. Yugoslavia is the pacesetter for these countries.[7] When it abandoned the Soviet type of planning apparatus, money began to play an important role in economic activity. The former concept of the money supply, defined in such a way as to include only coin and paper money, was inadequate in a country that considered decentralization seriously. By the beginning of 1952 a new definition more consistent with the new economic system was agreed upon. Since 1952 the money supply has been defined to include all monetary means that can be used directly as a means of payment, such as coin, paper money, transfer accounts of enterprises, liquid assets in investment funds, and other monetary assets such as savings deposits that can be readily converted. Such a definition, however, does not establish a clear-cut division between liquid and nonliquid assets. The vast middle ground between these few types of assets is a growing source of concern for the country's money managers.

Few will quibble with the idea that monetary policy ought to foster economic growth. The less-developed countries in Africa, Asia, and Latin America have many characteristics in common, including a relatively undiversified and inelastic productive system which responds only slowly to demand activated by an expansionary monetary policy. In these countries a very thin line indeed exists between inflation and the loss of international reserves on the one hand and a slow rate of growth on the other. Within these limits, however, monetary policy does play an important role.

In many developing countries, demand by borrowers for credit tends to be insensitive to small changes in interest rates. An alternative to pushing interest rates to exorbitant levels is, according to some, to resort to direct allocation of credit. Unfortunately, such action typically implies the imposition of direct controls.

As an instrument of monetary policy, open market operations is not effective in developing countries owing to the absence of an adequate securities market. Rediscount policy may be effective in those countries where banks are accustomed to borrow from the central bank. It is also used in many countries to influence and guide the flow of credit to "desired" ends. A central bank may grant favorable treatment or it may limit rediscounts to the refinancing of certain types of loans encouraging banks to lend for these purposes.

Changes in reserve requirements may also prove effective. However, in many of the developing countries liquidity ratios tend to be stable and in some the purpose of changes in reserve requirements appears to be to direct credit toward certain users by recognizing their debt instruments as liquid assets.

Role of Fiscal Policy

In the economists' tool kit, *fiscal policy* means changes in government expenditures, taxation, and manipulation of the budget. It is a tool preferred by Keynesians and reform liberals. Fiscal policy in its most general sense deals with the effects of changes in the levels of government receipts and expenditures and with the effects of changes in the budget deficit or surplus. In its detailed sense it examines effects on economic activity of the composition of revenues and expenditures, as well as the effects of such activity of fiscal policies of various levels of government.

Discussion before the Congressional Joint Economic Committee and the privately appointed Commission on Money and Credit has cast up surprising unanimity on the role of fiscal policy in promoting the objectives of the Employment Act of 1946.[8] In terms of fiscal policy, the objectives of the Act appear to be twofold: the maintenance of high levels of employment, and stability in the general level of prices. Accordingly, fiscal policy should mitigate fluctuations in aggregate demand so as to prevent the economy from developing high unemployment rates and upward pressure on the general level of prices. In effect, fiscal policy is concerned (in the short run at least) with adjusting aggregate demand to the objectives of high employment levels and stable prices.

Most expenditures and receipts of government, however, are undertaken for reasons other than the promotion of high employment rates and general price stability. This serves to complicate the tasks of fiscal policy which must resolve the immediate objectives of individual expenditure and receipt programs with those of the Employment Act. A case in point is defense expenditures and military buildup programs, which must be undertaken but may well be inconsistent with economic stability. Moreover, the changing requirements of various governmental programs have the effect of exerting varying degrees of pressures on employment and prices.

At times a distinction is made between fiscal policy aimed at promoting high levels of employment and price stability on the one hand and economic growth on the other. This distinction, however, is overdrawn. Maintenance of high levels of employment with a growing labor force usually means an expansion in a country's total output. Avoidance of inflation and deflation is usually conducive to capital formation and so to increases in a country's productive capacity.

More recently, emphasis is increasingly placed on the role of fiscal policy in promoting and sustaining a high rate of economic growth. On this issue two opposing views of fiscal policy can be presented as demonstrating the issues involved.[9] Needless to say, neither view is strictly correct.

One view argues that the problem of economic growth rates turns on the levels of private saving and capital formation. When resources are assumed to be fully employed, they may be allocated either to capital formation or consumption.

The larger the share devoted to capital formation the more capital will be combined with labor, increasing the productivity of the latter. And as a consequence, the rate at which the economy is producing goods and services will be increased. Accordingly, the role of fiscal policy in increasing the rate of economic growth is to reduce consumption, increase saving, and so increase capital formation. This may be done by appropriate tax policies that discourage consumption and encourage saving. Another way is simply to raise general taxes so as to generate public saving in the form of a budget surplus that would, presumably, be made available to the capital market through government debt retirement or lending.

The other view argues that capital formation need not be private but can, in fact, be public. Moreover, resources withdrawn from consumption need not necessarily go to capital formation. According to the adherents of this view, public capital formation has already played singularly important roles and there is every reason to believe that it can do so in the future. Indeed, a fiscal policy aimed at reducing consumption for the sake of increasing private capital formation may in fact lead to unemployment rather than increased investment. In order to sustain investment at high and rising levels, a high and rising level of consumer demand must exist in order to justify increased productive capacity. In the long run, moreover, investment is unlikely to create its own demand even if credit terms are eased. Accordingly, the role of fiscal policy is to promote a high and rising level of consumer demand as a necessary prerequisite to an increased rate of economic growth.

Those who take issue with both views cite such evidence as economic depressions and recessions, when in fact saving has led to decreases in output and unemployment rather than an increase in investment as expected. Indeed, the performance of the American economy during most of the 1950s is taken as an example of the incorrectness of the first view. During this period the American economy developed excess capacity, increased rate of unemployment, and general retardation in output performance.

They also point out, however, that the second view is not strictly correct, either, as an examination of available evidence quickly indicates. For example, one of the causes of increases in labor productivity over the long run has, in fact, been growth of the capital stock.

Clearly, choices must be made between consuming today and postponing some consumption for the sake of a larger share in the future. This is an issue common in all economies. It is also clear that this choice can be influenced by government action in its taxing and expenditures policies. The decisions as to the amounts allocated to consumption and investment is at times and in some countries left to the private sector. At other times, and in other countries, government takes a direct role in such decisions.

PROMOTING STABILITY

As a first approximation, government expenditures can influence the level of aggregate demand, provided that compensating changes do not occur in private expenditures because of taxes imposed by government. When few resources are idle, an expansionary fiscal policy will positively influence aggregate demand and so raise the general level of prices. It may, perhaps, even raise output, depending on how fully utilized are the economy's resources.

If fiscal policy is to have neither a positive nor a negative influence on aggregate demand, the government must increase the budget surplus when it increases its purchases of goods and services and conversely when its purchases are declining. The reason for this is that government purchases add, dollar for dollar, directly to aggregate demand whereas an equal amount of taxes will not necessarily reduce a taxpayer's expenditures dollar for dollar. Consequently, equal increases in government expenditures and taxes will positively influence aggregate demand, whereas equal decreases will negatively influence aggregate demand.[10]

It should be emphasized, however, that the state of the government's budget is not a very accurate measure of the stimulative or restrictive effects that fiscal policy will have in any specific period of time. In 1963, for example, the consensus was that tax rates were too high in spite of the fact that the budget was in deficit. The evidence, as cited, was the high rate of unemployment as well as a general economic slowdown in the period 1958–1963. Taxes were cut in 1964, and the economy picked up to the extent that the budget deficit eventually declined as a consequence of increased receipts. Conversely, it may be required to raise taxes during strong inflationary periods even though there is a surplus in the budget.

The basic aim of fiscal policy has evolved into trying to make total spending in the economy match productive capacity. Policy actions aimed at restraint or stimulus are based primarily on the state of the economy and not on the state of the budget.

Automatic stabilizers have helped to make fiscal policy more flexible. The fiscal structure has acquired features that result in automatic changes in receipts and expenditures in response to changes in income. Indeed, discretionary fiscal action taken to influence aggregate demand will be offset in part as a consequence of the trigger action it will have in setting off automatic changes in some fiscal components in the reverse direction. If a reduction in income occurs and is reflected in a fall in employment, it will lead to an increase in transfer payments in the form of unemployment compensation. It will also lead to a reduction in tax receipts at any given level of tax rates. And conversely, for an increase in income.

One very important problem in connection with automatic stabilizers is in the fact that taxes respond to changes in the level of prices as well as to changes in real output and employment. As long as all three variables move in the same direction, automatic stabilizers will operate so as to moderate fluctuations. If increases in the level of prices should coincide, for example, with decreasing employment, automatic stabilizers may result in restraint on the level of aggregate demand, resulting in a slippage from high employment rates.

The effectiveness of automatic stabilizers depends on the relative size of government expenditures, the level of tax rates, and the degree to which the tax base fluctuates with changes in national income. This has prompted investigation into the effectiveness of existing stabilizers. Such investigation reveals that during the postwar period the built-in flexibility of the Federal budget offset between one third to two fifths of the fall (or increase) in the GNP.[11] This remarkable performance in the postwar period has prompted attempts to improve automatic stabilizers and so bring about even more flexibility in the fiscal structure.

The Commission of Money Credit, for example, considered a number of modifications that would serve to improve the effectiveness of automatic stabilizers. It examined a variety of changes in the tax structure which would serve to strengthen it as an automatic stabilizer and conclude that no changes in the tax structure that would likely improve its functioning as an automatic stabilizer are feasible. On the other hand, the Commission argued that changing the structure of unemployment compensation by increasing the benefit levels holds promise for strengthening existing stabilizers.

The possibility of strengthening automatic stabilization through so-called formula flexibility was also examined. This device amounts to a provision for automatic changes in the level of certain tax rates whenever prescribed economic indicators change by specified amounts. Attractiveness of formula flexibility is to be found in the lack of bias that would result by lowering a selected tax rate in recession periods and raising it on the upswing on the basis of the same formula arrangement. This is in marked contrast to discretionary action, which would be subject to heavier pressure for tax cuts on downswing than for tax raises in the upswing. Drawbacks to formula flexibility are found in its unconventional nature, which retards ready acceptance. Another and perhaps more serious drawback is difficulty in choosing the appropriate set of indexes to which changes in tax rates would be related.

Discretionary fiscal measures are another important means available for influencing aggregate demand. Shortcomings of discretionary fiscal measures usually turn on two criticisms. One is the lack of accurate economic forecasts. Fiscal policy based on such forecasts may actually do more harm than good. On the other hand, this is simply a general criticism of a lack of forecasting methods which is equally applicable to the use of other discretionary policy measures.

The other is the legislative lag and deals with the general ability of Congress, or indeed other deliberative bodies, to act promptly in adopting discretionary fiscal measures. This inability vitiates considerably the use of such measures in stabilization policies where prompt action is necessary. Too much, however, can be made of this point.

For example, the Commission on Money and Credit in its report cites evidence to the effect that when Congress is presented with a straightforward situation, ways are found to accelerate the legislative process. Thus, simple tax extension measures convering excise and corporate income tax rates consumed less than a month's time from the initial action by the Ways and Means Committee; the excess profit in 1953 required less than 50 days; temporary extension of unemployment compensation in 1958 required 73 days, and its extension required only 18 days in 1959. Serious problems arise, according to the Commission's view, when attempts are made to change the basic tax structure and basic government expenditure programs for stabilization purposes.

Manipulation of taxes for purposes of promoting short-run stability is called for by some economists. If such manipulation is accepted as appropriate and effective, the problem exists of selecting the sectors and the components of private aggregate demand whose taxes are to be manipulated. Most people would argue that both the consumption and investment sectors would qualify as candidates.

A number of criteria exist with which to judge the appropriateness of taxes to be manipulated for short-run stability. Such criteria as certainty, compliance, effectiveness, and reversibility are considered as dominant in these judgments.

Those favoring tax changes point to the personal income tax as the top candidate meeting all the required criteria. Excise taxes, it is argued, have an undesired effect on demand. Consumers are placed on notice that soon items to be taxed will be more expensive to them and are thus encouraged to spend more and so raise demand at the very time when it should be lowered, and conversely for periods when aggregate demand is sluggish. Change in the corporate income tax rate is also considered a poor candidate, for the reason that such changes would increase business uncertainty. The same is true for changes in investment credits and depreciation allowances. Indeed, the Commission on Money and Credit, for example, urges that when discretionary tax adjustments are used to promote short-run stability, changes in the first bracket rate of the personal income tax should have first priority.

Available studies indicate, however, that one of the major obstacles to a more sensitive response of the income tax to changes in income is attributable to the present bracket structure itself. Before adopting changes in the first bracket rate, we would be well advised to consider, first, whether a different bracket structure would make the distribution of taxable income react more sensitively to income changes.[12]

Moreover, the demand effects of equal changes in various taxes may differ. For example, in the decade of the 1950s it is estimated that consumption expenditures would change by $700 million in response to a $1 billion change in personal income taxes brought about by a flat percentage cut in all bracket rates, $825 as a consequence of a $1 billion in excise taxes and $500 billion change in corporate income taxes.[13]

Change in government expenditures is another discretionary measure advocated as a means for promoting short-run stability. It is generally argued, however, that state and local levels of government are better able to promote short-run stability through adjustments in their expenditures than is the federal government. The latter has few expenditures programs which are sufficiently flexible to permit counter cyclical timing with any accuracy. Problems in administration and technology, moreover, compound those of timing, e.g., many projects cannot be shut down once started but must be finished.

Another criticism of discretionary changes in government expenditures is that government should concern itself with long-range requirements for public services. Those requirements may not be the same as those for short-run stability. Indeed, they may even be at odds. For example, purchases of goods and services by government for programs instituted during recessions may not be stopped during periods of prosperity and thus, in effect, the programs will be booming the boom.

It is suggested that one way to overcome some of these criticisms is to rank projects according to social priority and time required for completion. Accordingly, changes in government expenditures to combat recessions would be concentrated on projects with the highest social priority and in which a high ratio of spending would occur within the shortest time span. One objection is that the "social priority test" does not assure that the most useful expenditures will be made. It is more likely that the most politically expedient projects would receive priority.

Another method recommended for overcoming objections to discretionary changes in government expenditures would be to distinguish clearly between current and capital expenditures by government. The budget according to this argument should be divided into a capital budget and a current budget. Capital budget expenditures would be indicated on one side, and taxes and borrowing used to finance such expenditures on the other. Similarly, in the current expenditures budget, expenditures would be shown on one side and revenues on the other. This arrangement would better indicate the nature of government expenditures and debt. Increases in public debt, for example, backed by real assets, would correspond to an increase in an individual's debt backed up by real assets. Some of the reluctance to government expenditures would perhaps be overcome.

PROMOTING GROWTH

Economic growth can be encouraged or discouraged by tax policy. Which it will be depends very much on practical and administrative feasibility as well as on the ingenuity of tax technicians.

The federal tax structure has come in for particular attention as badly in need of overhaul. Much empirical work needs to be done on the taxes that should be changed, by how much, and the likely impact of such changes.

Attention in recent years has been focused on capital formation and its role in economic growth and the effects of changes in the tax structure on such for-mation.[14] The reported results indicate that expansion of the physical quan-tity of capital accounts for a relatively small part of the increase in output. Much of capital formation accounting for increases in output can be attrib-uted to that portion embodying technological advance.

Improvements in the *quality* of capital formation, in effect, are judged as the most important source of growth. One can argue, of course, that problems of technological advance and capital formation are really one and the same for the reason that research expenditures to advance the "state of arts" *are* capital formation. Also, it is only through new capital goods that new and improved methods can be introduced. Nevertheless, for purposes of tax policy it does make sense to make the distinction.[15]

Stimulation of innovations, research, and development are now given pref-erential tax treatment through rapid write-offs. Serious problems arise, how-ever, because of the difficulty in distinguishing clearly between expenditures that generate growth for the economy as a whole and those that simply increase product differentiation or raise the competitive position of a particu-lar firm.

Tax experts note with some justification that the economics of tax policy for growth are more complex than those for stabilization.[16] Formulating tax policy in order to raise both the level and quality of private capital formula-tion requires a careful balance between economic considerations on the one hand and strictly political considerations on the other.

An important issue in any discussion of tax policy and economic growth is the effect of taxes on incentives. Recent studies suggest a number of conclu-sions.[17] Changes in average and marginal tax rates have opposite effects on work incentives. Thus a decrease in the marginal rate improves incentives, while a decrease in average rates reduces incentives. In the case of individual incentives to undertake risky investments, the evidence indicates that it is not only the level of tax rates that is important but also the extent of the allow-ances for loss offsets.

Empirical findings indicate that the existence of income taxes does not appear to have adverse effects in the aggregate on incentives. One study, for example, presents an analysis of the relationship between labor force partici-pation rates (male, female, and both sexes combined) and the height of income tax rates for the United States (1890–1950), Great Britain (1911–1951), Canada (1911–1951), New Zealand (1896–1951), and Germany (1895–1950).[18] The results fail to show any systematic relationship between the two variables regardless of the time periods selected or within countries or between countries in those years when the tax rates were the highest.

Explanation of this rather surprising result can be attributed to the time periods selected. Income taxes were not an important burden on the majority of workers.

Another study undertaken in Great Britain for the postwar period also shows no systematic relationship between income taxes and incentives.[19] On the other hand, the results indicate that a sharp jump in tax rates does produce more tax disincentives.

British experience was also reviewed in an independent study which concludes that very high tax rates tend to reduce the amount of work done in certain segments of the labor force.[20] Another conclusion of some interest is that the most frequent type of incentive reported was postponement of retirement.

One incentive often overlooked by tax experts is the effect that income taxes have on the use of currency as opposed to bank accounts. Available studies for the United States and Canada indicate that income taxes encourage the use of currency as a means for evading tax payments.[21] There is, in fact, a direct and strong relationship between the currency money ratio and tax rates. As a consequence, bank reserves are placed under pressure from an often unexpected source. This is now the often cited phenomenon of the "underground economy."

It is generally agreed that government expenditures play an important role in promoting economic growth. The role itself involves two interrelated problems. One deals with the size and timing of total govermental expenditures. The other deals with the appropriate mix of governmental expenditures.

The Joint Economic Committee has devoted considerable attention to both problems.[22] Several contributors also presented considerations for directing government spending to promote growth. Some light was also shed on the connections between government spending, and saving and investing both by the public and private sectors. The conclusions to be drawn from these studies is that the effects of government spending have manifold influences on decision making far from the political arena.

For example, the ability of various pressure groups to influence expenditures has at times the effect of reducing the mobility of resources. Cases in point are various compensation payments paid by government in such industries as agriculture, shipping, mining, and oil. They are made, presumably, to cushion the effects of "technological changes." The net effect, however, may well be to slow down adversely the movement of resources.

In general, the problem of evaluating government expenditures is really one of judging whether the returns from such expenditures are equal to or greater than that which the public gives up in consumption and private investment. Returns from government expenditures typically involve two components: one is their contribution to productivity as measured by real GNP; the other is the nonmaterial return such as the benefits of education.

A SUPPLY-SIDE THEORY OF FISCAL POLICY: THE LAFFER CURVE

The upsurge of interest in "supply-side" economics promoted the conviction that American tax rates are so high as to discourage incentives and investment. Supply-siders believe that lowering taxes also calls for cuts in welfare spending. The net effect apparently will be to stimulate the economy. The process is summarized in the *Laffer Curve,* named by Jude Wanniski after Arthur B. Laffer in his guideline to supply-side theory, *The Way the World Works: How Economists Fail—And Succeed* (New York: Basic Books, 1978).

The Laffer Curve is so constructed that the government tax rate from 0 to 100 percent is plotted in the Y axis, and government revenue on the X axis. At the curve's lower end, if the government drops the tax rate to nothing, it gets nothing. And if it raises its tax rate to 100 percent, it also gets nothing. Why? Because in that case nobody will work for wages. If all income went to the state, people would revert to the barter economy. The exercise is to select an optimum point on the curve where taxes maximize government revenue.

Now, the heart of the supply-side argument is the conviction that the American economy is at a point on the curve above far too high from the optimum point. Lowering taxes will give the supply side of the economy such a shot in the arm that the United States will slide down the Laffer curve. As a result, tax revenues eventually will rise enough to take care of increased funding of the military; stagflation will end; dynamic growth will begin, and the budget will be balanced.

The trouble with the Laffer Curve is that, like the Phillips Curve discussed elsewhere, it is too simple to be of any service except as a symbol of a concept. In the case of the Laffer Curve, the concept is not new, and it is obvious— when taxes are too high they are counterproductive. The problem, of course, is to define *too high.* Few if any economists have any notion of what the Laffer Curve looks like except in the neighborhood of its end points. Even if they did know, few would be willing to say where to put the economy on it.

On the other hand, another study, *The Reindustrialization of America* (New York: McGraw-Hill, 1981) by six editors of *Business Week* argues that the Reagan administration's principal economic policy of cutting marginal taxes to stimulate investment is not sufficient to cure the American economy's problems. The culprits believed responsible for American economic troubles are misguided government, shortsighted management, and an outmoded collective bargaining system that fails to recognize the realities of international competition. *Business Week* editors suggest that a strong reindustrialization program should include a federal agency to allocate funds to ailing industries, targeted tax cuts for specific sectors of the economy, a sharp curtailment of the antitrust laws, and a collaboration by labor and management on quality-of-work programs to make these programs more productive.

EXPERIENCE IN OTHER COUNTRIES

Attempts to compare and contrast the importance of fiscal policy in promoting stability and growth in other countries is a very difficult task indeed. Most critical is the fact that considerable variation exists between countries in the items included in their budgets. As a consequence, the figures themselves are apt to be misleading.[23] The best that can be expected is an indication of whether the country used its intended overall balance anticyclically so as to promote short-run stability. Italy, Norway, the United Kingdom, and the United States in the period 1950–60 appear to meet the criterion of anticyclical use of their overall budget balances. In France, Belgium, Germany, Luxembourg, and the Netherlands, however, the evidence suggests that this was not the case during the same period.

Moreover, in Italy and Norway the overall budget surplus was also used to provide public savings for purposes of helping to finance a high level of investment and thus directly to promote economic growth.

To judge from available studies, the extent to which governments of various countries have been able to vary current and overall balances anticyclically has been limited.[24] Some limit is set in most countries by the fact that it is not easy to cut back government expenditures. In some countries a strong prejudice exists against government budget current deficits and surpluses, as well as against their use as instruments of fiscal policy.

To some people the specter of past runaway inflation is ever present. They place the blame for these inflations on irresponsible government expenditure. Accordingly, inflation can be avoided if the government keeps its budget in balance. This is, in effect, the traditional view of "correct" budget management.

Governments pursuing such a policy as, for example, Belgium in the early 1950s and Germany in the mid-1950s increase expenditures or reduce taxes in boom periods, and, conversely, during periods of economic contraction. The net effect is, of course, that aiming at such a policy simply reinforces both inflations and contractions. It is exactly the opposite of "proper" anticyclical policy.

Confusion also is created in many countries by people using the analogy of private debt to public debt, regarding all such increases as necessarily bad — resulting in burdens for future generations and threatening the country with bankruptcy. In Belgium, Italy, Luxembourg, and Germany governments were strongly against budget deficits. In France the situation during the 1950s was different. The French government's desire to keep down the size of the deficits was due more to the ever-present threat of inflation than to public opinion and professional skepticism against the use of budget deficits.

In developing countries fiscal policy is typically used in attempts to achieve a desired balance among competing investment demands, regulating the pattern of saving and maintaining a viable external account. One fiscal instrument growing in importance as a generator of savings in developing countries is profit of public enterprises. This is a change in attitude. Previously it was considered that a public enterprise should operate on a no-profit-no-loss basis. In situations where public sector investment of social overhead is concerned and external economies may be involved, the rule is perhaps a good one. Elsewhere, however, the rule may be inadequate. In view of the increasing expansion of the public sector, governments of developing countries would be well advised to insist that public enterprises make a profit through rational pricing policies.

An inefficient and inadequate machinery of tax administration in most developing countries results in a tendency to place taxes on wealth rather than on income. To be sure such taxes may help the authorities to restrict the spending power of relatively higher income groups as in various Asian and Latin American countries. The relatively low per capita income in these countries also discourages resort to indirect taxation as a method for raising aggregate savings.

Developing countries have hit on the effectiveness of taxation on establishing and promoting a "desired" pattern of investment. Through appropriate investment allowances, tax rebates, turnover taxes, and the like, the "desired" type of investment is encouraged and the "wrong" type discouraged. A tendency for such tax arrangements to become extremely complicated and cumbersome substracts considerably from their effectiveness.

The use of fiscal instruments to promote the foreign trade of developing countries is well known. An example is the subsidization of the production cost of goods to be exported. Such a practice is usually justified on the grounds that the exportable goods, particularly manufacturers of developing countries, cannot compete with those of the more developed countries owing to the divergence between the marginal social cost and the private social cost of producing new manufactures. These practices tend to receive "official approval" from such organizations as GATT. (General Agreement on Trade and Tarriffs).

Similar reasoning also is used to justify the taxation of certain exportable commodities of developing countries. This is the case when foreign demand is insensitive to price changes. These taxes serve to protect a developing country's terms of trade and thus its export earnings in terms of foreign exchange.

Taxation, of course, is also used by most developing countries as a means for regulating the amount and pattern of imports. This becomes particularly important in promoting the adoption of an appropriate degree of capital intensity. It is essential that the cost of imports not appear too low and thereby create an incentive for a developing country to adopt highly capital-intensive techniques completely inappropriate to its economy, and usually characterized by a redundant labor supply. This tendency can be rectified by placing high tariff duties on capital goods. The same thing, of course, can be accomplished by devaluation of the currency but the tax method is considered more desirable because of its selectivity.

Price and Wage Controls: How Effective?

ECONOMICS OF PRICE AND WAGE CONTROLS

Consider now the general question of price and wage controls as appropriate and effective stabilization policies.

As with taxes and government expenditures, price and wage controls are with us always. Minimum wages and minimum prices have been a major economic factor for many decades in most countries. Agricultural price supports in the United States are only the more popular examples of minimum prices. Not so obvious are minimum prices that are an indirect consequence of import tariffs designed to protect such high-cost American industries as shipbuilding and certain mineral industries by covering the differential between domestic and foreign production costs.

Maximum prices are illustrated by maximum interest rates for various types of loans and rent controls which flourish in many countries. There is also the practice of price but rather a specific price. Examples abound in such sectors of the economy as public utilities, transportation, and communication.

Consider some problems and consequences of prices for individual products and services (including wages). The effects of a fixed price for a product or service depend in the first instance on the level it is fixed and whether it is a minimum or a maximum price.

Let us suppose we set up an administrative agency to fix prices. Now suppose this agency fixed the price of a commodity or service precisely at the level at which it would fall relative to other prices if there were no price controls and the price is established by free market forces. In this case, the price control will have no effect, and our agency performed a needless exercise. And, of course, the administrative costs incurred by this exercise will be borne by the taxpayer.

Now suppose that our agency sets a fixed price which is a maximum price but that it sets the price at some level lower than what the price would be if it were determined by free market forces. In this case shortages will appear.

People will want to buy more of the commodity or service than they otherwise would, but less of the product or service will be produced than otherwise would have been produced. Why should less of the product be produced at this lower price? The reason is simply that at this lower price it becomes more profitable to produce other items whose prices are not fixed at this lower level. Now if more is demanded than is supplied, then some system determines who among the people is going to get the product or service in question. This can be done by attaching another office to our price-administering agency whose function will be to issue coupons, or the product or service can be given to old and regular customers of the suppliers, or it can be done according to the rule of "first come, first served." This is, of course, the familiar case of the queue with all the losses in time spent waiting one's turn.

If less of a product or service is produced because its price is fixed too low, it must be that fewer resources are employed in producing this product or service than were formerly employed. Now, what happened to those resources? They simply moved to other industries producing products and services whose prices were not controlled. And, ironically, since prices tend to be controlled in "essential" industries are not controlled in "unessential" industries, this means that price controls tend to cause fewer of the essential products or services to be produced and more of the unessential products or services.

But the above need not be the case at all, some will say, since the government can induce producers of the commodity or service in question to produce more at this lower price by offering them an incentive in the form of a subsidy. All this means is that, in effect, producers now receive a higher price, raised "artificially" by the government subsidy. The taxpayer in general will now bear not only the cost of the price-administering agency but also the additional cost of the subsidy.

Consider our last case in which a minimum price is fixed at a level higher than that which would prevail in a free market. Now there will be initial surpluses. At the higher price for the product or service more will be produced. Instead of rationing consumers, it will now be necessary to "ration" the production of the product or service among the many producers who would be willing to produce at this higher price. Again, as in the case of consumers, this can be done by attaching an office to our price administering agency whose function will be to allocate by quota production of the product or service in question.

This, in general, is the all too familiar problem in the past of American agricultural surpluses. In this case, the taxpayer as a consumer will very likely pay the higher price for the product or service as well as the cost of the administering agency.

Selective price controls, moreover, cannot avoid discrimination. If a producer's selling price is fixed, there is usually an obligation to control his costs. This means fixing more than the prices of a producer's more obvious inputs such as labor and raw materials. It also means that such items as taxes, interest costs, and business costs must also be fixed.

Control of labor costs, however is the most difficult. Such elements of labor costs as fringe benefits, compensation for overtime work, shift differentials, and paid leave serve to complicate the already difficult task of setting wage rates. The federal minimum wage example will suffice to illustrate the difficulties in setting wage rates.[25]

The inverse relation between changes in the minimum wage and substitution (capital for labor) effects one would expect from economic theory appears to be confirmed. When information on evasion and violations of the minimum wage law is taken into account, considerable light is shed on the complexities of wage fixing. In effect, an increase in the minimum wage is equivalent to a reduction in the price of evasion and avoidance. The price of evasion and avoidance is the cost of evasion and avoidance minus the benefits of evasion and avoidance. The benefit has increased with the increase in the minimum wage. And, other things equal, one would expect evasion and avoidance of the minimum wage to increase. This also appears to be confirmed by the evidence.[26] In addition, scattered evidence suggests that the minimum wage reduces the price of discrimination against blacks and teenagers.

The minimum wage has had adverse effects on wage differentials.[27] These differentials serve a useful purpose in allocating labor services into various occupations. They are, in fact, an essential part of the price mechanism. When they are subjected to an autonomous shock in the form of a government fiat, a compression of wage differentials occurs. The wages of those directly affected by the rise in the minimum wage rise more than wages of those not so directly affected. Since it is not as easy to allocate labor services as it is other services and goods, the problem of production adjustments is aggravated.

Matters are further complicated by difficulties in defining exactly what it is that is being controlled. Failure to specify accurately the end product or service leads to the inevitable tendency to increase profit margins by cutting quality, particularly where shortages already exist. The problem, moreover, is not simply one of quality deterioration. There is also the tendency for the variety of products to be reduced.

In the face of domestic price and wage ceilings, there is always the tendency for a producer to sell abroad at a higher price. When the producer is allocated fewer productive resources than he desires, he may seek to increase his supply by imports. This inevitably leads to price controls and physical controls over imports, such as foreign exchange controls, import and export quotas. The general direction into which a country adopting such controls is pushed forces its government and bureaucracy into a position as the sole judge on the volume and direction new investment will take. Government, and more specifically its bureaucracy, dominates the field of new investment through its policies regarding profits and sales.

The actual costs of price control are only imperfectly known. If we draw on American experience and the Office of Price Administration during World War II, some insights are possible. In fiscal year 1942 OPA's initial budget of $22.4 million mushroomed into $185.7 million in fiscal year 1945. In terms of manpower, OPA was probably the largest of the civilian war agencies. The agency employed almost 64,000 persons in 1945. Of these, little more than 4,000 were employed in Washington. To this must be added the large corps of unpaid volunteers on the local boards.

The Office of Price Stabilization (OPS) during the Korean war offers additional examples of the costs of controls. For the fiscal year 1952 the government's plans required 19,000 permanent positions in OPS alone. Price controls themselves accounted for about half of the requested stabilization appropriations of $238.8 million.

The time and talent required to comply with requirements of controls on the part of the private sector of the economy are indeed significant. It has been estimated that about 10 percent of the management's time was devoted to interpreting control measures and directing business accordingly. This does not include the additional time and costs incurred as a consequence of attempting to get adjudications from control boards and agencies in litigation. These costs, of course, were not allowed in computing ceiling prices under original ceiling price regulations.[28]

Price controls, of course, encourage the development of a "black market" and the exchange of goods and services at prices above the legally established ceilings. Experience both in the United States and in other countries contain numerous examples of declining production, shortages, and diversion of outputs into black markets. Producers are typically forced into violation of legally established prices in order to obtain raw materials to maintain their firm's output. Still others now find it profitable to incur the risks inherent in trading at above-legal prices. One study dealing with black market experience in the United States during World War II indicates that two out of three concerns investigated during 1944 were found to be in violation of logically established prices.[29]

Controlled economies and those which resort to considerable economic planning may actually encourage the development of a "black market" or "free market" alongside a "controlled market" as a way of introducing some flexibility into the economy. Indeed, in recent years a pronounced trend is observable on the part of formerly rigidly planned and controlled economies to adopt systems of flexible prices.

Some idea of the differences between past and most recent trends is the case of Yugoslavia.[30] Before 1952, when centralized planning was in force, the completed annual plan weighed over 3,300 pounds. Over 215 ministers on the federal and republic levels were issuing orders to enterprises, and the Federal Planning Commission employed a staff of 700 people. The amount of paper work imposed on the enterprises is indicated by the fact that each year they were required to submit from 600 to 800 reports per enterprise to the central authorities. Daily reports were requested from enterprises and these were then teletyped at the end of each workday by the local authorities to the appropriate ministries in Belgrade. These ministries would then consolidate their reports and send them along to the Federal Planning Commission.

WAGE AND PRICE GUIDELINES: "NONCOERCIVE" CONTROLS?

While some countries in EasternEurope are shedding the more extreme rigidities of economic planning and price and wage controls for more flexible prices as a way of improving the performance of their economies, other countries are experimenting with such supposedly "noncoercive" controls as wage and price guidelines or more commonly "incomes policy."

The countries already committed heavily into such a policy are Britain, France, and Belgium. Implementation of the "incomes policy" differs from country to country. Basically, however, the general procedure envisioned seems to be as follows. As part of an overall long-term plan the government will calculate the expected increase over that period in average productivity per period. Government will then decide how big a rise in wage rates, prices, and profits is compatible with avoiding inflation, achieving balance of payments equilibrium with high levels of employment. Finally, it will attempt to obtain the cooperation of all groups, including labor and management, to stick to these figures.

In the United States the guidelines policy attempts to affect wages and prices by persuasion and thus prevent inflation in times of strong demand.[31] Similar to the guidelines policy are programs of persuasion regarding investment plants, export or capital, and other economic decisions. The government's wage guideposts set an upper limit on negotiated wage increases of a given percent a year. In the case of prices, industries are supposed to act according to their individual productivity experience, with no average upward change.

If effectively implemented, such a policy could be used in given circumstances to bring down money costs and not merely prevent them from rising. Serious doubt is expressed, however, that such policy can in fact be made effective.

In the first instance it is necessary to obtain the cooperation of labor unions. While "optimism" is expressed in the case of British "incomes policy," which is equivalent to the American guideposts because of increasing acceptance there by both management and labor, observers agree that it would be some years before the policy would be able to break the high rate of wage increases in Britain.

In the second instance, support of labor unions can probably be obtained only on the condition that profits are also controlled. And, of course, control over dividend payments is inadequate since retained profits, which may be increased by a policy of wage moderation, belong to the owners of the property in question and serve to increase the value of such property. But controlling profits will probably mean in the end controlling prices.

In the third instance, the government must supervise movements in individual wage rates and prices if it is not simply to freeze the structures of relative wages and prices by following the simple rule of always raising all wage rates and prices by the same percentage. For all practical purposes, the market mechanism is eliminated.

Finally, there is the issue of the type of monetary and fiscal policy that must accompany an incomes or guidepost policy. An inherent part of any such policy, or indeed central plan, must be a monetary and fiscal policy that limits aggregate demand within appropriate noninflationary limits. Failure to do this and allow excess aggregate demand to develop, then a reduction in the price level (at least in the "official" price level) can be achieved only by the introduction of rationing. Neither an incomes nor a guidepost policy contemplates such a possibility. In effect, an incomes policy is not really much of a substitute for appropriate monetary and fiscal policies.

Austrian experience, for instance, is instructive in judging the usefulness of incomes policy. In 1957 Austria created a Price-Wage Commission consisting of representatives from government, management (employers) and labor organizations.[32] The Commission had a basis in law but no authority in the sense that it is a voluntary institution. Every planned price increase is presented to the Commission for "approval," which is given only if justified on "essential" cost increases. Similarly, requests for salary and wage increases are submitted to management only after the Commisssion has checked the amount of increase against possible price increases.

The Austrians apparently have been able to obtain cooperation on the part of both labor and management. The more critical issue, however, is whether the commission had been successful in its anti-inflationary policies. To judge from the opinion of most experts viewing the practice of the commission in handling hundreds of cases, the consensus is that the commission at best achieved a delaying action. It was unable to prevent the strong inflationary pressures in the Austrian economy which subsequently developed. Indeed, considerable concern on the part of the government prompted the institution of more restrictive monetary and fiscal policies.

The Netherlands is often cited as an example of an "effective" incomes policy. The Board of Arbitration has far-reaching powers regarding wage rates and working conditions. It is composed of experts appointed by the government and permanently advised by a so-called Labor-Foundation. The advisory body has a special wage committee to which the central employer and labor organizations send experts. Recommendations of this committee are passed on to the Board of Arbitration. It is also important to note, however, that though labor and management have a strong influence on wage policy in the Netherlands, collective bargaining autonomy does not exist there in the sense that it does, for example, in Sweden, France, Great Britain, Austria, or the United States.

The EEC, however, has collected data on wage costs in its various member countries which bear on the success of the wage policy in the Netherlands, which for all practical purposes is a government wage policy. For example, the increase in wage costs from 1954 to 1961 in Germany and in the Netherlands were almost the same, even though Germany did not have a government wage policy.

More important, it is also obvious to most observers that actual wages in the Netherlands differ signficantly from those established by the government and tied to growth in productivity. The actual or market wages which do reflect economic conditions in the Netherlands are substantially above those planned by the government. The government has undergone what appears to be a useless exercise in price fixing.

Experience in the United States which guideposts suggests that the policy has had no effect on wages, and has affected only a limited number of prices, such as those of steel, aluminum, copper and molybdenum. Some economists would transform the guideposts into a joint attack by government, labor, and management on inflationary pressure in specific "bottleneck" sectors of the economy, for example, construction, transportation, and medical and hospital services.

Notes

1. See, for example, James Tobin, "Friedman's Theoretical Framework," *Journal of Political Economy,* September/October 1972, pp. 852–63; Warren L. Smith, "Neo-Keynesian View of Monetary Policy," in Federal Reserve Bank of Boston, *Controlling Monetary Aggregates,* June 1969, pp. 105–26; Ronald L. Teigen, "A Critical Look at Monetarist Economics," *Review* (Federal Reserve Bank of St. Louis, January 1972), pp. 10–25; A. S. Blinder and R. M. Solow, "Does Fiscal Policy Matter?" *Journal of Public Economics,* November 1973, pp. 319–37; James Tobin and Willem Buiter, "Long-run Effects of Fiscal and Monetary Policy on Aggregate Demand" (Lowes Foundation Discussion Paper No. 384, 13 December 1974); John Kenneth Galbraith, *A Life in Our Times* (Boston: Houghton Mifflin Co., 1981); George Macesich, *The Internatinal Monetary Economy and the Third World* (New York: Praeger Publishers, 1981); and George Macesich and H. Tsai, *Money in Economic Systems* (New York: Praeger Press, 1982); the New York University debate between Milton Friedman and Walter Heller printed in *Monetary Versus Fiscal Policy* (New York: W. W. Norton, 1969).

2. R. Alton Gilbert and Michael E. Trebing, "The FOMC in 1980: A Year of Reserve Targeting," *Review* (Federal Reserve Bank of St. Louis, August/September 1981), pp. 2–22.

3. M1B = (currency + private demand deposits at commercial banks excluding deposits due to foreign commercial banks and official institutions + other checkable deposits, e.g., negotiable order of withdrawal accounts, automatic transfer service accounts, credit union share drafts, and demand deposits at mutual savings banks).

M2 = M1B + savings and small-denomination time deposits at all depository institutions, shares in money market mutual funds, overnight repurchase agreements issued by commercial banks, and overnight Eurodollar deposits held by U.S. residents at Caribbean branches of U.S. banks. Ibid., pp. 5, 16. See also Thomas D. Simpson, "The Redefined Monetary Aggregates," *Federal Reserve Bulletin* (February 1980), p. 100; *Improving Monetary Statistics* (Washington, D.C.: Board of Governors of the Federal Reserve System, 1978).

4. .*The Economist,* 14 November 1981, pp. 102–3. The British monetary target since 1978 is defined as sterling M3 = notes and coin circulation + sterling current account held by British private sector + sterling deposit accounts held by all British residents.

5. Ibid., p. 103.

6. Macesich and Tsai, *Money in Economic Systems.*

7. See also D. Dimitrijević and G. Macesich, *Money and Finance in Contemporary Yugoslavia* (New York: Praeger, 1973); Macesich and Tsai, *Money and Economic Systems;* George Macesich, *Yugoslavia: Theory and Practice of Development Planning* (Charlottesville: The University Press of Virginia, 1964), chap. 9; George Macesich, "Major Trends in the Postwar Economy of Yugoslavia," in Wayne S. Vucinich, ed., *Yugoslavia: Twenty Years of Socialist Experiment* (Berkeley and Los Angeles: University of California Press, 1969).

8. See *Compendium,* the Report of the Commission on Money and Credit, *Money and Credit:*

Their Influence on Jobs, Prices, and Growth (Englewood Cliffs, N.J.: Prentice-Hall, 1961), and *Tax Changes for Shortrun Stabilization,* Joint Economic Committee, 89th Congress, 2d sess. (Washington: U.S. Government Printing Office, 1966). Concern about stabilization policy has been focused primarily on monetary and fiscal policies of the federal government. Many analysts would agree that this focus in federal policy is not misplaced, since stabilization policy is not a major responsibility of state and local governments. The rationale behind this distribution of government functions among levels of government is discussed in Richard A. Musgrave and Peggy B. Musgrave, *Public Finance in Theory and Practice* (New York: McGraw-Hill, 1973), chap. 26. See also *Achieving the Goals of the Employment Act of 1946, Thirtieth Anniversary Review,* Joint Economic Committee, 94th Cong., 2d sess., 3 December 1976.

9. See, for example, *Compendium,* Report of Commission on Money and Credit; L. H. Meyer, "The Balance Sheet Identity, The Government Financing Constraint and the Crowding-Out Effect," *Journal of Monetary Economics,* January 1975, pp. 65–78; A. S. Blinder, R. M. Solow, et al., *The Economics of Public Finance* (Washington, D.C.: The Brookings Institution, 1974).

10. A good discussion of the balanced budget theorem can be found in W. A. Salant, "Taxes, Income Determination, and the Balanced Theorem," *Review of Economics/Statistics,* May 1957, pp. 152–61. For an interesting review of fiscal policy, see J. M. Buchanan, *The Public Finances,* rev. ed. (Homewood: Richard D. Irwin, 1965); Otto Eckstein, *Public Finance,* 3d ed. (Englewood Cliffs, N.J.: Prentice-Hall, 1973).

11. See *Compendium,* Report of the Commission on Money and Credit.

12. See, for example, E. C. Brown, "The Personal Income Tax as an Automatic Stabilizer," *Tax Revision Compendium,* Committee on Wages and Means, House of Representatives, Congress of the U.S. (Washington: Government Printing Office, 1959), pp. 2357–62; G. F. Break and J. A. Pechman, *Federal Tax Reformers: The Impossible Dream* (Washington D.C.: The Brookings Institution, 1975); J. A. Pechman, *Federal Tax Policy* (Washington: The Brookings Institution, 1977).

13. Richard A. Musgrave, "The Incidence of the Tax Structure and the Effects on Consumption," *Federal Tax Policy for Economic Growth and Stability,* Joint Committee on the Economic Report, 84th Cong., 1st sess. (Washington: U.S. Government Printing Office, 1959), pp. 194–205.

14. Robert M. Solow, "Technical Change and the Aggregate Production Function," *Review of Economics and Statistics,* August 1957, pp. 312–20; Norman B. Ture, "Growth Aspects of Federal Tax Policy," *Journal of Finance,* May 1962, pp. 280–88; George Macesich, "Mainsprings of Economic Growth and Development in the United States," *Review of International Affairs,* 5 March 1964.

15. See, for example, R. A. Musgrave, "Effects of Tax Policy on Private Capital Innovation," *Commission on Money and Credit, Fiscal and Debt Management Policies* (Englewood Cliffs, N.J.: Prentice-Hall, 1963), pp. 45–58.

16. Ibid.

17. George F. Break, "Income Tax Rates and Incentives to Work and Invest," *Tax Revision Compendium 3,* Committee of Ways and Means, H. R. (Washington: U.S. Government Printing Office, 1959), pp. 2247–56, and also his article "Income Taxes and Incentives to Work: An Empirical Study," *American Economic Review,* September 1957, pp. 529–49.

18. Clarence D. Long, "Impact of the Federal Income Tax on Labor Force Participation," in *Federal Tax Policy for Economic Growth and Stability* (Papers submitted by panelists appearing before the Subcommittee on Tax Policy of the Joint Economic Committee on the Economic Report, 84th Cong., 1st sess.), pp. 153–66.

19. Royal Commission on the Taxation of Profits and Income, *Second Report* (London: Her Majesty's Stationery Office, 1954), App. I, pp. 91–124.

20. See footnote 17.

21. For the United States, see Phillip Cagan, *The Demand for Currency Relative to Total Money Supply,* Occasional Paper 62 (New York: National Bureau of Economic Research, 1950). For Canada, see George Macesich, *Money and the Canadian Economy,* chap. 7, and "Demand for Currency and Taxation in Canada," *The Southern Economic Journal,* July 1962, pp. 33–38.

22. *Federal Expenditure Policies for Economic Growth and Stability,* Joint Economic Committee, Congress of the United States (Washington: U.S. Government Printing Office, 1957).

23. See, for example, A. H. Gantt, "Central Government: Cash Deficits and Surpluses," *Review of Economics and Statistics,* February 1963, for a comparison of cash deficits and surpluses in

France, Germany, and United Kingdom and the United States; Michael W. Keran, "Monetary and Fiscal Influences of Economic Activity: The Foreign Experience," *Review* (Federal Reserve Bank of St. Louis, February 1970), pp. 16–28.

24. E. S. Kirschen, et al., *Economic Policy in Our Time* (Chicago: Rand McNally, 1964), pp. 38ff.

25. See, for example, George Macesich and Charles T. Stewart, Jr., "Recent Department of Labor Studies of Minimum Wage Effects," *Southern Economic Journal,* April 1960; Marshall R. Colberg, "Minimum Wage Effects on Florida's Economic Development," *Journal of Law and Economics,* October 1960; John M. Peterson, "Recent Needs in Minimum Wage Theory," *Southern Economic Journal,* July 1962; Yale Brozen, "Minimum Wages and Household Workers," *Journal of Law and Economics,* October 1962; and L. G. Reynolds, "Wages and Employment in the Labor-Surplus Economy," *American Economic Review,* March 1965.

26. Macesich and Stewart, "Recent Department of Labor Studies," pp. 288ff.

27. George Macesich, "Are Wage Differentials Resilient? An Empirical Test," *Southern Economic Journal,* April 1961.

28. I am indebted to Drs. Marshall R. Colberg and Charles T. Stewart, Jr., for a number of the following observations regarding these costs. For another view, see Galbraith, *A Life in Our Times.* See also K. Brunner and A. H. Meltzer, eds. *The Economics of Wage and Price Controls,* supplement to *Journal of Monetary Economics* 2, 1976.

29. Marshall C. Clinard, *The Black Market: A Study of White Collar Crime* (New York: Rinehart and Company, 1952), p. 37.

30. Macesich, *Yugoslavia: Theory and Practice of Development Planning.*

31. See, for example, Charles E. Rockwood, "What's Wrong with the Wage Guideposts?" *Business Horizons,* Spring 1966, pp. 25–34.

32. See, for example, the remarks of Professor Theodor Putz, University of Vienna, before the "Seventh Bergedorf Round Table," 15 October 1962, Hamburg, Germany.

6

In Quest of Prosperity and Stability: Revolution and Counterrevolution

American Supply-Side Record

It is useful now to review the American economy's supply record since the early postwar years. The evidence should indicate whether in fact the economy has performed as poorly as argued by critics. It should also suggest whether removal of disincentives, presumably accumulated during the reform-liberal years, could significantly affect the economy. There is little disagreement that since at least 1973 the growth of American output has slowed as a consequence of poor productivity. A good part of the poor performance can be attributed to the supply-side shocks administered by energy price increases relative to other prices and consequent losses in economic capacity. In effect, energy price increases have produced an inward shift of the economy's production possibility frontier.

Consider, first, civilian labor force growth. Between 1948 and 1965 the American labor force has expanded to a 1.2 percent annual rate of growth.[1] From 1965 to 1980 labor force growth accelerated to a 2.3 percent rate. Capital stock rate accelerated at about the same rate up to about 1973. From 1948 to 1965 the stock of plant and equipment rose at a 4.1 percent. It spurted to a 4.9 percent rate from 1965 to 1975, then dropped to a 3.0 rate from 1975 to 1980.

These figures thus suggest that there has been no major deterioration of resource growth rates. As a matter of fact, the supply of available resources expanded much faster during the period 1965–1975 than in the earlier period.

To be sure, the evidence does suggest that the unemployment rate associated with full employment conditions has risen since the 1950s, as we noted earlier. It has not reversed the pattern of accelerated labor force growth indicated by data on "labor force participation rate." Even more important, the growing unemployment rate does not seem to be significantly associated with growing supply-side disincentives.[2] Of course, some policies do produce a withdrawal from the labor force, for example, minimum wages which reduce opportunities especially for the young and inexperienced, and social security arrangements which encourage older and more experienced workers to retire earlier. Changes in demographic composition of the labor force appear to account for much of the increase in the full-employment unemployment rate.

An expanded government sector which draws resources from the private sector where productivity tends to be higher appears to have peaked in 1973–75 in terms of federal, state, and local government purchases of goods and services, as well as in the share of employment as a percentage of the civilian labor force. It is thus difficult to show that government has constrained output growth by altering the allocation of resources away from the private sector.[3]

The most likely candidate as a major source of disincentive for production and growth is the significant and rapid increase in government transfer payments.[4] This is also the most serious area of contention between reform-liberals who argue that tax increases to pay for increased transfer payments do no more than redistribute purchasing power with no real effects on demand, price, or aggregate output. Critics disagree. In their view, increased transfers and taxes create disincentives to supplying resources in the market.

On balance, the supply-side record for the American economy does not suggest that radical supply-side policies will produce spectacular results. More likely, the effects on resource availability, growth, and efficiency will be modest. Reduction in marginal tax rates may remove disincentives on work effort. Supply-side-oriented policies may also encourage, at least temporarily, investment and productivity growth. Only in the area of recent capital formation is there clear resource supply shortfall, and this is explained by energy price increases rather than strictly government policy actions. In fact, it appears that the principal determinants of stagflationary developments since 1973 and 1979–80 have been the sharp supply-shocks generated by increases in the relative price of energy.[5] Indeed, they appear also to account for most of the post-1973 decline in capital formation.

To the extent that the American economy was successful for the first twenty-five years after World War II, reform-liberals are entitled to some of the credit. Insofar as things have gone wrong since then, they would not wish to shift all of the blame to others.

What is of more interest are those people who have come to recognize the changing nature of the economy in the 1970s and 1980s. Central to their preoccupations are the shocks applied to the economy on the supply side. Related to them is the decline in the underlying growth rate caused by such things as high energy costs, lower investment, and a new lack of belief in growth. The evidence also supports the conclusions that monetary policy should be formulated with a longer-term focus. Such a focus implies that inflation, rather than unemployment, should serve as the primary guideline for aggregate demand policy. This does not mean that policymakers should ignore unemployment; rather, long-term benefits to society will be greater if stabilization policies hold to a relatively stable path of monetary growth, as Monetarists urge.

Failure of Fine Tuning

Interventionist or active monetary and fiscal policies advocated by reform-liberals and Keynesians, and characterized as "fine tuning," are now viewed not as a solution to the stabilization problem but as the problem. The slow-down in real growth carrying with it rising unemployment suggests that monetary and fiscal policies should be stimulative. The quickening and persistence of inflation in the 1970s and 1980s, on the other hand, seems to call for monetary and fiscal restraint. This conjunction of developments, called *stagflation* as we have noted, thus poses a dilemma in policy matters.

This dilemma is summed up, as discussed, in the Phillips Curve, whereby inflation and unemployment are viewed as symmetrical problems—too stimulative an economic policy brings inflation while one too restrictive increases unemployment. Stabilization policy is "fine-tuned" to provide just the right growth of total demand so that neither inflation nor unemployment occurs. Events of the 1970s quickly demonstrated that the Phillips Curve fell short of providing an adequate explanation. Inflation persisting in the face of rising unemployment runs counter to predictions based on the Phillips Curve. These events cast doubt that there exists a "right" amount of total demand that will permit the achievement of both full employment and price stability.

Indeed, our discussion elsewhere is consistent with the evidence summarized and presented by D. R. Francis of the St. Louis Federal Reserve Bank, which suggests that a sustainable "low level of unemployment *cannot* be obtained for the purchase price of a higher rate of inflation—for short periods the relationship between inflation and unemployment may exist but the experience of the last four or five years has provided evidence casting serious doubt on the validity of the Phillips Curve relation over the long run."[6]

According to the evidence presented by Francis, for the U.S. from early 1952 to the fall of 1962, when monetary growth averaged 1.8 percent, unemployment averaged 4.9 of the labor force; from the fall of 1962 to the end of 1966, when money accelerated to a 3.8 percent rate of growth, unemployment also averaged 4.9 percent. Starting in 1966, however, when money increased to 6 percent a year, unemployment also increased, averaging 4.7 percent. Since the late sixties, the evidence indicates that accelerating money growth is accompanied by accelerating inflation. This suggests that the unemployment rate may not be a very useful guide to monetary policy.[7] If the focus of policy is on the price level, other policies may well be required to deal with the problems of unemployment.

Our discussion indicates that essentially two principal views emerged in the 1960s and 1970s on the issue of simultaneously slowing price increases and maintaining employment growth. One stresses the short-run trade-off between prices and unemployment, and the other emphasizes the absence of a stable long-run relationship between varying rates of anticipated price changes and the level of unemployment.[8]

The "trade-off" view does not focus on unemployment as a determinant of prices directly. The view argues that unemployment and the rate of change of unemployment influence money wages and wage changes, and, in turn, bring about changes in the level of prices. According to this view, several factors such as profits, cost-of-living, and additional employment pressures determine wage changes, though unemployment pressures appear to be the most significant determinant. Of particular importance for policy purposes is the stability of the Phillips Curve and prices (wages) employment relationship. The evidence suggests that, in fact, such stability does not exist.

The principal argument of the "long-run equilibrium view" is that trade-offs between wages or prices and unemployment are a transitory phenomenon. Once other factors have completely adjusted to the trend in spending growth, no "trade-off" exists. To be sure, in the short run there can be a discrepancy between expectations and actual price or wage changes, but not in the long run. After the discrepancies between expected and actual values have worked themselves out, the only relevant magnitudes are "real," or price deflated.[9] As soon as a new price trend becomes stabilized and fully anticipated, nominal and real wages will coincide and unemployment will fall to its natural rate. In other words, an inflationary policy is neither a necessary nor a sufficient condition for the attainment of high levels of employment.

Both views recommend that other policy tools are required to deal with problems of unemployment and thus complement monetary and fiscal measures. Employment policies geared toward improving the efficiency of operation of labor markets are recommended. Economists espousing both views recommend that steps be taken to improve job skills and facilitate the dissemination of information relating to job openings. Certain structural impediments to the efficient operation of labor markets should be removed or modified, such as minimum wage laws and restrictions on occupational mobility. They also recommend that the system of unemployment compensation receive additional study to see if, in fact, the system actually diminishes the incentive to work.

The futility of such a general measure as the 1978 Humphrey-Hawkins Full Employment and Balanced Growth Act is but a case in point. This law requires government to set five-year goals for the American economy. The goals are to be stated in numerical terms each year, and the President is to present a program for achieving these goals. Furthermore, the act specified that the first "economic plan" have as goals, for five years later in 1983, an unemployment rate of 3 percent for most workers and 3 percent also for the rate of inflation as measured by the CPI.

Some of the rhetoric at the time of the act's passage seemed to suggest that Congress had by its action delivered to those wanting jobs abundant employment opportunities and to those worried about inflation a reasonably stable price level. The evidence is that it had nothing of the sort. The unemployment goal rate for 1983, for example, has moved upward from 4 percent set at the beginning of 1979, to 7.9 percent set as that year's target in January 1982. And the goal for 1983's rate of inflation moved from 3 percent put forward at the beginning of 1979, to an 8.2 percent goal set in January 1981, to 5.2 percent set early in 1982. There is little in this record to suggest confidence in the ability of Congress to mandate unemployment and inflation rates.

Declining Influence of Reform-Liberals and Keynesian Ideas

Reform-liberals drawing on Keynes' intellectual contributions to political economy provided the necessary revolutionary zeal that spread the gospel through the English-speaking world, and after the war to continental Europe and Japan. The ideas of full-employment and how to achieve it through interventionist and discretionary monetary and fiscal policies by the central government were high on the agenda of reform-liberals and their intellectual allies abroad.

In the United States, as we discussed earlier, the Employment Act of 1946 dedicated federal power to the achievement of "maximum employment, production, and purchasing power." Indeed, by 1947 the federal government had assumed responsibilities for all sorts of social insurance and safety net schemes designed to ensure national prosperity and stability. Keynesian ideas do not necessarily support or oppose various "welfare-state" measures even though, as we noted, Keynes was confident that the more serious shortcomings of capitalism such as unemployment and arbitrary and inequitable distribution of wealth and income could be overcome by judicious application of the ideas and policies he advocated.

It was left to reform liberals to articulate these ideas into practice in the postwar period. These ideas were most forcefully advanced by Nobel prizewinner Professor Paul Samuelson. He is the principal architect of the synthesis of Keynesian and neoclassical ideas that became the American mainline economics in the postwar era. Accordingly, the country can have full employment, growth, and stability — all with a degree of the income-redistributing taxation it ethically desires. Capitalism can work within egalitarian policies. It no longer must fear the business cycle and the periodic breakdowns whose solutions perplexed classical and neoclassical economists for over 200 years.

Not everyone, of course, shared the optimism of Keynes, Samuelson, and like-minded reform-liberals. Those to the political right and left of reform liberalism doubted the validity of these claims, even when for two and a half postwar decades events seemed to justify the optimism. By the late 1950s and mid-1960s, their anxieties increased. General disillusionment set in with the stagflation of the 1970s—the combination of high inflation and high unemployment.

For an answer, some economists turned to Professor Friedrich Hayek, leader of neoliberalism and recipient of the Nobel prize in 1974. Professor J. R. Hicks writes that it is easily forgotten that Hayek's ideas rivaled those of Keynes in the early 1930s.[10] The issue was unemployment, but since Hayek's theories also included the likelihood of rising prices, attention was focused on Keynes' ideas of inadequate aggregate demand and interventionist government policies.

Inflation, according to Hayek, is caused chiefly by government control and manipulation of money.[11] In fact, writes Hayek, "Government's everywhere and at all times have been the chief cause of depreciation of the currency. Though there have been occasional prolonged falls in the value of a metallic money, the major inflations of the past have been the result of governments' either diminishing the coin or issuing excessive quantities of paper money."[12] Manipulation of money by government is encouraged by extensive debt financing undertaken for various political reasons, including providing more social services to its citizens.

Government support of labor unions—whereby they are "permitted" to force up wages and thus create unemployment—is irresponsible exercise of political authority. For once unemployment is so created, government must step in to remove it by increasing the money supply and thus validating union action. As a result, the government is little more than a monetary hostage to union desires.

The problem of inflation can be avoided, according to Hayek, by stabilizing the rate of growth of the money supply. This may be accomplished along lines suggested by Friedman, although Hayek has other proposals, one of which we discuss in this study. The objective is to remove monetary policy actions as a source of uncertainty to private decisionmakers, while at the same time lessening inflationary pressures. As noted elsewhere in this study, Hayek's views on the monetary organization are in keeping with those of the Austrian School. The money supply and the monetary organization are not candidates for manipulation, any more than are a society's legal institutions. On this issue the Austrians are more rigid than Chicago Monetarists.

Hicks finds Hayek's scenario of rising prices and unemployment possible under certain conditions. For instance, unemployment can occur owing to a decline in the marginal productivity of labor. If labor fails to accept a decline in real wages, unemployment could increase simultaneously with rising general level of prices. Several circumstances may produce a fall in the marginal productivity of labor, and so a decline in real wages. Rapid population growth, destruction of capital through war or political upheaval, and unfavorable foreign trade conditions are the more obvious causes which can produce a fall in the marginal productivity of labor.

Indeed, Hicks writes,

> It is by no means excluded that it should happen for Hayek's reason: in the aftermath of an attempted expansion greater than the economy was able or willing to afford . . . so that it has been abortive. If shortages develop for such a cause, prices will rise. . . . There may be rapid inflation; but if it is to be kept down to a finite rate of inflation, there must be unemployment. This is the Hayek 'slump'. To such conditions the Keynesian prescription is irrelevant, as irrelevant as Hayek's was in 1931.[13]

The evidence does suggest that in the quarter century after World War II, the economy was overstimulated for a number of years. To be sure, in the postwar period, discretionary monetary and fiscal policies had a mixed record in reducing cyclical fluctuations that were indeed mild by historical standards. By the 1970s these discretionary policies oscillated between attempts to combat inflation and attempts to combat unemployment, with poor timing and with, for the most part, indifferent and perverse results. In effect, the turbulent 1970s were dominated by discretionary policies and by seemingly uncontrollable inflation, recessions, sharp declines in real wages, unemployment, energy problems, as well as various raw materials shortages. They stand in marked contrast to the comparatively prosperous early postwar years, which appeared to justify the optimism of reform liberals.

The "stagflationary" disappointments of the 1970s, the high rates of unemployment, inflation, and interest, the depressed stock market, the slowdowns of productivity and growth and capital formation discredited reform-liberalism and ushered in a political and ideological counterrevolution spearheaded by Monetarism and neoliberalism in the form of "Reaganomics" in the United States and "Thatcherism" in Great Britain. Just as Keynesian theory inspired the revolution, so a wave of professional reaction to the synthesis of Keynesian and neoclassical doctrines that became orthodoxy in the 1950s and 1960s sustains the counterrevolution. We have discussed elsewhere the important intellectual role of Milton Friedman, the Monetarists, and the Chicago School in bringing about the counterrevolution. Suffice it to say here, the doctrines of reform liberalism considered new at the turn of the century and into the Depression are discredited, and now challenged, by the doctrines of neoliberalism and monetarism of more than a hundred years ago. These doctrines now appear to be guiding philosophies of Congress, Parliament, president and prime minister. To be sure, there are many divergencies in economic theory, popular ideology and actual policy. Nevertheless, the counterrevolution has compelled a debate on the economic assumptions of the last two generations. It has at the same time questioned the growth of government power and intervention in economic and political affairs.

Central Banks and Monetary Targets

We have already called attention to the issue of means and ends raised in several countries regarding the methods of monetary control. How can a central bank control monetary growth? One approach is through interest rates. The other is by controlling the monetary base directly. Interest rates affect the demand for money, as suggested elsewhere. But the interest rate effects may be overwhelmed by other effects. This suggests that the central bank is better advised to operate more directly on the supply of money through the monetary base. These magnitudes can be controlled. As a result, monetary growth can be affected in more predictable ways than through interest rates.

Monetarist preference for a "monetary aggregate target" rather than a "money market target" as the appropriate target for monetary policy is closely associated with their view of the control of nominal and real rates of interest. As we discussed earlier, Monetarists hold that the authorities are at best able to fix the nominal rate of interest.[14] Their theory on the real rate of interest emphasizes the importance between the nominal market rate of interest and the real rate of interest. Only if the expected rate of inflation is equal will nominal and real rates of interest be zero.

The choice of an indicator that will quickly and accurately give the direction and magnitude of monetary policy is also closely associated wih the Monetarist preference for a "monetary aggregate target." A useful indicator must possess such characteristics as a high degree of correlation with the target variables; accurate and reliable statistics on the indicator, quickly available to authorities; and exogeny rather than endogeny — monetary authorities should be capable of controlling the variable. Indeed, Anna J. Schwartz eliminates the distinction between targets and indicators.[15]

In fact, the ideal target, Schwartz argues, ought to be judged on three criteria: (1) Is it measurable? (2) Is it subject to control by central banks? (3) Is it a reliable indicator of monetary conditions? On the basis of data for the U.K., Canada, and Japan, Schwartz concludes that the money stock is the best "target-indicator." Similar conclusions are reached in other studies."[16]

I have presented results elsewhere suggesting that central banks only rarely succeed in hitting monetary targets.[17] When they miss, it is nearly always in overshooting, creating "base-drift." The base-drift problem occurs if the supply of money ends up above its ceiling, raising the issue of what should be used as the starting point for the next target. By unsettling financial markets, "base-drift" creates additional difficulties for the monetary authority in its effort to achieve longer-term monetary goals.

How seriously, then, should governments react to such signals? If the monetary target is a single measure, there is little choice with which to judge policy. In low inflation countries — Japan, Switzerland, West Germany — this would not seem to be a problem. Their narrow and broad definitions of money have been moving closely in line with each other. When they decide to change target rates, the choice is clear. The United States uses several target definitions so as to assure itself that a broad thrust of policy is correct. If all targets are missed, then clearly something is wrong and presumably something else is required.

Our discussion of the rational expectations theory suggests at least one reason for lack of better performance in target practice on the part of central banks. Another is the public's diminished credibility in the monetary authorities and the central bank to behave in a consistent fashion.[18] For these reasons, among others, monetary authorities are urged to abandon short-term stabilization attempts altogether and to pursue instead a credible long-term steady state policy. One such policy is a constant money growth rule proposed by Milton Friedman and the Monetarists. It is an idea that has been widely discussed for years. We shall trace its evolution in the next chapter, for it is an important weapon in the Monetarist arsenal.[19]

Evidence also suggests why central banks have not adopted a "fixed monetary rule." It may well be, as some economists argue, including this writer, that discretionary policies serve the established bureaucracies. Such a policy permits them to take credit when economic conditions are good and allow for disclaimers of responsibility when economic conditions deteriorate.

Another reason for such reluctance may be in the degree of "independence" possessed by central banks.[20] Such independence depends on (1) the method of appointment of governors; (2) the length of time that they serve; (3) whether they have legislated objectives clear enough to be a barrier to government intervention; and (4) whether their constitutions provide the bank or the government with the final authority for monetary policy. In practice, central banks may have rather less, or rather more, freedom than their charters suggest. This is likely to depend on tradition as well as on the personalities involved.

Only the German Bundesbank has final authority for monetary policy. The governor, moreover, is not directly appointed by the government. The National Bank of Yugoslavia is an independent federal institution, established by federal law. The bank is managed by the governor, who is appointed by the Federal Assembly on the recommendation of the Federal Executive Council. He is responsible to both of these institutions for the implementation of bank operations and targets. The Federal Assembly and the Federal Executive Council decide monetary policy targets, and the National Bank is responsible only for their implementation. In policy formation the National Bank, nonetheless, plays a significant if not dominant role in monetary policy, thanks to ready acceptance of its proposals by policy makers.

The central bank of the Netherlands has a clearly defined objective of price stability built into its constitution. On no other score could it be considered independent. In fact, the world's two oldest central banks, Riksbank of

Sweden (1668) and the Bank of England (1694) are clearly subservient to their governments in the formation of monetary policy. In the United States and Germany, central bank control rests with a board composed of the heads of the several regional banks, thereby allowing for greater "independence" from the central government.

It is not surprising that central banks find themselves in the uncomfortable position where monetary and fiscal policies meet. They must meet the requirements of their governments. This means ensuring that the government is able to function smoothly in meeting its financial obligation. In many countries, government borrowing in the 1970s has resulted in regular deficits, and debt has risen as a proportion of gross national product.

Concern with inflation calls attention to the growth in the money supply. Governments have reacted by setting formal targets for monetary growth. Since central banks must now try and achieve monetary targets while at the same time ostensibly financing much larger public sector borrowing, their job is made all the more difficult. Their lack of enthusiasm in embracing monetarism is understandable. Such an embrace would impose severe constraints on the exercise of discretionary monetary authority. On the other hand, a clearly defined policy of rules would remove central banks from the political quagmire in which they now find themselves stuck while in pursuit of illusory goals.

Notes

1. The supply-side figures in this section are from J. A. Tatom, "We All Are Supply-siders Now," *Review* (Federal Reserve Bank of St. Louis, May 1981), pp. 18–30.

2. D. Hamermesh, "Transfers, Texas, and the Nairu," in Laurence H. Meyer, ed., *The Supply-Side Effects of Economic Policy* (St. Louis Center for the Study of American Business and Federal Reserve Bank of St. Louis, 1981). NAIRU is the nonaccelerating inflation rate of unemployment and is comparable to the "natural rate of unemployment" or the full employment rate.

3. In fact, Tatom reports, "Other forms of capital formation, including government, show the same slowing as that in the business sector. From 1960 to 1973, the growth of the federal government capital stock was at a 1.1 percent rate; from 1973 to 1980, this growth rate declined to a 0.4 percent rate. For state and local governments, the decline was from a 4.8 percent to a 2.0 percent rate from 1973 to 1980." (Tatom, "We All Are Supply-siders Now," p. 27.)

4. See for example, Macesich, *The International Monetary Economy and the Third World*.

5. See J. A. Tatom, "Energy Prices and Capital Formation: 1972–1977," *Review* (Federal Reserve Bank of St. Louis, May 1979), pp. 2–11. For a discussion of the optimal monetary policy response to energy supply shocks, see A. S. Blinder, "Monetary Accommodation of Supply Shocks," *Journal of Money Credit and Banking*, November 1981, pp. 425–38.

6. D. R. Francis, "Inflation, Recession—What's a Policy Maker To Do?, *Review* (Federal Reserve Bank of St. Louis, November 1974), p. 17.

7. Milton Friedman, "The Role of Monetary Policy," *The American Economic Review*, March 1968, p. 10; Albert Rees and Mary T. Hamilton, "The Wage-Price-Productivity Perplex," *Journal of Political Economy*, February 1967, p. 70; E. S. Phelps, "Money-Wages Dynamics and Labor Market Equilibrium," *Journal of Political Economy*, July/August 1968, p. 686.

8. See, for example, R. W. Spence, "The Relation Between Prices and Employment: Two Views," *Review* (Federal Reserve Bank of St. Louis, March 1969), pp. 15–21. See also I. M.

McDonald and R. M. Solow, "Wage Bargaining and Employment," *American Economic Review,* December 1981, pp. 896–908; G. A. Akerlof and B.G.M. Main, "An Experience-Weighted Measure of Employment and Unemployment Durations," *American Economic Review,* December 1981, pp. 1003–11.

    9. Friedman, "Role of Monetary Policy," p. 10.

    10. J. R. Hicks, *Critical Essays in Monetary Theory* (London: Oxford University Press, 1967).

    11. F. A. Hayek, *The Constitution of Liberty* (Chicago: University of Chicago Press, 1960).

    12. Ibid., pp. 327–28. See also F. A. Hayek, *Monetary Theory and the Trade Cycle* (London: Jonathan Cape, 1933), *Prices and Production* (London: George Routledge & Sons, 1946), and *Profits, Interest and Investment and Other Essays on the Theory of Industrial Fluctuations* (London: George Routledge & Sons, 1939),

    13. Hicks, *Critical Essays in Monetary Theory,* p. 215.

    14. See George Macesich, *Monetarism: Theory and Policy* (New York: Praeger Publishers, 1983).

    15. Anna J. Schwartz, "Short-Term Targets of Three Foreign Central Banks," in Karl Brunner, ed., *Targets and Indicators of Monetary Policy* (San Francisco: Chandler Publishing Co., 1969).

    16. Macesich, *Monetarism: Theory and Policy.*

    17. George Macesich and H. Tsai, *Money in Economic Systems* (New York: Praeger Publishers, 1983).

    18. For a discussion of the credibility hypothesis, see William Fellner, *Toward a Reconstruction of Macroeconomics: Problems of Theory and Policy* (Washington, D.C.; American Enterprise Institute, 1976) and Macesich, *Monetarism: Theory and Policy.*

    19. See also Macesich, *Monetarism: Theory and Policy.*

    20. See Macesich and Tsai, *Money in Economic Systems.*

7

Monetary Rules and Discretionary Authority

Appeal of Discretionary Monetary Authority

Central bankers view their conduct of monetary policy as an "art," which thus leaves the policy system conveniently undefined and open to their discretionary control. They will not voluntarily give up their discretionary authority for that of a monetary policy defined and constrained by the behavior of the money supply as urged by Monetarists. This is understandable. There is, after all, a problem of power.[1]

Monetary Rules and Their Proponents

In a broad sense, an ancestral lineage could be established between today's proponents of a monetary rule and such time-honored challengers of convention and banking school ideas as, for example, the Currency School or the Bullionists. In a stricter sense, however, the origin of monetary rules is usually dated and personified more precisely: the year given is 1936, the author quoted is Henry C. Simons.[2]

Simons' proposal of 1936 was not altogether new. In its underlying theoretical analysis, the importance of the development of the quantity theory of money from John Locke to Irving Fisher is clear. The proposal's affinity with the earlier "100 Percent Reserve Plan" is also clear.[3] Simons' first mention of monetary rules is contained in a 1934 pamphlet, where a rule or rules are part of a larger program for bank reform better known today as the Chicago Plan, and economic reform in general.[4] Among five proposals presented "in a descending scale of relative importance," the proposal with reference to banking and currency ranks second only to the "elimination of private monopoly in all its forms":

Establishment of more definite and adequate "rules of the game" with respect to money, through

1. Abolition of private deposit banking on the basis of fractional reserves
2. Establishment of a completely homogeneous, national circulating medium, and
3. Creation of a system under which a federal monetary authority has a direct and inescapable responsibility for controlling (not with broad

discretionary powers, but under simple, definite rules laid down in legislation) the quantity (or, through quantity, the value) of effective money.[5]

At the same time, Simons states that "the adoption of one among the several definite and unambiguous rules . . . is more important than the choice among them."[6] An observation which most subsequent proponents of monetary rules have not only accepted but emphasized as well.

The kinds of rules that Simons is referring to include on one end of the spectrum a constant quantity of money and on the other a rule based on the stabilization of some price index. While Simons in his final position accepted a rule expressed in terms of a price index, he nevertheless felt "that his earlier persuasion as to the merits of the rule of a fixed quantity of money was fundamentally correct."[7] But the latter rule cannot be implemented, Simons argues, because we have not attained what he calls the *ideal financial structure.*[8] *This structure should include a "sharp differentiation between money and private obligations" in order to increase the power "of the central government . . . to create money and effective money substitutes."[9] In more specific terms, his argument against the rule of keeping the quantity of money constant in practice is based on what is today known as the Gurley-Shaw Thesis;*[10] the possibility, that is, "of sharp changes on the velocity side" due to "the perverse variability in the amounts of 'near-moneys.' "[11]

The stabilization of some price index thus represents the second-best, though unsatisfactory, solution to Simons:

> If price-level stabilization is a poor system, it is . . . infinitely better than no system at all. And it seems now highly questionable whether any better system is feasible or possible at all within the significant future.[12]

On this score Simons agrees at least in principle with other economists and Congressional committees of his time.[13] With them he sees one reason for the second-best nature of price stabilization in the difficulties presented by the definition of a particular index.[24] More important, according to Simons, is another disadvantage of rules in terms of some price index:

> All these schemes . . . define programs in terms of ends, with little discussion of appropriate means; they call for an authority with a considerable range for discretionary actions, and would require much intelligence and judgment in their administration; and they would leave us exposed to continuous legislative (if not administrative) tinkering.[15]

Here it becomes obvious that Simons' "underlying position may be characterized as severly libertarian or, in the English-Continental sense, liberal," with, he points out, the "emphasis upon liberty as both a requisite and a measure of progress."[16]

This is important, since the major emphasis in Simons' political-economic program is not placed on specific or even quantitative economic targets but on the ethical values of liberty or freedom. This inherent liberal persuasion thus entails one of the distinctive features of Simons' approach and argumentation.

Another early proponent of a monetary rule, though not talking in terms of rules, is Carl Snyder, who concludes from his empirical analysis:

> As trade and production as a whole grow at a fairly fixed and definite rate, then for the maintenance of price stability the volume of the media of exchange or bank credit must increase at the same rate.[17]

In contrast to Simons, Snyder derives his conclusion from a target-oriented, quantitative analysis. With this approach and his proposal in terms of "controlling the volume of bank credit, maintaining its increase at a fixed and predetermined rate per annum,"[18] he is in surprisingly close proximity to some of today's proponents of monetary rules.

Another contemporary and close colleague of Simons, Lloyd W. Mints, is usually associated with the former in his ideas as to the proper management of monetary policy.[19] The existing differences between Mints and Simons are more a matter of emphasis than of substance. Both believe in the inherent stability of the "free" economic system; both feel that some rule would be better than none; both mention the desirability of, and at the same time similar difficulties concerning, a constant quantity of money; and both conclude that price-level stabilization may be the most feasible—even if difficult to implement—guide for monetary policy.

Some differences do exist in the valuation of objectives or targets. Mints seems to place greater emphasis on monetary stability per se as compared to Simons' ultimate objective of liberty. And in the degree of special analysis concerning some details, Mints analyzes some of the questions under more technical aspects. He discusses, for example, various indexes in terms of stabilization, and concludes that "an index of wholesale prices is probably the best guide for monetary action".[20] He then expands this discussion by also considering international aspects of the questions involved;[21] and, following a suggestion by Milton Friedman, he analyzes the possible effect of lags, concluding tentatively that "the evidence then . . . affords no confirmation of the contention that lags in the effectiveness of changes in the stock of money might accentuate fluctuations in the level of prices."[22] Again, however, there is not detailed description of how the guide of price level stabilization may be translated into a simple monetary rule.

Starting from rather similar bases but different dispositions, Clark Warburton and Milton Friedman both come up with at least superficially similar conclusions and proposals, the differences in which, though not trivial, are mostly more a matter of specific detail than of general substance.[23] Clark Warburton, like Friedman, arrived at his final conclusion only after extensive empirical studies.[24] These studies led to two important findings. First:

Scrutiny of . . . quarterly measures of quantity and circuit velocity of money, adjusted for trend, showed that the quantity of money led and its circuit velocity lagged at the turning points of business cycles. In fact, the departure in the quantity of money from a reasonable rate of growth occurred during the preceding boom phase of the cycle, and thus not only preceded a reduction in the rate of use of money but also the top of the boom. It was these observations which led to the emphasis . . . on an erratic money supply as the chief originating factor in business recessions and not merely an intensifying force in the case of severe depressions.[25]

And second:

The influence of Federal Reserve action, together with monetary policies such as the Treasury price of gold, has been so overwhelmingly dominant that it is a realistic and truthful statement to say that the supply of money in the United States is the result of the *de facto* monetary policy of the United States government. The conclusion cannot be avoided that federal government agencies, particularly the Federal Reserve authorities, have been responsible for the drastic and erratic variability of the quantity of money in the United States since the close of World War I.[26]

From these findings and inferences Warburton derives his conclusion and proposal for monetary policy: a constant rate of growth in the quantity of money.[27]

At least in principle, this is the same conclusion as the one reached by Friedman. However, Friedman arrives at his proposal following a different road, which in part, in its beginning, seems to have been staked out by Simons and Mints. Friedman is an early critic of discretionary monetary policy.[28] Through his research with Anna J. Schwartz at the National Bureau of Economic Research, he too arrives at the rule "that the stock of money be increased at a fixed rate year in and year out."[29] His subsequent research and studies helped to underpin his initial conviction and to enlarge and specify the proposal.[30]

A more precise delineation of the characteristics of the two proposals by Warburton and Friedman can probably best be achieved by comparing some of the major issues involved. The first issue is the general background of, or reason for, the proposal. As mentioned before, Friedman started out with a fairly strong inclination for some rule and against "the uncertainty and undesirable political implications of discretionary action by government authorities."[31] At the same time, however, he emphasizes a possible other, more pragmatic disadvantage of discretion — lags in response: "Long and variable lags could convert the fluctuations in the government contribution to the income stream into the equivalent of an additional random disturbance."[32] These initial premonitions about lags later became a conviction through his research on the lag in the effect of monetary policy, and the corresponding argument in favor of his proposal achieved importance. Friedman thus believes that the "contribution to economic stability" by the rule "is the most that we can ask from monetary policy at our present stage of knowledge," though, as he points out, "other forces would still affect the economy . . . and disturb the even tenor of our ways.³³

Warburton, on the other hand, while not disregarding the possible effect of lags, places less emphasis on them, "and their existence is not crucial to his proposal."³⁴ At the same time, he seems to consider—even more so than Friedman—"monetary . . . policy as the overwhelmingly important originating factor in serious economic disturbances".³⁵ Or, as Richard T. Selden states; "Warburton comes close to accepting a monetary theory of business cycles, for mild and severe cycles alike."³⁶

The second issue refers to the general framework surrounding the proposal. For Warburton, the only statutory change of major importance is the directive concerning the implementation of the rule itself. While he is in favor, for example, of retirement of the Federal Reserve stock, reduction in the number of members of the Board of Governors, abolishment of Regulation Q, and some of the changes with regard to reserve requirements, he emphasizes "how admirable the central banking machinery, with the existing type of banking institutions, could serve . . . if given the proper directive by Congress."³⁷

He therefore takes issue with Friedman, who regards the rule as the most important part, but as one part only, of the desirable change in the monetary system. Among his many recommendations are the elimination of fractional-reserve banking, of the discount window, of the prohibition of interest payment on demand deposits, and of Regulation Q.³⁸ As incisive as these changes may be, they are not indispensable.

> The problems of the organization of the Federal Reserve System are extremely important so long as . . . two guidelines . . . are not in effect. If these guidelines were put into effect, the problem of organization would become of little importance because the present power of the Federal Reserve System to introduce instability into the economy would be eliminated.³⁹

The two guidelines Friedman is referring to here are a constant rate of growth of the money supply and competitively determined interest rates.

The third and last issue concerns the more pragmatic or technical aspects of the rule—the question of the definition of money, seasonal adjustment, specific rate of growth in the money supply, and the general flexibility of the rule.

Both Friedman and Warburton are in favor of using an expanded version of the conventional definition of money. Whereas Friedman's proposal is in terms of currency held by the public, plus adjusted demand and time deposits in commercial banks, Warburton considers several other concepts as well.⁴⁰

Differences in emphasis seem to exist between Warburton and Friedman as to the question of whether allowance ought to be made in the proposal for seasonal variation. Warburton tends to favor seasonal adjustment, while Friedman, after initial doubts, reaches the "tentative conclusion to dispense with seasonal adjustments" because "there is no seasonal to adjust until a decision is made what seasonal to introduce."[41]

The remaining two questions — the actual growth rate of the money supply, and its flexibility — are closely related. In their respective answers, Friedman and Warburton have developed what appear to be rather marked differences. Friedman has suggested growth rates between 3 and 5 percent per year, and on more theoretical grounds a growth rate of 2 percent.[42] However, in his own words, "I have always emphasized that a *steady* and known rate of increase in the quantity of money is more important than the precise numerical value of the rate of increase.[43]

Warburton has proposed similar growth rates, with possible slight variations depending on the concept of money used. He arrived at these rates the same way Friedman did — by allowing for a certain percentage decrease in secular velocity.[44] But Warburton's emphasis seems to be more on an average range for the rate of growth in money than on its absolute constancy. When he states that aside from seasonal adjustments, "adjustments . . . may be needed on account of . . . any other conditions which have been demonstrated to require variations from the calculated line of growth in the quantity of money in order to maintain stability of prices of final products,[45] he creates some uncertainty as to the specific content of his proposal. Compared to Friedman, who believes in a much more rigid application of the rule, Warburton seems to be closer to supporters of what might be called *formula flexibility.*"

In discussions of monetary rules, the proposal made by Edward S. Shaw is usually associated with Friedman's rigid rule, which has become known as the "Friedman-Shaw proposal." A reasonable degree of similarity seems to exist with but one major exception: Shaw's preference as to the definition of money, though flexible, seems to lie with the conventional concept.[46] Two other supporters of what Shaw calls "the principle of 'look-Ma-no-hands' in money management" are Robert L. Crouch and Leland Yeager.[47]

James W. Angell has suggested a monetary rule which may initially appear akin to Warburton's proposal, at least as far as the degree of flexibility is concerned.[48] However, Angell would apply the rule to the achievable money supply or indirectly to the commercial bank reserve base. Considering his additional proposals, which include more frequent use of stronger selective controls, "it is obvious that Angell does not look with favor on the Warburton-Friedman proposals.[49] Phillip Cagan, on the other hand, seems to be in almost complete agreement with Warburton.[50]

Several other economists have suggested rules in terms of formula flexibility.[51] The element that all their various proposals have in common as compared to Warburton's rule, for example, is a built-in adjustment mechanism, leading to automatic adjustments in the rate of growth of the money supply whenever certain specified changes can be detected in the economy. These changes, and the frequency with which they are to be considered, represent the distinguishing elements of the proposals within this group.

For instance, Hosek favors a rate of growth of the money supply at "a rate that is equal to the expected rate of growth in potential GNP . . . after the money supply is initially raised to the full employment level."[52] Bronfenbrenner, on the other hand, suggests that "the growth rate of the money supply should equal the sum of the growth rates of the labor force and average labor productivity, less the growth rate of the velocity of circulation of money.[53] Adjustments based on observations of the past should be made every month or quarter. In addition, Bronfenbrenner also favors setting upper and lower limits to the annual rate of growth of the money supply in the vicinity of 8 percent and 1 percent "regardless of the formula's occasional vagaries."[54]

It is this kind of a range or band which quite a few economists have adopted as the centerpiece of their proposals. Representatives of this group include Karl Brunner, Gregory C. Chow, Carl F. Christ, Thomas Mayer, Jacques Melitz, and the Joint Economic Committee.[55] Generally based on the observation of "wild gyrations in the growth rate of the money stock,"[56] the guidelines usually involve a range of about 2 to 6 percent per annum, sometimes with the possibility not only of adjustments in the band but of exceptions to it as well. Some of these proposals evidently seem to be supporting discretionary action more so than "automaticity."

Finally, no two rules are alike. The range covers the complete spectrum from almost perfect rigidity to guidelines coming very close to supporting the existing degree of discretion. This diversity within the "Rules Party" may help to explain the sometimes almost scornful reception by the opposition of some of the proposals.

Monetary Rules and Their Detractors

Consider now some of the major points against monetary rules raised by their detractors.[57] Two major points in dispute are the concept of money and the mechanism that links monetary and other economic variables.

The debate over the definition of money includes the issues of what is to be regarded as money now, and the issue of the changing "moneyness" of assets, because "a fixed rule freezes the definition over time."[58] The first issue is debated not only between advocates of the opponents to rules but within each group as well and among monetary economists in general. As the proposals indicate, various concepts of money have been included, and most advocates of rules are of the opinion that a rule applied to any definition is preferable to the existing degree of discretion. Thus it seems that the definition of money per se is not really a vital issue in the theoretical debate. This issue of the flexibility, over time, of the concept of money may be more important, but it is obviously also a matter of the degree of specific flexibility built into the rule. No proposal is regarded "as the be-all and end-all of monetary policy for all time."[59]

The link between the stock of money and income is discussed in terms of the velocity of money, and more specifically in terms of the variability or stability of the velocity. Proponents of rules believe in a relatively stable and predictable velocity, whereas opponents tend to regard velocity as subject to erratic variations.[60] Without analyzing all the details and individual differences here, suffice it to say that these differences are no longer as sharp as formerly. Moreover, the evidence discussed and cited elsewhere in this study indicates that the argument is overdrawn.

A similar statement could be made about the second major issue over time lags. This issue centers around three elements — the definition or measurement of lags, their length or distribution, and their variability. Typically, long and variable lags are associated with proponents of rules, short lags with opponents to rules.[61] Friedman is the only one among the proponents who makes explicit allowance for the variability of lags.[62] Also, while a few proponents seem to share the belief in at least the possibility of relatively long lags, any dividing line, if it is to be drawn, does not follow the established rules-versus-discretion discussion.[63] The haziness appears to be mainly a consequence of the lack of definitude in the theoretical issues. We have enumerated some of these issues elsewhere in this study.

Another issue raised by critics and discussed in the last chapter concerns the best indicator of monetary policy. Analyzing monetary rules, Arthur M. Okun concludes:

> It takes . . . a big jump to go from the proposition that quantities deserve emphasis to the position that quantities alone should be the criteria of monetary policy. It is still another leap to the proposal that the only quantities that should count are those relating to one particular financial variable defined as money.[64]

It appears, however, that for once Okun is not speaking for the majority. In a survey of more than 70 American monetary economists, "by a more than 2-to-1 majority, respondents favored making the growth of the money supply or its cognate, base money, the target of monetary policy."[65] The discussion of this question is presented at some length elsewhere in this study.

A similar issue raised by critics refers to the ability of the monetary authority to achieve a prescribed change in the money stock:

> The difficulty is that the money hinges on the willingness of business and individuals to borrow, the asset preferences of individuals and nonbank institutions — all of which are subject to only imperfect control by the Federal Reserve.[66]

Although the control of the money stock under the present system is subject to adequate forecasting by the Federal Reserve, the issue of effective control is not restricted to monetary rules: once the money supply is accepted as indicator or subtarget, any rational monetary policy implies effective control of the money supply as a prerequisite. Whether the present Federal Reserve System complies with this prerequisite is therefore a broader, much more basic question of monetary policy.

The essence of the differences between critics and proponents of monetary rules can perhaps be cast in another question: Can the target(s) be achieved more effectively and precisely by rules or by discretion? Two specific arguments can be usefully noted: the often-heard critique that monetary rules are characterized by the "implicit precept: Ignore fiscal policy,"[67] and the obstacle to rules "is several ends are in complex and unstable rivalry or conflict with each other."[68]

The first argument appears overdrawn. Proponents of "rules" simply do not ignore fiscal policy. Whereas quite a few supporters appear to rely more heavily on monetary policy, this cannot be interpreted as a subscription that "only money matters"; on the other hand, as Selden points out, "Even if it were true that money does not matter, we should nevertheless try to make it behave in the manner most consistent with economic stability."[69]

The second argument implies the hypothesis that conflicting objectives can be served more effectively by a monetary authority which is "to use its best judgment each time that a decision of some sort is called for as to the relative weight to be given to the objectives."[70] Aside from the question, whether this kind and degree of discretion is compatible with the economic and political system, the intuitive nature of the argument hinges on another, more institutional, issue: the relative fallibility or infallibility of the monetary authority.[71] The evidence on the fallibility of the monetary authority and its agent, the central bank, is impressive.

Empirical Evidence from Several Countries

The first attempts to compare the hypothetical performance of rules with other policy alternatives were made simultaneously with some proposals and their rebuttals.[72] Friedman, for example, compared the actual change in the quantity of money with his 4 percent rule and scored the difference as being in the "right" or "wrong" direction, using criteria such as " 'leaning against the wind,' namely, that the stock of money should grow at a slower than average rate during business expansions and at a higher than average rate during business contractions."[73] Applied to the United States on a monthly basis for periods of almost 32 years, the results show actual monetary policy as "right" or "better" than the rule in 40 to 55 percent of the months considered. Even before presenting the rather inconclusive results, however, Friedman declares the attempt a failure because of the difficulties in defining generally acceptable criteria of judgment.[74]

The first explicit tests of monetary rules were performed by Martin Bronfenbrenner.[75] His tests include four strategies of monetary policy: the "judgment" rule, or actual monetary policy; two "inflexible" rules with an annual growth rate of the money supply of 3, respectively 4 percent; and a "lag" rule, whereby the growth rate of the money supply is determined by the rate of change in real output and velocity during the past year or quarter. Defining the ideal growth rate of the money supply as the actual growth rate minus the rate of change in the price level, he explicitly assumes a constant aggregate income and velocity for each time interval; and he also accepts price level stability as the only target and comparative criterion of monetary policy. The actual tests were initially performed using annual data for the period 1901 to 1958, excluding the years of World War II; further tests using quarterly data for the period 1947-I to 1958-IV were added later. The data include two concepts of money—the "conventional" and an "expanded" concept; and two price indexes—wholesale and consumer. Though the results vary with different data and subperiods, they seem to suggest, according to Bronfenbrenner, the possible superiority of the inflexible rule (particularly the 3 percent rule using annual data) and the lag rule (using quarterly data) over the judgment rule.

Entirely different conclusions were reached by Donald P. Tucker, when he repeated Bronfenbrenner's computations for the annual version, excluding, however, the years of World War I as well.[76] The results, so obtained, show the judgment rule superior to all other rules, indicating, as Tucker concludes, "how sensitive the conclusions are to changes in the underlying assumptions."[77]

Less obvious are the results obtained by Charles Schotta, who applied the Bronfenbrenner tests, with the exception of the lag rule, to annual Canadian data from 1927 to 1961, again excluding the years World War II.[78] Overall, both the judgment and the 3 percent rule seem slightly superior to the 4 percent rule; but the margin varies and is hardly decisive. Schotta cites the possibility of different and changing objectives of Canadian monetary policy as perhaps the major reason for the difference in his result as compared to Bronfenbrenner's and concludes by questioning "the applicability of American monetary history to the economic experience of other nations."[79]

Another test of monetary rules has been conducted by Franco Modigliani.[80] The basic procedure is similar to Bronfenbrenner's. Modigliani also tries to determine what he calls the "target money supply," considering, however, not only price stability but also full employment as a target. The determination of full employment income assumes a proportional relationship between income and employment. Full employment is defined as a 4 percent rate of unemployment; price stability as no increase in the

GNP deflator. Again, velocity is assumed to be constant for each time interval, in this case six-month periods.

Several concepts of money and various rules are examined. Aside from the conventional and expanded money supply, Modigliani also first adds time deposits in mutual savings banks and the postal saving system, and then outstanding deposits in savings and loan associations to the expanded definition of money. The main rule examined is a steady 3 percent annual increase in the respective money supply; another rule first adjusts the money supply to the full employment level of the preceding period and then adds a fixed growth rate; a third alternative, the "switch" rule, has the most inclusive concept of letting money grow at 3 percent whenever current income is greater than or equal to the previous peak level, and switches to the second rule with the conventional concept of money whenever current income is below the previous peak level.

Modigliani evaluates the performance of various monetary strategies by calculating the deviation of the actual money supply, and the money supply according to the described rules, from the target money supply for the period beginning with the second half of 1947 and ending with the second half of 1962. The often-quoted results state that overall discretionary policy has outperformed all rules, except the switch rule, no matter what concept of money is chosen. This is particularly true for the subperiod 1952 to 1960. The much poorer performance in the other subperiods stems from the fact that, according to Modigliani, during these periods the monetary authority was seeking to achieve targets other than price stability and full employment.

Concluding his study, Modigliani writes:

> As I see it, the inference to be drawn from the test is . . . that (1) on the whole the evidence supports the use of discretion over a rule, but that (2) there is room for some limitations in the use of discretion, particularly in the form of spelling out more precisely the goals to which the discretionary powers should be directed, and the procedures by which these goals are to be changed.[81]

Rather different results were obtained from two other tests conducted on the basis of Modigliani's approach. Richard Attiyeh changed two of Modigliani's assumptions: Following the research by Arthur M. Okun, he chose a 1-to-3 relationship between employment and income rather than 1 to 1; and taking up another suggestion by Modigliani, he defined price stability to be consistent with 1 ½ percent increase in the GNP deflator.[82] Using the same data as Modigliani, but restricting the tests to the subperiod 1952 to 1960, he found the second rule to be markedly closer to the target than discretionary policy. Attiyeh concludes that Modigliani's test results are very sensitive to the definition of the target money supply and evidently also to the period selected for anlaysis.

Introducing lags into Modigliani's procedure by letting the target money supply lead by one or two periods has been attempted by Thomas Mayer.[83] Again the results are distinctly different from Modigliani's and over all more favorable for the rigid rule than for discretionary policy. Since empirical analyses "clearly suggest" the existence of a lag of at least one quarter, Mayer concludes that "Modigliani's claim to have established the superiority of discretionary policy must be rejected."[84]

In a recent study, Macesich and Tsai report test results on Bronfenbrenner's four monetary rules—judgment rule, 3 percent rule, 4 percent rule, and lag rule—as applied to Belgium, France, Germany, Italy, the Netherlands, United Kingdom, Sweden, Yugoslavia, Canada and the United States, for the years 1956 to 1980 (1958–80 for Yugoslavia) using annual data. We may draw on these results for the purposes at hand.[85]

The United Kingdom. To judge from the overall test results, the 3 percent rule performs best, and the judgment rule is the poorest performer in the United Kingdom during the period 1951–80. The 4 percent rule and the lag rule perform equally well. The judgment rule aside, there are no clear-cut results as to which might give the lower absolute deviations. An inflationary bias is revealed in all cases considered, irrespective of which price index or which definition of money is used.

Sweden. Similar tests are also conducted for Sweden, Canada, Yugoslavia and the United States. To judge from the overall test results, the 4 percent rule performs best in Sweden during the period 1951–80. The 3 percent rule suggests a slight deflationary bias, when a broader definition of money together with either wholesale or consumer price is used in the analysis. On the other hand, the judgment rule, the 4 percent rule, and the lag rule during the same period tend toward an inflationary direction. In all cases, the judgment rule is the poorest performer. The 3 percent is poorer than the 4 percent rule *only* when a broader definition of money together with wholesale prices is used. On the other hand, the lag rule is significantly poorer that the 3 percent and the 4 percent variants, regardless of which price index or which definition of money is used. Thus, the order of better performance is the 3 percent rule, and 4 percent rule, the lag rule, and the judgment rule.

Yugoslavia. In Yugoslavia the judgment rule does better than the 3 percent, the 4 percent, and the lag rule when wholesale prices are used, irrespective of which definition of money is used in the test. The 3 percent, 4 percent, and lag rules, in turn, are the better performers when consumer prices are used. The 4 percent rule performs slightly better than the 3 percent rule in all cases considered. However, there are no clear-cut results as to which might give the lower absolute deviations. On the other hand, the lag rule performs better than both the 3 percent and the 4 percent rule in the case which uses a broader definition of money together with wholesale prices.

A deflationary bias is revealed in the 4 percent and the 3 percent rules, while an inflationary bias is suggested in the judgment rule and the lag rule. However, the inflationary bias in the lag rule is relatively small compared to those of the judgment rule. The small negative algebraic deviation in the lag rule may be a statistical artifact as a result of fluctuation of annual data.

Canada. To judge from the overall test results the judgment rule appears superior during the period 1951–80, when narrow definition of money is used in the analysis.

The average absolute value of the deviations for the judgment rule is consistently lower than that of the other three rules when a narrow definition of money is used. The judgment rule, however, has a larger average value of the deviations than do these three rules when a broader definition of money and consumer prices is used in the test.

In the second set of tests, the results indicate a tendency toward an inflationary bias in the judgment rule, whereas a deflationary bias appears in the 3 percent and lag rules. The judgment rule aside, the absolute deviations tended to be smaller when consumer prices are used in the analysis. Again, the judgment rule aside, the use of a broader definition of money yields the lower absolute deviations.

The United States. To judge from the overall tests results, the judgment rule performs consistently poorer by comparison to the three rival rules regardless of the definition of the money supply or price index used. The average absolute value of deviations for the judgment rule ranges from .0618 to 0.626. The use of consumer prices seems to yield lower absolute deviations in all cases considered.

In the second set of tests, the results indicate a strong tendency toward an inflationary bias in the judgment rule, while a deflationary bias appears only in the 3 percent rule when a broader definition of money is used. However, these deflationary biases are too small to be significant. This might be a statistical artifact. In order of performance, it is the lag rule that scores better in the United States. It is followed by the 4 percent, the 3 percent and the judgment rule.

THE EEC

What implication can we draw from this evidence with respect to the longstanding debate on "rules versus discretion" and a supranational monetary authority for coordinating stabilization policies? From the point of view of the individual member EEC countries, that combination of forecasting ability, political pressure, and administrative routine which passes as "judgment" or "discretionary" monetary policy has a slight edge. The individual records in these countries seem favorable to such policy, at least in comparison to the other three rules considered, provided that the monetary authority makes use of its discretion in the pursuit of price stability as the stated goal. This is, of course, a serious constraint on the exercise of discretionary authority by central banks.

The evidence with respect to the other rules, though not spectacular, is not irrelevant. On the contrary, in the experience of all six original EEC countries, the 3 percent and 4 percent versions of the "inflexible rule" came close to the record registered by the "judgment rule." This is particularly significant for a supranational monetary authority. The formulation and implementation of a "judgment rule" by such authority for the entire community, so that the rule is compatible in all six countries, may very well overtax the ingenuity of such an organization. It would probably lead to oligopolistic reaction on the part of each of the countries and to squabbles which would undermine EEC as an effective organization. A useful alternative would be an obligation on the part of the EEC monetary authority to adhere to, say, a 4 percent increase in the money supply designed to serve the goal of price stability. This rule does perform reasonably well in most member countries. Its adoption would serve to defuse the explosive nature of the situation by making it unnecessary for a central monetary authority to thrash about in search of a judgment rule acceptable to all member countries, individually and collectively.

Rules can provide a useful guide to monetary management. Rules designed to serve specific goals nevertheless do focus attention on areas of conflict, and lay open to public debate both the goals and means for reaching them. This is particularly important in such a multinational and multistate organization as the EEC. A given rule at least avoids one of the principal objections to discretionary policy—that such a policy may be used to serve goals other than those agreed upon by all participants within the community.

Theory of Bureaucracy and Central Banks

Impressive as the case for rules over discretionary authority may be, we have it from the theory of bureaucracy that we can expect central bankers not to take seriously theory and empirical evidence that will constrain their activities. This has little to do with individual central bankers, many of whom are outstanding. At issue is the system itself and the incentives to which central bankers respond.

Central banks as government agencies exercise discretionary policy. It is thus important to have an independent evaluation of their performance in terms of explicit criteria. Central banks are loath to accept this constraint, since they view the exercise of monetary policy as an "art" that cannot be defined or measured in terms of any single variable. Their preference is to discuss monetary policy in terms of unmeasured variables such as the intentions of policymakers or the state of monetary restraint, or else in terms of a set of nonequivalent measuring variables among which the interpreter is free to choose as he wishes.

A case in point illustrating well the issues involved is the experience cited by Milton Friedman in his exchange with Federal Reserve authorities.[86] In describing a 1969 Federal Reserve conference on controlling monetary aggregate, he writes:

> Prior and subsequent to this time, outside persons were invited to meet with members of the board in Washington from time to time. I attended many such meetings of so-called academic consultants. They were interesting experiences, no doubt instructive to the many Federal Reserve personnel who sat around the sides of the boardroom, where the meeting was invariably held, without participating. However, I finally concluded that the meetings were called purely for window-dressing purposes. I was unable to detect any inference whatsoever exerted by the consultant's comments on the system's actions. Indeed, the choice of the particular consultants invited to attend seemed designed to guarantee offsetting and contradictory advice, leaving the Fed free to pursue its own devices. However, even on those rare occasions when something approaching a consensus emerged, I could detect no subsequent effect on policy.[87]

According to our theory of bureaucracy, this is what, in fact, we should expect.[88] Policymaking is an "art" that is heavily dependent on inside information and expertise. Consistent with the theory of bureaucracy, the Federal Reserve simply undercut and disregarded the knowledge that would constrain it. Thus in reply to a letter in 1969 from Friedman regarding Federal Reserve use of monetary aggregates as targets, Chairman William M. Martin writes:

> I seriously doubt that we could ever attain complete control (of monetary aggregates), but I do think it quite true that we could come significantly closer to such control then we do now — if we wished to make that variable our exclusive target. But the wisdom of such an exclusive orientation of monetary policy is, of course, the basic question.

Friedman's view of Martin's reply and what he later learned of the affair is certainly consistent with our theory. Thus:

> That's a very instructive statement (Martin's). First of all, it says what the Fed has repeatedly denied and was to deny throughout the rest of the period that I'm talking about, that it *could* control monetary aggregates. But second, the Fed didn't really mean it. The reply was simply designed to immobilize one — as I later learned from an economist in the Fed's Research Division, who boasted to me about his cleverness in constructing that reply. And of course, it did immobilize me. Why conduct a study to figure out how to do something the Fed already knew how to do?[89]

Again, as our theory suggests, it is the agency itself that is important and not individuals, distinguished though they may be. Thus in 1980, when Arthur Burns became chairman, Friedman writes, "Monetary growth was put first and money market conditions second. However, that change turned out to be pure lip service and was later de-emphasized."[90]

Congress passed Concurrent Resolution 133 in 1975, which expressed the sentiments of Congress that the Federal Reserve control monetary aggregates, and consult and report to Congress at regular intervals. This was a resolution strongly opposed by the Federal Reserve. When passed, the Federal Reserve pledged cooperation. Within two years the Federal Reserve undermined the resolution.[91]

If Congress has not been able to bend the Federal Reserve to its will, a recent study suggests that past Presidents have been more successful.[92] It is argued that since the Treasury-Federal Reserve accord of March 1951, American President's have been, in fact, the principal political influence behind Federal Reserve policy. According to the evidence cited in the study, Fed policy was significantly changed in 1953, 1961, 1969, 1971, 1974 and 1977, all years in which the presidency changed. This is consistent with our theory, since risk avoidance would push the Fed to pay closer attention to presidential desires than to those of Congress. It is the president and his administration that can directly threaten the Fed's status as an agency.[93] The President does have the power to name the chairman of the Federal Reserve Board and at least two other members of the board during each presidential term. There is, moreover, a close working relationship between the administration and the Federal Reserve Board.

It is significant, for instance, that during the important monetary policy changes between 1950 and 1970, the same individual, William M. Martin, was chairman. The strong presidential influence under which the central bankers of the Federal Reserve operate is suggested by events during the tenure of President Johnson (1963–69). These are also the years when market participants began to realize that significant changes were occurring in the country's monetary system away from a constrained specielike system to an unconstrained government fiat standard.

Additional confirmation of presidential influence on the Fed is provided by the Nixon administration (1969–74), when Arthur Burns served as chairman. In 1972, when Nixon was running for re-election, the old M1 definition of the money supply grew at almost 8.5 percent during the last quarter of 1972 and the first quarter of 1973, or at better than 6 percent during the period 1969–74. This is indeed a postwar record growth in the money supply. President Nixon also removed the country's last links with gold in 1971. To this may be added the administration's futile attempts to hold down inflation by price and wage controls and guidelines while promoting an expansive monetary policy.

During the Ford and the subsequent Carter years, monetary policy registered an indifferent performance. Ford succeeded in slowing monetary growth during his tenure (August 1974 to December 1976) by holding to his priority to bring down inflation. Arthur Burns was chairman of the Fed during this period.

Carter at first considered inflation a nonmonetary phenomenon and promoted monetary growth with the idea of lowering interest rates and encouraging investment. Arthur Burns continued to serve as Federal Reserve chairman until March 1978, when Carter appointed G. William Miller to the position. In November 1978 President Carter changed priorities from stimulating the economy to fighting inflation that spurted into double digits. From the previous high of over 8.5 percent rate of growth in the old M1 reached by October 1978, the money supply growth was slowed by March, 1979. Thereafter it again took off with M1B growing at a 13 percent annual rate between March and October of 1979.

Paul Volcker became Chairman of the Federal Reserve in August 1979. On October 6, 1979, he announced that the Federal Reserve would henceforth concentrate on directly controlling the money supply and de-emphasize interest rates as targets. We have discussed elsewhere the performance of American monetary policy since 1979. President Reagan's comments suggesting that it might be a good idea to put the Fed under Treasury supervision may well be a harbinger.

We should also expect that an agency such as the Federal Reserve in our example would push its own version of "history." Such activities can range from outright concealment of information that might be unfavorable to it or helpful to its critics, to pushing a general framework within which agency activities are interpreted so as to minimize the danger that it will be accused of making serious agency error.

On this score, it is interesting that the Federal Reserve undertook an extensive examination of its experience with monetary aggregates. In a massive two-volume study, the conclusion reached is that "the basic operating procedure represents a sound approach to attaining long-run objectives set for monetary standards."[94]

Quite a few observers will agree with Friedman when he writes, "I believe that the fundamental explanation for the persistence and importance of bureaucratic inertia in the Federal Reserve System is the absence of a bottom line."[95] In short, the Federal Reserve operates in a manner consistent with our theory of bureaucracy. It is such recognition that has prompted more fundamental proposals for monetary reform, which we discuss in the following chapter.

Notes

1. Culbertson puts the issues involved succinctly:

Concern for its own power and prestige will cause it to prefer policy systems discretion, which is to say agency control over actions, agency power. The more closely constrained the actions are by rules or performance criteria, the less the power and prestige of the agency, as it is demoted from the status of decision maker to that of a social errand boy. Its preference for such policy systems leads the agency to prefer economic models, or theories, that justify or support them. Since the class of policy system involves an undefined behavior of the instrumental variable, it is in general opposed by systematic theories — since these lead to defined optimal behavior of the instrumental variable (defined money-supply functions, for example), thus eliminating the rationale for agency discretion. The agency, thus, is led to prefer models in which the performance of the economic system is unknowable, indeterminate, to deny existence of such knowledge as would lead to decision rules that would undermine its power. The agency's risk avoidance impels it in the same direction. The more indefinite the state of knowledge, the less the likelihood that the agency will ever successfully be demonstrated to have committed a serious error, thus the greater is its security. [J. M. Culbertson, *Macroeconomic Theory and Stabilization Policy,* (New York: McGraw Hill Book Company, 1968), pp. 410–411]

See also A. Downs, *Inside Bureaucracy* (Boston: Little Brown, 1967); H. G. Johnson, "Problems of Efficiency in Monetary Management," *Journal of Political Economy,* October 1968, pp. 971–90; Keith Hebeson and John F. Chant, "Bureaucratic Theory and the Choice of Central Bank Goals: The Case of the Bank of Canada," *Journal of Money, Credit and Banking,* May 1973, pp. 637–55; P. Selznik, "Foundations of the Theory of Organizations," *American Sociological Review* 13 (1948), reprinted as F. E. Emery, ed., *Systems Thinking* (Hammondsworth: Penguin Books, 1969); O. F. Williamson, *The Economics of Discretionary Behavior: Managerial Objectives in a Theory of the Firm* (Chicago: Markham Publishing Company, 1964); Albert Breton and Ronald Wintrobe, *The Logic of Bureaucratic Conduct* (Cambridge: Cambridge University Press, 1982.)

2. Henry C. Simons, "Rules Versus Authorities in Monetary Policy," *Journal of Political Economy,* February 1936, pp. 1–30. This chapter draws in part on Ranier Stuper, "An Empirical Analysis of the Debate over Rules versus Discretion with Special Reference to the Monetary Management of the German Bundesbank from 1958 to 1970" (Ph.D. dissertation, Florida State University, 1973) and George Macesich, *Monetarism: Theory and Policy* (New York: Praeger Publishers, 1983). See, also, George S. Tavlas, "Some Initial Formulations of the Monetary Growth Rule," *History of Political Economy,* Winter 1977, pp. 535–47 and the references cited by Tavlas; Tavlas, "Some Further Observations of the Monetary Economics of the Chicagoans and Non-Chicagoans," *Southern Economic Journal,* April 1976, pp. 685–92; Tavlas, "The Chicago Tradition Revisited: Some Neglected Monetary Contributions of Paul Douglas, *Journal of Money, Credit and Banking,* November 1977; Thomas M. Humphrey, "Role of Non-Chicago Economists in the Evolution of the Quantity Theory in America 1930–1950, *Southern Economic Journal,* July 1971, pp. 12–18.

3. For a discussion of this and similar plans, see Albert G. Hart, "The Chicago Plan for Banking Reform," *Review of Economic Studies* (1935), pp. 104–16.

4. Henry C. Simons, *A Politive Program of Laissez Faire: Some Proposals for a Liberal Economic Policy,* Public Policy Pamphlet, no. 15, ed. H. D. Gideonse (Chicago: University of Chicago Press, 1934); reprinted in Henry C. Simons, *Economic Policy for a Free Society* (Chicago: University of Chicago Press, 1948), pp. 40–77.

5. Ibid., p. 57.

6. Ibid., p. 63.

7. Simons, "Rules Versus Authorities," p. 16.

8. Ibid.

9. Henry C. Simons, "The Requisites of Free Competition," *American Economic Review, Supplement,* March 1936, p. 69.

10. Cf. John G. Gurley and Edward S. Shaw, "Financial Aspects of Economic Development," *American Economic Review,* September 1955, pp. 515–38.

11. Simons, "Rules Versus Authorities," p. 5.

12. Ibid., p. 21.

13. See, for example, Irving Fisher, *Stabilizing the Dollar* (New York: Macmillan, 1920); U.S., Congress, Hearings before Committee on Banking and Currency, House of Representatives on H.R. 11806, 70th Cong., 1st sess., 1928; U.S. Congress, *Restoring and Maintaining the Average Purchasing Power of the Dollar,* Hearings before Committee on Banking and Currency, Senate, on H.R. 11499 and S. 4429, 72nd Cong., 1st sess., 1932.

14. Simons, "Rules Versus Authorities," pp. 12–13, n. 11.

15. Ibid., p. 12.

16. Henry C. Simons, "Introduction: A Political Credo," *Economic Policy for a Free Society* (Chicago: Univ. of Chicago Press, 1948).

17. Carl Snyder, "The Problem of Monetary and Economic Stability," *Quarterly Journal of Economics,* February 1935, p. 198.

18. Carl Snyder, *Capitalism the Creator: The Economic Foundations of Modern Industrial Society* (New York: Macmillan, 1940), pp. 220-21.

19. See, for example, Lloyd W. Mints, *Monetary Policy for a Competitive Society* (New York: McGraw-Hill, 1950), pp. 115-73; Mints, "Monetary Policy and Stabilization," *American Economic Review, Papers and Proceedings,* May 1951, pp. 188-93.

20. Mints, *Monetary Policy for a Competitive Society,* p. 136.

21. Ibid., pp. 143-59.

22. Ibid., p. 142.

23. For a comparative summary of the development of Warburton's and Friedman's proposal, see Selden, "Stable Monetary Growth," pp. 324-31. The following paragraphs rely partly on this study. An interesting and useful study by William Yohe, "The Intellectual Milieu at the Federal Reserve Board in the 1920s," presented at the annual Meeting, History of Economic Society, Duke University, May 25, 1982, sheds considerable light on the background of Federal Reserve policy making during its formative years.

24. See, for example, Clark Warburton, "The Volume of Money and the Price Level between the World Wars," *Journal of Political Economy,* June 1945, pp. 150-63; Warburton, "The Misplaced Emphasis in Contempory Business-Fluctuation Theory." *Journal of Business,* October 1946, pp. 199-220: reprinted in *Readings in Monetary Theory,* selected by a Committee of the American Economic Association (Homewood, Ill.; Richard D. Irwin, 1951), pp. 284-318; Warburton, "The Secular Trend in Monetary Velocity," *Review of Economics and Statistics,* March 1948, pp. 128-34.

25. Clark Warburton, "Testing a Hypothesis" (March 1951), p. 12 (mimeographed), quoted in Selden, "Stable Monetary Growth," p. 327.

26. Clark Warburton, "The Misplaced Emphasis in Contemporary Business Fluctuation Theory," p. 211.

27. See, for example, Clark Warburton, "How Much Variation in the Quantity of Money Is Needed?" *Southern Economic Journal,* April 1952, pp. 495-509; Warburton, "Rules and Implements of Monetary Policy," *Journal of Finance,* March 1953, pp. 1-21; U.S., Congress, House, Committee on Banking and Currency, *Compendium on Monetary Policy Guidelines and Federal Reserve Structure,* pursuant to H. R. 11, Subcommittee on Domestic Finance of the Committee on Banking and Currency, House of Representatives, 90th Cong., 2nd sess., 1968, pp. 634-44 (hereinafter referred to as *Compendium*).

28. See, for example, Milton Friedman, "A Monetary and Fiscal Framework for Economic Stability," *American Economic Review,* June 1948, pp. 245-64; Friedman, "Commodity Reserve Currency," *Journal of Political Economy,* June 1951, pp. 203-32: Friedman, "Price Income, and Monetary Changes in Three Wartime Periods," *American Economic Review,* Papers and Proceedings, May 1952, pp. 612-25.

29. Milton Friedman, *A Program for Monetary Stability,* The Millar Lectures, No. 3 (New York: Fordham University Press, 1960), p. 90. Results of his research at NBER can be found in Milton Friedman and Anna J. Schwartz, *A Monetary History of the United States,* National Bureau of Economic Research, Studies in Business Cycles, No. 12 (Princeton, N.J.: Princeton University Press, 1963). Milton Friedman and Anna J. Schwartz, *Monetary Trends in the U.S. and U.K. 1867-1975* (Chicago: University of Chicago Press, 1982).

30. Cf. Milton Friedman, "The Lag in Effect of Monetary Policy," *Journal of Political Economy,* October 1961, pp. 447-66; Friedman, *The Optimum Quantity of Money and Other Essays* (Chicago: Aldine Publishing Co., 1969), Ch. 1.

31. Friedman, "Monetary and Fiscal Framework," p. 263.

32. Ibid., p. 254.

33. Milton Friedman, "The Role of Monetary Policy," *American Economic Review,* March 1968, p. 17.

34. Selden, "Stable Monetary Growth," p. 331.

35. Statement of Clark Warburton, *Compendium,* p. 634.

36. Selden, "Stable Monetary Growth," p. 331.

37. Warburton, "Rules and Implements," p. 17; see also, for example, Statement of Clark Warburton, *Compendium,* pp. 639-40.

38. Cf. Friedman, *Program for Monetary Stability,* pp. 100-102.

39. Statement of Milton Friedman, *Compendium,* p. 204.

40. Warburton, "How Much Variation?" pp. 495–98; Statement of Clark Warburton, *Compendium,* pp. 636–37.

41. Friedman, *Program for Monetary Stability,* p. 92.

42. Milton Friedman, "Should There Be an Independent Monetary Authority?" *In Search of a Monetary Constitution,* ed. L. B. Yeager (Cambridge: Harvard University Press, 1962), pp. 242–43; Friedman, *Optimum Quantity,* pp. 45–48.

43. Friedman, *Optimum Quantity,* p. 48.

44. Cf. Warburton, "How Much Variation," pp. 498–500.

45. Warburton, "Rules and Implements," p. 7; as examples of such conditions, Warburton mentions changes in short-run velocity and changes in the rate of growth of population and productivity; see Warburton, "How Much Variation," pp. 502, 506–8.

46. Edward S. Shaw, "Monetary Stability in a Growing Economy," *The Allocation of Economic Resources,* Essays in Honor of B. F. Haley (Stanford, Calif.: Stanford University Press, 1959), pp. 218–35.

47. Ibid., p. 233. Statement of Robert L. Crouch, *Compendium,* pp. 119–27; Statement of Leland Yeager, *Compendium,* pp. 651–57.

48. James W. Angell, "Appropriate Monetary Policies and Operations in the United States Today," *Review of Economics and Statistics,* August 1960, pp. 247–52.

49. Selden, "Stable Monetary Growth," p. 333.

50. Statement of Phillip Cagan, *Compendium,* p. 106.

51. Martin Bronfenbrenner, "Monetary Rules: A New Look," *Journal of Law and Economics,* October 1965, 173–94; statement of William R. Hosek, *Compendium,* pp. 304–13; statement of Allan H. Meltzer, *Compendium,* pp. 488–91; statement of George R. Morrison, *Compendium,* pp. 493–501.

52. Statement of William R. Hosek, *Compendium,* p. 307.

53. Bronfenbrenner, "Monetary Rules," p. 179.

54. Ibid., p. 182.

55. Statement of Karl Brunner, *Compendium,* pp. 100–103; statement of Gregory C. Chow, *Compendium,* pp. 106–9; statement of Carl F. Christ, *Compendium,* pp. 109–15; statement of Thomas Mayer, *Compendium,* pp. 46–72; statement of Jacques Melitz, *Compendium,* pp. 479–88; U.S., Congress, Joint Economic Committee, *Standards for Guiding Monetary Action,* Report of the Joint Economic Committee (Washington, D.C.: Government Printing Office, 1968), pp. 16–20.

56. Statement of Thomas Mayer, *Compendium,* p. 465.

57. See, for example, Abba P. Lerner, "Milton Friedman's 'A Program for Monetary Stability': A Review," *Journal of the American Statistical Association,* March 1962, pp. 211–20; reprinted in *Monetary Policy: The Argument from Keynes' Treatise to Friedman,* ed. William Hamovich (Boston: D. C. Heath and Company, 1966), pp. 102–17; Jacob Viner, "The Necessary and the Desirable Range of Discretion to Be Allowed to a Monetary Authority," *In Search of a Monetary Constitution,* ed. L. B. Yeager (Cambridge: Harvard University Press, 1962), pp. 244–74; Daniel S. Ahearn, *Federal Reserve Policy Reappraised, 1951–1959* (New York and London: Columbia University Press, 1963), pp. 225–33; Paul A. Samuelson, "Reflections on Central Banking," *National Banking Review* 1 (September 1963), pp. 15–28; Charles E. Walker, "Fact and Fiction in Central Banking," *Essays in Monetary Policy in Honor of Elmer Wood,* ed. P. C. Walker (Columbia, Mo.: University of Missouri Press, 1965), pp. 109–29; Lyle E. Gramley, "Guidelines for Monetary Policy—The Case Against Simple Rules," *Readings in Money National Income, and Stabilization Policy,* rev. ed., ed. W. L. Smith and R. L. Teigen (Homewood, Ill.: Richard D. Irwin, 1970), pp. 488–95; Erich Schneider, "Automatism or Discretion in Monetary Policy," *Banca Nazionale del Lavoro Quarterly Review,* June 1970, pp. 3–19.

58. Ahearn, *Federal Reserve Policy,* p. 226.

59. Friedman, *A Program for Monetary Stability* (New York: Fordham University Press, 1959), p. 98.

60. Cf. Samuelson, "Reflections on Central Banking," pp. 17–18.

61. Selden, "Stable Monetary Growth," pp. 347–52.

62. Milton Friedman, "The Lag in Effect of Monetary Policy," pp. 447–66.

63. Thomas Mayer, "The Lag in Effect of Monetary Policy: Some Criticisms," *Western Economic Journal,* September 1967, pp. 324–42.

64. Arthur M. Okun, *The Political Economy of Prosperity* (Washington, D.C.; The Brookings Institution, 1970), p. 116.

65. Staff Report, *Compendium*, p. 13.

66. Ahearn, *Federal Reserve Policy*, p. 226.

67. Ibid.

68. Viner, "Necessary and Desirable," p. 249.

69. Selden, "Stable Monetary Growth," p. 354.

70. Viner, "Necessary and Desirable," p. 259.

71. Charles R. Whittlesey, "Rules, Discretion, and Central Bankers," *Essays in Money and Banking in Honour of Richard S. Sayers*, ed. C. R. Whittlesey and J. S. Wilson (London: Oxford University Press, 1968), pp. 252-65.

72. See, for examples, Shaw, "Monetary Stability," pp. 221-31; Minks, *Monetary Policy*, pp. 139-42; Walker, "Fact and Fiction," pp. 119-22.

73. Friedman, *Program for Monetary Stability*, p. 95.

74. Ibid., pp. 95-98.

75. Martin Bronfenbrenner, "Statistical Tests of Rival Monetary Rules," *Journal of Political Economy*, February 1961, pp. 1-14; Bronfenbrenner, "Statistical Tests of Rival Monetary Rules: Quarterly Data Supplement," *Journal of Political Economy*, December 1961, pp. 621-25. See also George Macesich, "Monetary Policy in the Common Market Countries: Rules Versus Discretion," *Weltwirtschaftliches Archiv*, Band 198 (1972), pp. 20-52; George Macesich, *Geldpolitik in einem gemeinsamen europaischen Market* (Money in a European Common Market), Baden-Baden; Nomos Verlagsgesellschaft, 1972); George Macesich and H. Tsai, *Money in Economic Systems* (New York: Praeger Publishers, 1982).

76. Donald P. Tucker, "Bronfenbrenner on Monetary Rules: A Comment," *Journal of Political Economy*, April 1963, pp. 273-79.

77. Ibid., p. 178.

78. Charles Schotta, Jr., "The Performance of Alternative Monetary Rules in Canada, 1927-1961," *National Banking Review*, December 1963, pp. 221-27.

79. Ibid., p. 227.

80. Franco Modigliani, "Some Empirical Tests of Monetary Management and of Rules Versus Discretion," *Journal of Political Economy*, June 1964, pp. 211-45.

81. Ibid., p. 244.

82. Richard Attiyeh, "Rules Versus Discretion; A Comment," *Journal of Political Economy*, April 1965, pp. 170-72.

83. Mayer, "Lag in Effect," pp. 331-35.

84. Ibid., p. 334.

85. Macesich and Tsai, *Money in Economic Systems*, chap. 10.

86. Milton Friedman, "Monetary Policy: Theory and Practice," *Journal of Money, Credit, and Banking*, February 1982, p. 98.

87. Ibid.

88. Ibid., p. 106.

89. Ibid.

90. Ibid.

91. Ibid., p. 108. James L. Pierce, whom Friedman cites for evidence on this score, writes:

> The evidence clearly points to the conclusion that the Federal Reserve has *not* placed greater emphasis on monetary aggregates in its actual–as opposed to stated–policy making. In fact, the evidence suggests that the Fed has placed even greater reliance on stabilizing the money market, frequently at the cost of losing control over the monetary aggregates, since House Concurrent Resolution 133 was passed. Upon examination, one finds that the range for the Federal funds rate is almost always hit and the targets for the monetary aggregates apparently left for later attention. That is to say, stabilizing the money market in terms of keeping the Federal funds rate within a prescribed range takes precedence. [James L. Pierce, "The Myth of Congressional Supervision of Monetary Policy," *Journal of Monetary Economics*, April 1978, reprinted in Thomas M. Havrilesky and John T. Boorman, eds., *Current Issues in Monetary Theory and Policy*, 2d ed. (Arlington Heights, Ill: AHM Publishing Company, 1980), p. 482]

92. Robert E. Weintraub, "Congressional Supervision of Monetary Policy," *Journal of Monetary*

Economics, April 1978, pp. 341–62. See also Robert D. Auerbach, *Money, Banking and Financial Markets* (New York: Macmillan Publishing Co., 1982), pp. 362ff.; Thomas M. Havrilesky "The Economist's Corner: The Politicization of Monetary Policy," *The Bankers Magazine,* Spring 1975, pp. 101–4. In fact, Havrilesky writes, "The politicization of the Federal Reserve System is rather an accomplished fact. With monetary policy so hamstrung by the political constraints and regulations of its own leadership, it is no surprise that the Federal Reserve spokesmen to the interference for wage and price controls and continually repeat the tired litany which attacks economic theory for its lack of (political) realism, and thereby defends its own obscurantism." Ibid., p. 104. See also Nathaniel Beck, "Presidential Influence on the Federal Reserve in the 1970s," *American Journal of Political Science,* August 1982, pp. 415–45.

93. On the ownership issue and the Fed independence, see George Macesich, "Stock and the Federal Reserve System," U.S., Congress, House, Subcommittee on Domestic Finance of the Committee on Banking and Currency, *Compendium on Monetary Policy Guidelines and Federal Reserve Structure,* 90th Cong., 2d sess. (Washington: U.S. Government Printing Office, December 1968) and Macesich, "Central Banking, Monetary Policy and Economic Activity," pp. 437–54.

94. *New Monetary Control Procedures,* Federal Reserve Staff Study, vols. 1 and 2 (Washington, D.C.: Board of Governors of the Federal Reserve System, February 1982). For a review of these studies, see Stephen M. Goldfeld, "New Monetary Control Procedures," *Journal of Money, Credit and Banking,* February 1982, pp. 148–55. See also JMCB Debate "Is the Federal Reserve's Monetary Control Policy Misdirected?" *Journal of Money, Credit, and Banking,* February 1982, pp. 119–47.

95. Friedman, "Monetary Policy: Theory and Practice," p. 124.

8

The Issues of Monetary Reform:
Private Monetary Arrangements and
Constitutional Constraint

Private Monetary Arrangements and American Nineteenth-Century
Multi-Currency Experiences

PROPOSALS FOR PRIVATE MONETARY ARRANGEMENTS

Dissatisfaction with monetary arrangements has promoted consideration of various alternative proposals, including the elimination and/or constitutional constraint of government monopoly on the provision of money.[1] Hayek, for instance, a prominent neo-liberal (libertarian) argues that inflation is the inevitable consequence of government monopoly over a country's monetary arrangements. He advocates a free choice in money. Hayek sets the philosophic tone and direction to proposals for a free and competitive monetary arrangement.

Benjamin Klein also discusses such competitive monetary arrangements, arguing that it is a fallacy to argue that with free competition in money private producers would issue and exchange their monies for goods and services at such a rapid rate as to push the price level toward infinity.[2] According to Klein, private money producers who wish to remain in business can do so only by issuing quality money which will retain its purchasing power. Failure to do so would result in the money-producing firms losing customers, incurring losses, and ultimately going bankrupt. Klein's monetary arrangement is based in part on commodity money.

Stephen Morrell focuses on issues involved in a competitive money supply by posing the following questions to influential (neo-liberal) libertarian scholars:[3]

(1) What is the proper role of the State, if any, regarding money?
(2) Is the private production of money a viable alternative to State monopolization of money?

(3) If private money production comes to exist, (a) what form should it take? (b) what form do you think it will take?

(4) What changes, if any, in the legal framework of the United States would be necessary for a private monetary system to work?

(5) What issues should libertarians address themselves to with regard to money?

The answers Morrell received suggest that not only is such a monetary arrangement theoretically sound, but it is practically possible — if only to those of libertarian persuasion. Morrell, concludes that "to many individuals the concept of a private monetary arrangement is an alien one. Varied inter-action of the concept would therefore be necessary to get there from here."[4]

In fact, a private monetary arrangement is what in essence the United States had for almost the first one hundred years of its history as an independent nation. It is useful, to draw together the various threads of American monetary experience for the answers they suggest to Morrell's questions. Such a comparison is all the more useful in view of neo-liberal responses to Morrell's questions.

The dominant response to the first question is that there is no role for the state, other than the enforcement on money producers of the same laws regarding fraud and the enforcement of contracts which apply to other private firms. Or, as Rothbard succinctly replied, "The only proper role of the state in money is to disappear."[5]

The replies to the second question on the viability of the private production of money include examples of where private monetary systems thrived, such as in Scotland from 1716 to 1845 and the Suffolk Bank System in Massachusetts between 1825 and 1858. Morrell notes that it is useful to distinguish between pure commodity money such as gold and silver coin, which circulates as private money, and private token coinage, which has flourished when government coinage has been insufficient. Private bank notes, however, appear to be the center of controversy.

Gordon Tullock's reply on Chinese experience states that it may be useful to separate the medium of exchange and store of value functions of money. The medium-of-exchange function may be a natural monopoly — a conclusion Tullock apparently believes to be "weak, empirical, and subject to technological change." In the Chinese hyperinflation, according to Tullock, government currency continued to circulate, while record keeping by both firms and individuals was carried out on a unit-of-account basis. Individuals and small firms kept accounts in dollars or silver coins, while large firms maintained their own indexes — for the most part in terms of their own supplies.

Answers provided to the second part of the third question, as to the forms that private money production will take, the consensus appears to be that it will be based on some form of commodity money, with fractional reserve banknotes redeemable either into the commodity money or into some "market basket" collection. Gold was the commodity most often mentioned as one which would form the basis of a private monetary system.[6]

In response to the fourth question, most agreed that the existing monetary-legal arrangement, is based on statutory rather than common law, should be abolished. Hayek is straightforward in arguing: "Deny politicians all influence over the supply of money." *(Denationalization of Money)* specifically, the Federal Reserve System is to be abolished, legal tender laws repealed, restrictions on entry into banking are to be relaxed, power of government to restrict private contracts revoked. In short, everything standing in support of government monopoly over the money supply is to be removed.

Constitutional power of Congress to coin money and regulate its value may present a problem. It can be argued that Congress as a result of its power over coinage has power to establish a monopoly legal tender and the right to refuse to accept other monies in payment of taxes. One consequence is that the federal government appears to possess advantages in money production not available to private producers.

In fact, however, no Constitutional changes may be required. One respondent, Charles Baird, argues that all that would be necessary to establish a private monetary arrangement is for the government to declare itself out of the fiat money business. In his view, government could continue to issue paper money, which could continue to serve as money only to the extent people chose to use it as such.

Finally, responses to "What issues should libertarians address themselves to with regard to money?" enables Morrell to set up a working agenda grouped around three issues. One issue deals with steps necessary to establish a gold-based monetary system. The preference is for a private or mixed public and private monetary arrangement based on gold. The second issue deals with demonstrating how and why government control of money is dangerous. The third issue focuses on Hayek's desire for moving with dispatch to a free monetary arrangement.

AMERICAN NINETEENTH-CENTURY MULTI-CURRENCY EXPERIENCES

Morrell is certainly correct that "people will not reject State monopoly money, however unsatisfactory it may seem, unless we can make a positive case for private money." American pre–Civil War experience with a largely private monetary arrangement based on specie (gold and silver) is suggestive. The historical record is mixed. The fact is that the notes of hundreds of banks circulated in any American community. Some were "as good as specie"; some worth half their face value; some counterfeit. Indeed, the differences between "legitimate" paper issue was one of degree and not of kind. The existence of "bank-note detectors" suggests the nature of the "quality" problem with the circulating media.[7]

Undoubtedly some counterfeiting went on—for why else counterfeit detectors? On the other hand, it was an easy matter to enter into legitimate banking during this period, so that legal "counterfeiting," which was preferable, made the illegal kind less widespread. Indeed, Hepburn writes,

> Notwithstanding the strength of the State Bank of Indiana, the state itself was for a time the favorite place for incubating banks (note issuing) without capital, banking offices, or furniture. A circular letter issued, offering aid to anyone desiring to start such a bank, stated that the sole cost necessarily incurred in starting a $100,000 bank would be $5,000 for plates to print the notes and expenses, including compensation to the promoter, and $5,000 as margin to carry the necessary bonds to be deposited. The owner of such a bank could as well reside in New York as Indiana.[8]

The operations of "strictly private" bankers are not included in any official estimates of banking operations.[9] They were not required to report to any authority. In function the private bankers varied considerably and were usually somewhat different from chartered state banks. They were not banks of issue, though they sometimes circumvented or openly violated laws against note issue. For example, the existence of "George Smith's money" is a case in point. These notes were issued by the Wisconsin Marine and Fire Insurance Company, which was controlled by George Smith. The company clearly had no right to issue circulating notes, but these notes were convertible into specie at all times with such absolute certainty that they passed at par everywhere, and for years constituted the best currency in the Northwest.[10] The later development of private bankers in the deposit field can be partly attributed to the stricter regulations imposed on state banks by the various states.[11]

Moreover, counterfeit notes as well as those of broken banks, until discovered, added to the money supply and so tended to raise prices imposing a self-administered tax on cash balances. The revenue, however, did not go to the government. It went to counterfeiters. Phillip Cagan notes that "when the economy lingered at less than full employment, new issues of notes helped stimulate recovery; consequently, from the modern view, skillful counterfeiters who would double their efforts during hard times should be acclaimed public benefactors."[12] We have noted the direct costs to society elsewhere. The advantages of a uniform currency to the rapid development of industry and commerce in the United States was repeatedly underscored.

Partly in response to the American public's demand for a uniform currency, and partly out of the Treasury's desperate need to meet war requirements, the federal government assumed its long-neglected Constitutional monetary powers, effected first in the Legal Tender Act of 1862 and then in the Sherman Act of 1863, establishing the National Bank System. They were exercised again in 1865 but less successfully when Congress put a prohibitive tax on state bank notes in an effort to force state banks to shift to the national system.

One result, of course, was to promote the use of deposits and checks by state banks and elsewhere.

One can argue that the bank note problem was never the principal concern of reformers. For instance, while many state banks did make the shift to the National Bank System, a substantial and growing number did not, demonstrating that the "bank note issue was not essential; it was not even of great importance, and it was no more than a mirror source of profit even when accounted to be of value as advertising."[13] Difficulties in financing the war and concern over its unexpected duration were undoubtedly more important. The Treasury's longstanding policy in compliance with the Department of Treasury Act of 1846 of accepting payment in specie only, and its insistence that the first large war loan for which it arranged conform with its specie policy, drained bank specie reserves. As a result specie payments were suspended in December 1861. The Treasury thereafter insisted on payment in its own Greenback notes authorized by the Legal Tender Acts of 1862.

Greenback notes, however, were not at first issued in a quantity adequate to handle large sales of U.S. bonds. It was argued that issue of Greenbacks should be restricted so as to limit bank reserves and further issues of bank notes. President Lincoln's Secretary of the Treasury, Salmon P. Chase, proposed a new, uniform currency backed by U.S. bonds to replace state bank notes. Congress would not even consider it. By 1863 matters were different. Victory appeared a long way off, and government expenditures were mounting. The ability of the Treasury to function under such conditions was seriously questioned. Chase's proposal for a unified national currency became attractive as a war measure. Even so, the bill was passed by only a narrow majority. The fact is that none of the provisions of the various banking legislation were really new. In one form or another they were already in practice in some states.

American experience with private bank notes suggests also that poorer banks showed more interest in putting out notes and keeping them out. The better banks cultivated deposit business. From about 1850 on, deposits exceeded bank notes in public hands. One reason bank deposits received little interest in early reports is that the relationship between deposits and loans was hazy and often omitted from banking statistics. Bank notes, however, received considerable public attention.

Public sentiment favored open banking with few of the restrictions of other businesses. Indeed, "free banking" was taken to mean, as pointed out by the Comptroller of New York in 1849, that anyone was "freely permitted to embark in it, upon compliance with certain conditions." The early framers of American banking legislation insisted on differentiation of banks from corporations. In New York, for instance, attempts were made to designate "free banks" authorized as "associations" to differentiate them from corporations. The state constitution required to be valid any act of incorporation to be adopted by a two-thirds majority of all legislators — a majority that could not be obtained. The problem was avoided by substituting the word *association* for *corporation,* and the bill was passed. Subsequent New York court decisions cast doubt on the constitutionality of the distinction. A new state constitution defined *corporation* to include *association.*

Free banking in New York appeared to work well, as it did in the other northeastern states. Banks were free to issue notes in return for depositing bonds with the state as security for the notes. Apparently, established wealth and a generally conservative financial atmosphere accounted for its success. So, too, in the South, banks in such centers as New Orleans were sound. Free banking made little headway in the commercial centers of the region. It was in the West and parts of the South, however, that the experiment went out of control, casting doubts on "free banking."

Indeed, my own estimates suggest a respectable average reserve ratio for reporting banks of about 22 percent for the period 1834–60. Even in the absence of required legal reserve requirements in some areas, it cannot be assumed that in practice banks maintained inadequate reserves. For instance, Clearing House banks in New York City maintained reserves of 20 percent against deposits in 1858, and raised this to 25 percent in 1862.

As a matter of fact, from 1791 to 1811 the First Bank of the United States served to maintain the "quality" of bank notes, and from about 1820 to 1836 the Second Bank of the United States performed the same service; the Suffolk Bank of Boston did much the same for bank notes in New England almost up to the Civil War, while in the rest of the country currency conditions ranged from good to poor.

Resentment and envy were created by the Bank of the United States in its role as depository of the Treasury and its self-assumed role of currency regulator. The bank kept pressure on the state banks' reserves, thus limiting their credit extension and expansion of their deposit and note liabilities. These feelings were reinforced by states' rights, fear of increasing federal power, and growing monopoly in the country's monetary arrangement. The stage was prepared for the struggle for monetary supremacy which has characterized a good deal of American monetary and financial history. One effect of this struggle was to generate considerable public uncertainty over money and the country's monetary system.

Thus, the First Bank's charter was allowed to expire in 1811, and its offices became state banks. In 1814 a general suspension of specie occurred, and for the next five years American circulating bank notes (in terms of specie) left much to be desired. The Treasury found its operations made difficult, thanks to the varying rates of discount in the bank notes of state banks. These difficulties prompted another attempt at national banking. In 1816 The Second Bank of the United States was chartered for twenty years. Once again the Bank collided with local banks and states' rights politicians.

As we noted, the Suffolk Bank in Boston which Hayek recommends as a model for a private monetary arrangement served New England well as a regulator of currency. Unlike the Bank of the United States, however, which performed its regulatory function as the creditor of local banks, the Suffolk Bank, like the Federal Reserve Banks, performed its regulatory role as their debtor. Nor did the Suffolk Bank have its constitutionality challenged as did the Bank of the United States in 1819 in the now-celebrated Supreme Court decision in *McCulloch* v. *Maryland.* Its constitutionality assured, which its detractors denied, freed from prohibitory taxation by states in which it had offices, the Second Bank of the United States enjoyed a brief period of prosperity — a period during which it managed to improve the country's currency circulation while at the same time alienating important sections of government on whose good will its survival depended. This is an early illustration of the illusory nature of central bank independence.

President Jackson's administration, which began in 1829, ushered in a new phase in the continuing and growing struggle for monetary supremacy. Matters were complicated by the fact that the Second Bank of the United States was located in Philadelphia, whose dominant economic role was overtaken by New York. Moreover, New York was the source of the bulk of Federal Customs receipts. These receipts went to Philadelphia for deposit, with the Second Bank providing considerable irritation to New York merchants and underscoring again the issues of states' rights. The issue was soon brought to national attention when Martin Van Buren, an influential New Yorker, became advisor to President Jackson. Since the Bank's charter was to expire in 1836, the New Yorkers set about getting the deposit of federal funds moved to New York City. This was not difficult to do in view of the political temper of the times. To be sure, the Bank's opponents on Wall Street kept their own counsel; the agrarian and states' rights interests and President Jackson were cultivated to their side. They won. In 1832 President Jackson vetoed the new charter passed by Congress. A few months later Jackson was re-elected with a sizable majority. Anticipating the Bank's demise in 1836, Jackson began transferring government deposits to selected state banks.

Thereafter came the Specie Circular of 1836, and the Deposit Act, which called for distribution of the federal surplus among the several states. The distribution was to be made in 1837 in four installments. Only the first installment was paid in full, and within a year of the Van Buren administration the Treasury was in deficit more than $5 million. The New Yorkers, however, did not get their "Big Bank." Instead, the opponents of banking pushed through the Independent Treasury System in 1846. Under this system the banks were denied all federal deposits, the Treasury was required to hold all its funds in its own vaults in gold and silver, and all payments to and by the Treasury were required to be made in coin only.

THE SECOND BANK OF THE UNITED STATES AND THE MONEY SUPPLY: AN EARLY ATTEMPT AT CENTRAL BANKING BY DISCRETIONARY AUTHORITY AND ITS LIMITS

It is held by contemporaries and more recent students that the Second Bank of the United States represented an early central bank which had three distinctive methods with which to exercise its discretionary authority and thus affect "favorably" the money supply:[14] it was the depository of federal funds; it possessed numerous branches; it exercised "proper restraint" in its dealing as a private bank.

By skillfully employing these methods, it is held, the Bank was able to wield control over state banks and through them on the money supply.[15] The process of control was simplicity itself: the Bank merely presented the bank notes of the state banks for payment when they fell into its hands. Contemporaries emphasized that the stability of the country's currency depended almost exclusively on this measure.[16] As to the effects of these operations, evidence is presented that state bank notes prior to 1834 had been either driven out of circulation or made redeemable in specie.[17]

Thus, Bray Hammond, after defending the Second Bank, comments on its destruction:

> After much painful experience the achievements of the Jacksonians in the banking field were repudiated in the administrations of Abraham Lincoln, Woodrow Wilson, and Franklin Roosevelt, and the monetary order they destroyed was in principle restored. In reflecting on the stupidity, self interest, and cost of the Jacksonian blunder, one may well remember how intelligently Nicholas Biddle played his responsible part in the order and how, loyally, though not so intelligently, he tried to prevent its destruction.[18]

This is indeed a harsh and serious indictment of the Jacksonians. It is all the more harsh and serious since it is not at all clear that the Second Bank and its president possessed the control over the money supply that Hammond and others attributed to them. In the first instance Hammond's argument in defense of discretionary monetary control exercised by the Second Bank is overdrawn. For example, he writes:

> Mr. Biddle's conduct of the Bank was very careful. Nothing impressed him more than the delicacy and the complexity of the economy; and whatever stimulation or pressure was required should be administered with care and lenity. The word "gentle" and "gently" were always coming from his quill.[19]

It should be pointed out, however, that if the Second Bank could affect the money supply and the economy by "skillfully" employing the methods at its disposal, it could just as well affect the money supply and the economy by "unskillfully" employing the same methods. It does little for the defense of discretionary controls to argue that such controls will always, or even often, be employed "skillfully." And indeed there is little comfort to be found in the ability of "skillful" employment of discretionary controls even by so august a figure as Nicholas Biddle. Thus Hammond, commenting on the reasons for the fall of Nicholas Biddle, writes:

> I should ascribe his fall, perhaps the most dramatic and consequential in American history, to four things which are not matters of morals but are, very clearly, matters of judgment, of temper, and of calculation. The first was his temperamental inability to cope with the assault upon the government bank which terminated the early and better part of his career; the second was his poor business judgment; the third was his having too much to do with the agricultural South and too little with the industrial North; the fourth was his predilection for easy money and the long-term capital market.[20]

Furthermore, even the methods available to the Second Bank for controlling the money supply are subject to several criticisms. In the first instance, the possession of numerous branches might simply have resulted in the circulation of the notes of the Second Bank instead of the notes of state banks. This does not mean that the availability of a relatively uniform currency might not have been economically advantageous. It does mean, however, that the possession of numerous branches is consistent with little or no effect on the total money supply. In the second instance, the exercise of "proper restraint" in its dealings as a private bank is asserted as a method for keeping state banks in debt to the Second Bank. By keeping state banks in debt, it is said, the Second Bank restricted their operations with a threat of a call for specie. The serious employment of this method, however, would almost certainly have resulted in making the Second Bank a smaller institution. Indeed, if it made no loans and issued no notes it would simply go out of business. The real method of control over state banks seems to have stemmed from the Bank's position as a depository for federal funds.[21] In its position as a federal depository, a state bank in all payments to the government had to satisfy the Bank of the United States that its notes were equivalent to specie before the government would receive them and if the government refused them, a source of extensive circulation was closed. In this matter, the Bank could face a state bank with the alternative of operating on a specie paying basis or having its business severely restricted and the credit of its notes destroyed.

However, in order to see what the real effects of the Bank's actions were on the money supply, one must see what its effect was on international economic movements. The reason for this becomes obvious when one recalls that the United States was on the international specie standard with fixed exchange rates. Under these circumstances a country's first monetary duty is to obey the well-known rules for the operation of that standard. There is little room indeed for a central bank—albeit a primitive one such as the Second Bank—to exercise discretionary authority and to pursue an independent course of action.

Under a specie standard the exchange rates are fixed within specie points, with the result that the internal price level and income in the United States are at first determined by the external events. Thus the internal price level must be of a value relative to the external price level, such that payments, including capital flows, balance. Consequently, the internal money supply is determined by external conditions, but its composition may be affected by internal monetary circumstances. A special explanation for domestic disturbances can arise only if internal prices move differently from external prices.

Domestic conditions can affect the internal price level and incomes appreciably only insofar as they affect the conditions of external balance. For example, suppose internal monetary (bank credit) expansion threatens suspension of specie payments. A price level sufficiently low relative to the external price level must occur so that a surplus will arise which finances the capital outflow.

If the country is not on a specie standard and fixed exchange rates, the situation is different. Internal monetary changes affect income, the price levels, and exchange rates. Income and the internal price level are no longer rigidly linked to external events.

The primacy of external events on internal income and price levels is important because much of the monetary upheaval in the United States during the nineteenth century may have been simply manifestations of disturbances more fundamental in nature. Erratic capital flows into and out of the United States, which characterized important periods of the nineteenth century, are but cases in point. The increase in capital inflows required an increase in the internal stock of money in the United States. The only question was how. An expansion of bank note issues and deposit credit would not be a reason for an increase in the money supply; it would be only one form of a rise that would have occurred in one way or another. And, of course, the opposite would occur for periods of world deflation and cessation of capital imports.

Consider, for instance, the sharp decline in the United States from 1839 to 1843.[22] External prices also declined, and the required internal price fall in the United States was further intensified by the cessation of the capital inflow of earlier years and by some repatriation of foreign investment. This contraction had important effects on the banking structure of the United States, namely the destruction of the Second Bank in 1841 (then under Pennsylvania charter), a 25 percent decrease in the number of banks from 1840 to 1843, and about a 30 percent decrease in the stock of money. The collapse of the banking system was one of the forms by which an adjustment, forced by other circumstances, worked itself out. The price decline abroad, cessation of the large capital inflow of earlier years, repudiation of obligations, suspension of specie payments by some banks, and distrust both at home and abroad in the maintenance of the specie standard by the United States made a sizable decline in prices the only alternative to the abandonment of the specie standard and depreciation of the dollar relative to other currencies. Given the maintenance of the specie standard, such an adjustment was unavoidable; if it had not occurred partly through the banking collapse, it would have done so in some other way, for example, by the export of specie. Along with the rest of the country, the less developed areas such as in the southern states of Alabama, Mississippi, Florida, Arkansas, Louisiana, Georgia, and the Carolinas contributed their share to readjustment by banking collapses and repudiation of both domestic and international debt.

Reactions to these various necessary adjustments took many forms, including those already discussed. On the national level, Andrew Jackson's "hard currency" schemes and the Specie Circular of 1836 are perhaps the best illustrations of reaction against adjustments generated by external factors which required an expansion of the money stock in the United States.[23] On the local levels, prohibition against banking in some states is characteristic of the extreme form reaction took to the necessary contraction in the money stock, which was partly manifested in the banking collapse of the later 1830s and early 1840s. Singularly harsh, these attempts are but examples of efforts to tighten the country's monetary straitjacket and to force its monetary radicals to dance to the tune of the specie standard.

The amount of confusion and mischief spread by some historians and others who fail to grasp the realities of the specie standard game is best illustrated in the commotion over the Second Bank of the United States. Arthur M. Schlesinger, Jr., for example, argues that the Second Bank was a menace to representative government, and its alleged destruction at the hands of Andrew Jackson fully justified.[24] This eliminated, presumably, the concentration of power over loans and currency circulation from the hands of a relatively small group of men. Thus Professor Schlesinger would have us believe a dangerous obstacle to American economic expansion was removed. Bray Hammond, on the other hand, as noted, defends the Bank in a harsh and serious indictment of the Jacksonians.

Much of the confusion, as noted, arises out of the methods ostensibly available to the Second Bank for controlling the money supply. Some of the contemporary reviews attributed the direct "cause" of the rise in prices in 1834–36 and subsequent difficulties to the operations of "speculators." Friends of the federal administration and supporters of the Second Bank of the United States freely exchanged acrimonious charges, each blaming the other for the country's economic plight. Others simply blamed all three, the speculators as well as the two contestants for monetary supremacy. All groups agreed that something was "wrong" with the money system of the country, but of course disagreed what that "something" was. For example, the federal government emphasized "monopoly" in banking, and sought to eliminate such "monopoly" by the removal of government deposits from the Second Bank of the United States and by the elimination of the Bank as a national institution. In addition, government sought to institute a "hard currency" in the place of existing "bank rags," i.e., bank notes. The supporters of the Second Bank of the United States, on the other hand, argued that the new method of handling government deposits was the cause of the surplus which accumulated in the Treasury by 1836. The distribution of this surplus in 1837, they argued, precipitated the crisis of that year and the difficulties that followed. As a solution to the country's economic plight, they called for a recharter of the Second Bank, or a similar institution, the return of government deposits, and a "well-regulated" bank currency." The term *well-regulated* was usually interpreted to mean according to the "needs of trade."

For almost a decade the struggle for monetary supremacy continued. And, of course, so did the uncertainty about the ultimate outcome.

In respect to the struggle for monetary supremacy, it is worth emphasizing the contrast between the arithmetic and the economics of the situation. The rapid rise in the internal stock of money, prices, and the physical volume of trade in the period from 1834 to 1836 was coincident with the general external expansion. Coupled with the external expansion was the substantial inflow into the United States of both short-term and long-term capital. Although the capital inflow varied, owing partly to the uncertainty created by the struggle for monetary supremacy, it did not cease completely with the difficulties of 1837 but continued into 1839.[25] Under these external conditions, internal adjustments were required on the part of the United States. The only question is how. If, for example, banks expand or contract their deposits and notes in circulation, this is not, under the assumed conditions, the reason the money supply rises or falls— it is only the form that is taken by a rise or a fall that would have occurred one way or another. This is the difference between the arithmetic and the economics of a situation. Thus the withdrawal of government deposits from the Second Bank and the use of state banks as depositories for government funds may well have increased money, prices, and surplus in the Treasury, but only because external circumstances in this period required an internal expansion. As was indicated, this does not mean that internal disturbances cannot affect the money supply and prices; they can, but only insofar as they affect the conditions of external balance. It could be, for example, that the internal monetary expansion, coupled with the distribution of the surplus, threatened suspension. This, in turn, would have promoted a capital outflow that would be deflationary.

During the period of suspension, 1837–38, the situation in the United States was different. Internal monetary changes affected the internal price level, and through it the exchange rate, so the price level was no longer rigidly linked to external price levels. Although to a first approximation the changes in the internal stock of money were determined by the requirements of external balance, the particular way in which changes in the money stock were achieved reflected domestic monetary influences.

We may summarize the pre-1860 American monetary experience with a method devised by Phillip Cagan for analyzing changes in the money stock.[26] Cagan views the stock of money as having three proximate determinants within an identity relationship.

The proximate determinants of the money supply are high-powered money (specie), the currency-money ratio (specie-money), and the reserve ratio specie to bank notes and bank deposits in public hands. The reserve ratio referred to is not a legal requirement set by monetary authorities, but the existing ratio of reserves to deposits. Since all high-powered money must be either currency in public hands or reserves held by banks, these variables account completely for changes in high-powered money, with shifts in the composition of cash balances between currency and deposits, and with changes in bank-created deposit and notes outstanding.

Cagan formulates these relationships into the identity

$$M = \frac{H}{C/M + R/D - (C/M)(R/D)}.$$

The variation in M due to changes in the determinants may then be calculated by the formula

$$\frac{d}{dt} \ln M = \frac{d}{dt} \ln H + \frac{M}{H}(1 - R/D)\frac{d}{dt}(-C/M) + \frac{M}{H}(1 - C/M)\frac{d}{dt}(1R/D).$$

Multiplying each component of the right-hand side by $\dfrac{100}{\frac{d}{dt}\ln M}$ yields the effect expressed as a percentage.

The results of the investigation summarized in Tables 8.1 and 8.2 indicate that over the entire 1834–60 period, the most notable roles are played by, first, changes in the reserve ratio; second, changes in specie-money ratio; third, changes in high-powered money.

Let the variable which contributes the largest short-term effect of the three in any given year be called the "most significant variable" for that year. The evidence indicates that this most significant variable was not the same throughout the 26-year period under the review. Of the three, the banking reserve ratio appears to be the most significant. In an index presented in

Table 8.1   Money Stock, National Income, Velocity and Prices in the
United States, 1834-1860 (in thousands of dollars)

Year	Original Money Stock[a] (000)	Midyear Money Stock[b] (000)	Velocity[c]	National Income (000)	Warren-Pearson Price Index (Base 1830)
1834	152,052	156,939	7.12	1,117,405	99
1835	161,826	189,783	7.34	1,393,007	110
1836	217,741	220,876	7.40	1,634,482	125
1838	220,473	225,065	7.06	1,588,959	121
1839	229,658	216,557	7.65	1,656,661	123
1840	203,457	195,153	7.38	1,440,229	104
1841	186,849	180,314	7.13	1,285,539	101
1842	174,730	162,066	6.80	1,102,049	90
1843	149,252	165,369	6.70	1,107,972	82
1844	181,487	191,836	6.78	1,330,648	85
1845	202,190	214,732	6.84	1,468,767	91
1846	227,274	239,732	6.88	1,649,356	91
1847	252,171	259,757	6.97	1,810,506	99
1848	267,343	263,137	6.83	1,797,226	90
1849	316,349	347,609	6.65	2,311,600	92
1851	379,270	393,859	6.67	2,627,040	91
1852	408,449	429,878	6.68	2,871,585	97
1853	451,303	478,122	6.70	3,203,417	107
1854	504,936	506,750	6.72	3,405,536	119
1855	508,565	521,535	6.49	3,384,762	121
1856	534,505	554,471	6.96	3,859,118	115
1857	574,436	525,755	6.53	3,443,180	122
1858	477,073	511,915	6.12	3,132,920	102
1859	546,858	556,161	6.46	3,592,800	104
1860	565,165	565,465	6.80	3,845,162	102

[a]Money Stock, from Table 8.2, page 142.

[b]Midyear money stock derived by the arithmetic average of each two years in succession.

Source: Velocity and National Income: George Macesich, "Money Stock National Income and Velocity in the U.S. 1834-60" (working manuscript);Warren-Pearson Wholesale Price Index: G. R. Warren and F. A. Pearson, *Wholesale Prices for 213 Years, 1720-1932* (Ithaca: Cornell University Press, 1932), Part 1, pp. 8-9.

Table 8.3, where one indicates least significant, the variables score as follows: $H = 1.88$; $C/M = 1.92$; $R/D = 2.23$. These results give substance to concern over internal monetary and banking stability raised by writers of classical and neoclassical persuasion, even though the disturbances themselves are basically of external origin and the ones to which banks were reacting. Such concern ostensibly prompted the passage of the National Bank

Act of 1863 and significant federal government intervention into the economy. As noted above, financing the Civil War by the federal government, however, may well have had a greater weight attached to it than requirements of banking reforms and/or providing a uniform currency for the country. In conclusion, it is interesting to note that contrary to the views of contemporaries and those of more recent students, the monetary damage done by the initial struggle for monetary supremacy, and the uncertainty generated by making a large specie stock desirable, rather than producing too rapid a rise in the money supply, kept the money supply from rising as much as it otherwise would have. All of this, however, was played out against a background of fluctuating capital imports and a specie standard with fixed exchange rates.

Accordingly and to a first approximation, it seems reasonable to conclude that the internal struggle for monetary supremacy was a surface manifestation of a deeper disturbance — the general worldwide expansion and subsequent contraction coupled with a substantial inflow of capital. The consequent adjustment to the external disturbance at first permitted the internal struggle to continue. For example, the capital inflow enabled the Second Bank to stand against the partisans of "hard currency." At the same time, the inflow of specie enabled the partisans of "hard currency" to press for the elimination of the Bank. However, the internal struggle set in motion forces which in themselves were important.

American experience tends to leave most people skeptical about extension of the "free market" to monetary arrangements — even if workable. As the experience underscores, monetary affairs are seldom left alone. Indeed, they readily become critical political issues of a very explosive nature. Proper institutional constraints are necessary. The international specie standard and fixed exchange rates seemed to keep the American experience within prescribed bounds. Even so, it did not always work well.

The Classical Gold Standard, Managed Fiduciary Standard, and Economic Performance Since 1834: A Summary View

Available evidence appears to suggest that economic performance in Great Britain and the United States was better under the classical gold standard than under the managed fiduciary standard. For instance, both the price level and real economic activity were more stable in the pre-1914 period under the gold standard than in any period since. The unfortunate coincidence of troubles which produced the collapse of the international monetary and financial framework, and the subsequent deflation, real output instability, and high unemployment which characterize this period, account for much of the poor performance. These results underscore our earlier discussion of the profound political, philosophic, economic, and social changes that have occurred in the world since the early years of the twentieth century.

Table 8.2 Proximate Determinants of Money Stock in the United States, 1834-1860

Year	M[a] (000)	H[b] (000)	C/M[c]	RR[d]	DH[e]	DC[f]	DR[g]	DM[h]	ΔM[i]
1834	152,052	41,000	.104	.185				101.6	9,774
1835	161,826	51,000	.044	.284	350.3	256.8	-505.6	99.8	55,915
1836	217,741	65,000	.115	.208	61.7	-58.9	77.1	99.9	6,270
1837	224,011	72,300	.154	.200	374.9	-350.5	75.5	99.9	-3,538
1838	220,473	86,474	.233	.208	-1124.5	1118.1	115.3	108.9	9,185
1839	229,658	85,731	.177	.239	-21.1	277.7	-156.8	99.8	-26,201
1840	203,457	82,309	.242	.215	33.6	106.9	-40.6	99.9	-16,608
1841	186,849	78,586	.234	.243	54.4	-16.6	62.3	100.0	-12,069
1842	174,780	79,795	.294	.230	-22.9	155.4	-32.5	100.0	-25,528
1843	149,252	89,620	.376	.360	-73.5	71.5	106.0	103.9	32,235
1844	181,487	99,442	.273	.378	53.2	57.9	-11.1	100.0	20,703
1845	202,190	95,432	.253	.293	-38.1	24.1	114.7	100.7	25,084
1846	227,274	96,253	.239	.243	7.3	20.4	72.5	100.3	24,897
1847	252,171	116,893	.324	.206	186.9	-144.1	57.4	100.2	15,172
1848	267,343	108,898	.234	.226	-121.3	279.2	-57.8	100.2	-8,412
1849	258,931	118,016	.287	.236	-251.5	298.7	53.8	101.0	57,418
1850	316,349	148,680	.326	.213	115.3	-32.8	17.5	100.0	62,921
1851	379,270	176,355	.337	.194	94.1	-9.5	15.4	100.0	29,179
1852	408,449	190,469	.348	.182	103.9	-26.4	22.5	100.0	42,859
1853	451,308	217,308	.377	.168	132.1	-51.0	18.9	100.0	53,628
1854	504,936	219,706	.318	.172	9.8	96.4	-6.0	100.1	3,629
1855	508,565	230,523	.347	.162	671.2	-778.9	207.8	100.0	25,940
1856	534,505	230,082	.319	.163	-3.8	105.7	-1.8	100.0	39,932
1857	574,437	240,863	.318	.149	63.4	5.9	31.6	100.0	-97,364
1858	477,073	248,173	.364	.245	-16.1	43.6	74.0	101.5	69,785
1859	546,858	244,187	.255	.257	-11.9	124.2	-12.0	100.3	18,307
1860	565,165	232,691	.264	.201	-146.4	-46.2	292.8	100.1	

[a] Money Stock: George Macesich, "Money Supply in the United States, 1934–60." (working manuscript)

[b] High-powered Money: Total specie less specie in the Treasury. In this computation, all Treasury holdings are assumed to be in specie.

[c] Currency -Money Ratio: Specie in public hands divided by the Money Stock in (1).

[d] Reserve Ratio: Specie in banks divided by deposits plus bank notes held by the public.

[e] Adjusted relative influence of the change in High-powered Money (expressed as a percentage) on 100 percent of the change in the Money Stock.

[f] Adjusted relative influence of the change in the Currency-Money Ratio (expressed as a percentage) on 100 percent of the change inthe Money Stock.

[g] Adjusted relative influence of the change in the Reserve Ratio (expressed as a percentage) on 100 percent of the change in the Money Stock.

[h] Algebraic total of (5), (6), and (7). It shows total change in the Money Stock accounted for by the three variables.

[i] Absolute change in M.

Note: All figures are shown to the date nearest January 1 of the year reported.

Table 8.3   Most Significant Single Determinant

	H	C/M	R/D	Size of ΔM
1835	2	3	1	+ S
1836	1	3	2	+ L
1837	1	2	3	+ S
1838	1	2	3	− S
1839	3	1	2	+ S
1840	3	1	2	− L
1841	2	3	1	− M
1842	3	1	2	− M
1843	3	2	1	− L
1844	2	1	3	+ M
1845	2	3	1	+ M
1846	3	2	1	+ M
1847	1	2	3	+ M
1848	2	1	3	+ M
1849	2	1	3	− S
1850	1	2	3	+ L
1851	1	3	2	+ L
1852	1	2	3	+ M
1853	1	2	3	+ L
1854	2	1	3	+ L
1855	2	1	3	+ S
1856	2	1	3	+ M
1857	1	3	2	+ M
1858	2	3	1	− L
1859	3	1	2	+ L
1860	2	3	1	+ M

Note: See Table 8.2 for explanation of column heads.

According to evidence presented by Bordo, a slight downtrend on the average of 0.14 percent per year in the price level is registered in the United States during the period 1834–1913.[27] The exceptions in this trend are the sharp price rises during the 1830s, substantial capital imports into the United States, and again price rises from 1861–1866 during the American Civil War when the United States was off the gold standard. The rapid price deflation from 1869 to 1890 was necessitated by American return to the gold standard in 1879.

Price stability does not characterize the period since World War I. In fact, in the United Kingdom, the United States, and elsewhere, price levels have on the average been rising. Short periods of price stability occurred during the 1920s under the Gold Exchange Standard, the 1950s and early 1960s under the Bretton Woods System. For the period 1914–79, price levels in the

United States registered an annual rate of increase of 2.2 percent and for the U.K. an average annual increase of 3.81 percent.

Overall the record does indicate more long-term price stability during the gold standard era than in the years since departure from that standard. The tendency for price levels to revert toward long-run stable value under the gold standard ensured a measure of predictability with respect to the value of money. There could be short-term price rises or declines; inflation or deflation however would not continue.

Long-term price stability encouraged people to enter into contracts on the expectation that changes in prices for commodities and factors of production would reflect real changes and not changes in the value of money brought about by inflation or deflation. One consequence of departure from the gold standard and lack of constraint in general prices is to generate confusion, as between changes in price levels and changes in relative prices. This confusion increases the possibility for people to misjudge market signals and so incur major economic losses.

The evidence on real per capita income for the U.S. and the U.K. suggests that it was more stable under the gold standard than in any period since World War I. For the United States the mean absolute values of percentage deviations of real per capita income from trend is 6.64 percent from 1879 to 1913, and 8.97 percent from 1919 to 1979 (excluding 1941–45). For the U.K. the figures are 2.14 percent from 1870 to 1913 and 3.75 percent from 1919 to 1979 (excluding 1939–45). There is, moreover, in the U.K. a permanent break in trend in 1919, so that in subsequent years real per capita income is almost always below trend.

Unemployment, too, is on the average lower in the pre-1914 period in both the U.S. and the U.K. than in the post-World War I period. For the United States, average unemployment for 1890–1919 is 6.78 percent, and for 1919–79 (excluding 1941–45) it is 7.46 percent. For the U.K. the average unemployment rate over the period 1888–1913 is 4.30 percent, and for the period 1919–79 (excluding the World War II years 1939–45) it is 6.42 percent.

The evidence thus tends to support the view that the classical gold standard is associated with more economic stability than the managed fiduciary standard by which it was replaced. The problem with the comparison is that it includes the interwar period when the international monetary and financial organization collapsed.

The evidence presented by Bordo takes this into account. Accordingly, three time periods are compared: the pre–World War I gold standard period, the interwar period, and the post–World War II period. In point of fact, both World War years are omitted for comparison. Overall prices are more variable under the gold standard than in both post–gold standard periods. The least variability occurs in the post–World War II period. For the U.S., average annual percentage change in prices for the period 1879–1913 is 0.1 percent, and the coefficient of variation of annual percentage changes in the price level is 17.0. For the U.K. during the period 1870–1913 prices drift downward at an annual percentage change of – 0.7 percent and a coefficient of variation of – 14.9. For the period 1919–40 the U.S. records an annual percentage change in price of 2.5 percent with a coefficient of variation of – 5.2. For the U.K. and the period 1919–38, the average annual percentage change in prices is – 4.6 percent with a coefficient of variation of 3.8. The post–World War II years 1946–79 for the U.S. showed an average annual percentage rise in the price level of 2.8 percent with a coefficient of variation of 1.3. For the U.K. the average annual percentage rise in prices is 5.6 percent with a coefficient of variation of 1.2.

The stability of real output is suggested by the coefficient of variation of year-to-year percentage changes in real per capita output. The evidence suggests for the United States a coefficient of variation of 3.5 for the period 1879–1913; 5.5 for the period 1919–40; 1.6 for the period 1946–79. For the U.K. this coefficient is 2.5 for the period 1870–1913; 4.9 for the period 1919–38; 1.4 for the period 1946–79. In sum, real output is considerably less stable in both countries during the interwar years to the post–World War II years in both countries when higher rates of inflation and lower variability in output and unemployment are registered. It demonstrates the apparent policy preference away from long-term price stability toward full employment and suggests the reason, described earlier, behind the strong inflationary pressures in the postwar years. It is on the basis of such evidence that the public recognized that a specielike monetary system no longer existed and began to arrange their affairs accordingly.

The evidence also suggests that a fiduciary money standard based on a monetary rule for steady monetary growth could provide the benefits of the gold standard without its costs. A prerequisite for success, however, is a firm commitment on the part of government to maintain a monetary rule as well as to incorporate as one of its goals long-run price stability.

In any case, the fact is that the international specie or gold standard cannot be restored. It requires a return to the set of economic, political, and philosophic beliefs upon which that standard is based and which we have discussed. This is unlikely. It is probably easier to deprive the government altogether of its monopoloy over money. The magnitude of such a task, however, should not be minimized. The sensitive issue of national sovereignty is involved. For this reason, among others which we have discussed, governments will not voluntarily abdicate their power over money. These difficulties, therefore, permit an alternative approach in the form of Constitutional monetary constraints designed to restrict government manipulation of the money supply.

A Monetary Constitution

The constitutional approach to restricting the government's money role is viewed by many people, including this writer, as realistic.[28] In essence, it sets aside the assumption that governments are "benevolent despots." It assumes that politicians are not above self-seeking and have tended throughout the ages to abuse their money-creation authority. Accordingly, unrestrained monetary monopoly is the institutional explanation of the great postwar inflation which picked up pace in the 1970s and as such requires institutional reform. "It is the *monetary regime,* not *monetary policy,* that must be modified."[29]

Several schemes are proposed whose rules, in effect, amount to a form of constitution. The objective is to constrain the money monopoly powers of government. Brennan and Buchanan list and discuss four such regimes:[30] (1) free market in money, with no governmental role; (2) governmental money issue, but competitive entry; (3) pure commodity money, with governmental definition of value; (4) fiat money issue constrained by constitutional rules.

The first regime is similar to our foregoing discussion. The government simply has no role in money. It would not define the medium of exchange; it would not print money; it would not regulate private printing of money or bank notes; it would not regulate banking or credit. Such money as would emerge would be private money without government guarantees. Government would collect taxes in the money of its choice.

Even under such a free market arrangement, Brennan and Buchanan point out, "the government would be limited to minimal or protective state functions, involved largely in enforcing property rights and contracts among private parties."[31] Shortcomings of such a "free market" arrangement include the tendency to overexpand or overcontract the money supply. The "market failure" analysis of free markets would suggest a role for government. The advisability of such a role depends on the likelihood of its degenerating into an unconstrained monopoly of money issue. If one is pessimistic regarding ultimate government behavior, the other three monetary regimes are then ruled out as well. It does not rule out, however, a constitutional constraint on keeping the government completely out of monetary affairs.

The second regime is similar to Hayek's proposal for the denationalization of money, discussed above. The constitutional arrangements would involve a guarantee of free entry into the money-creating business and the freedom to hold balances, executive payments, and make contracts in money of holder's choice. Unlike the free-market arrangement, in this regime the government may offer some protection from booms and busts in private money creation.

The third regime is the more familiar specie/gold standard discussed elsewhere in this study. To maintain a strict commodity standard requires considerable effort. There is a tendency to convert commodity money into reserves upon which derivative bank and government paper money is issued. This would require that considerable "government regulation over and above the value of the monetary unit would have to be laid down in the constitution."[32]

Finally, the fourth regime would empower government to issue fiat money and allow a monopoly to specifically define rules that limit the powers of the money-creation authority. These are the now familiar rules advocated by Milton Friedman and earlier by Irving Fisher and Henry Simons, as we discussed elsewhere in this study.

What the several advocates share is the agreement that a monetary constitution is necessary and desirable. The specifics and content of such a constitution remain to be developed. On this score Brennan and Buchanan argue persuasively "that constitutional restraints, not advice, are the only effective discipline on politicians." "We cannot, and should not, expect the decision makers in the Bank of England or the United States Federal Reserve Board to behave 'as if' they are bound by a nonexistent constitutional rule for money issue. They will behave in accordance with such a role only if it exists. As the 1980s commence, more and more economists are coming to realize that unrestrained monopoly is the constitutional explanation of the great inflation of the 1970s. Institutional explanation suggests institutional reform. . . . It is the *monetary regime,* not *monetary policy* that must be modified."[33]

Our discussion of the theory of bureaucracy and central banks suggests the important role that the growing body of research results in the field of "public choice" can make to analysis of government.[34] It is now generally agreed that governments and their agencies have an internal dynamic of their own and are often insensitive to the wishes of their citizens. Few will now argue with confidence that electoral controls over politicians really work. Even fewer will now accept with confidence the pronouncements of central bankers that monetary policy is an "art" and as such is best managed by themselves according to their own lights. Indeed ". . . the differences, on balance, between nominally democratic regimes — as in the USA or UK, etc. — and nominally nondemocratic regimes — as in the Latin American military dictatorships — seem considerably less relevant, at least for monetary and budgetary policy, than they might at one time have appeared."[35]

Events in most countries in the post–World War II period underscore the difficulties in successfully operating a "democratically constrained" model of politics. It is made all the more difficult by the ability of bureaucrats to set the agenda for legislative actions with close support of politicians whose immediate political interests may be so served. Organized groups may well thwart public interest in pursuing their own narrow interests, as we have occasion to note in this study. It is suggested in the exercise of discretionary policy by central banks and it is particularly manifest in the use of government fiscal and regulatory measures for the benefit of special groups. Indeed

Buchanan puts it well when he points out that modern man, in the struggle to escape from the clutches of bureaucracy, can rely only on himself or on others like him.[36] The same is true in monetary affairs. In fact, it is also true irrespective of the socioeconomic and political system in place in a country. It holds for a market-oriented economy, a worker-managed economy, and a socialist economy.

On the international level, one solution to the monetary problem for countries constitutionally restricting government's money role is to tie the countries at the economic level with flexible exchange rates.[37] Such an agreement permits each country to develop its economy within the confines of its territory according to its own appraisal of possibilities. Flexible exchange rates provide an "automatic" trade balancing mechanism, thereby eliminating the necessity for trade and exchange controls. At the same time, the individual nations are freed from having to coordinate monetary (and fiscal) policies and economic development programs with other nations. Encroachment into the delicate area of national sovereignty is minimized.

By promoting what would partially deputize for competitive price flexibility, flexible exchange rates would increase the effectiveness of the price mechanism and thus contribute to legitimate international economic integration. Such an arrangement provides a means for combining international interdependence among countries through trade, with the greatest possible amount of internal monetary and fiscal independence; no country would be able to impose its mistakes of policy on others nor would it have their mistakes imposed on itself. Every country would be free to pursue policies for internal stability according to its own appraisal of possibilities. If all participating countries succeeded in their internal policies, reasonably stable exchange rates would prevail. The chances for such success presumably would be all the greater if each country constrained its government's monopoly over money. Each country, moreover, is left free if it so chooses to design whatever monetary constraints best suit its circumstances.

On the other hand, critics of a system of flexible exchange rates argue that an exchange rate left to find its own level will not necessarily trace out an optimum path through time. An *optimum*, at that, is very difficult to define, since its criteria hinge on expectations that can never be guaranteed.[38] Nevertheless, there is no necessity in the market to yield such a reasonably satisfactory rate. In small undiversified and less developed countries, which are members of the world market, a lack of sophisticated individuals with a heterogeneous outlook and sufficient capital may impair the working of a competitive market in foreign exchange.

Another criticism is that exchange rate adjustments will not necessarily insulate the level of domestic activity while correcting an internal balance. Exchange rate adjustments are particularly desirable where price levels have moved out of line. The exchange rate correction will restore the terms of trade to their original position and leave the volume and balance of trade and real income in each country at their original levels. The units of measurement will simply be changed. This is no longer true where the sources of disturbance are structural changes in trading countries with different rates of full employment growth and cyclical income fluctuations. In effect, repercussions on domestic employment and output can be reduced, but apparently they cannot be eliminated by flexible exchange rates.

Critics of constitutional constraint on money monopoly of government interpret such efforts as reflecting a profound mistrust in the institutions of American democracy. They argue that it is more than a retreat for "fine tuning." It is, rather, a desire to abjure all discretionary management of the economy.[39] This is reinforced by recent research investigating the interaction between political and economic forces, as in the theory of the political business cycle. Accordingly, it suggests the possibility that elected policymakers will manipulate economic policy in ways that exacerbate business cycles. Thus, attempts to substitute imperfect but binding rules for procedures that are in principle optimal but in practice prove manipulable are very likely worse than fixed rules and may be worse than constitutional constraints. Such arrangements are summed up by critics as the lame leading the sometimes wicked.

One rejoinder to such critics is that there is more to the idea of constitutional constraint than simply economic and political expediency, however important. As we discussed elsewhere there is a fundamental difference in the philosophy of money held by many of these critics. This view is put well by Frankel: "A monetary economy depends on a vast number of circumstances arising out of the history, mores, beliefs, and political and economic experience of society as a whole. It cannot be separated from them. That is why a dependable and free monetary order is a relatively rare phenomenon in the history of nations."[40] I would add that monetary order and money are important irrespective of a country's political system.

Monetary manipulation designed to decrease uncertainty has actually increased it by destroying faith in the monetary order. In the process, it threatens not only democracy itself but worldwide stability. There may be, indeed, better institutional arrangements than imposing rules and constitutional constraints. Thus far, however, they have not been forthcoming, thanks in part to government and bureaucratic restriction on experimentation with alternative monetary arrangements.[41]

Notes

1. See, for example, F. A. Hayek, *Denationalisation of Money* (London: Institute of Economic Affairs, 1976); H. G. Brennan and J. M. Buchanan, *Monopoly in Money and Inflation: The Case of a Constitution to Discipline Government* (London: Institute of Economic Affairs, 1981); S. O. Morrell, "In Search of a New Monetary Order: An Open Discussion on Aspects of a Freely Competitive Monetary Arrangement," *Institute Scholar*, vol. 1., no. 1 (1980), pp. 1–2; M. Bronfenbrenner, "The Currency-Choice Defense," *Challenge*, January/February, 1980, pp. 31–36.

2. Benjamin Klein, "The Competitive Supply of Money," *Journal of Money, Credit, and Banking,* November 1974; see also James R. Edward, "Monopoly and Competition in Money," *The Journal of Libertarian Studies* 4, no. 1 (Winter 1980), pp. 107-17.

3. Morrell, "In Search of a New Monetary Order," pp. 1-2.

4. Ibid., p. 2.

5. Ibid., p. 1.

6. Ibid., p. 2.

7. George Macesich, "Counterfeit Detectors and Pre-1860 Monetary Statistics," *Journal of Southern History,* May 1961, pp. 229-32.

Says W. G. Sumner in his *Banking in the United States* (New York: Journal of Commmerce and Commercial Bulletin, 1896), p. 455:

The bank-note detector did not become divested of its useful but contemptible function until the national bank system was founded. It is difficult for the modern student to realize that there were hundreds of banks whose notes circulated in any community. The bank notes were bits of paper recognizable as a species by shape, color, size, and engraved work. Any piece of paper which had these came with the prestige of money; the only thing in the shape of money to which people were accustomed. The person to whom one of them was offered, if unskilled in trade, had little choice but to take it. A merchant turned to this "detector."

Advertisements for the notes of broken banks appeared regularly in the financial sections because these notes could be used as claims against the existing capital of the broken banks. Thus Bicknell continually issued the following form. In 1835 he advertised:

Broken Bank Notes Wanted

The subscriber having received an order for the following sum in notes of Broken Banks, will purchase same, in lots, at the following prices:

$5,000 Bank of Maryland	at $.20	on	the	dollar
4,000 Susquehanna Bridge, payable at Md. Savings inst.	" .40	"	"	"
1,000 Bank of Alexandria	" .80	"	"	"
500 Bank of New Brunswick	" .20	"	"	"
500 Farmer's Bank	" .30	"	"	"
500 Salisbury Bank	" .50	"	"	"
250 Comm. Bank Milling	" .90	"	"	"
250 Westmoreland Bank	" .75	"	"	"

Robert T. Bicknell

No.2 Philadelphia Exchange

[Bicknell's *Counterfeit Detector,* Vol. 3, No. 1, April 1835]

8. A. B. Hepburn, *A History of Currency in the United States* (New York: Macmillan Company, 1915), p.164.

9. In addition to various reports submitted by state chartered banks, the primary source of monetary statistics for this period is the U.S. Comptroller's Report of 1876. The Comptroller in turn compiled his information from Congressional documents bearing serial numbers 385, 576, and 684, and Elliot's Funding System (28th Cong., 1st sess., Executive Document No. 15).

10. George Macesich, "Sources of Monetary Disturbances in the U.S. 1834-45," *Journal of Economic History,* September 1960; Hepburn, *Currency in the United States,* p. 164. See also Henriette M. Larson, "E. W. Clark and Co. 1837-57: The Beginning of an American Private Bank," *Journal of Economic and Business History,* IV (1931-32), pp. 488ff; R. H. Timberlake, Jr. "The Significance of Unaccounted Currencies," *Journal of Economic History* 41 (December 1981), pp. 853-66.

11. International impact of American "free banking" is suggested in the following report by Niles' *Weekly Register:*

On Wednesday night, four persons were arrested at a boarding house in Courtland Street, on suspicion of being counterfeiters. It appeared that about a week ago the gentlemen located themselves in the attick, where they were busily employed striking off bank bills, purporting to be on the Ottawa Bank of Montreal. The suspicions of the landlady being excited, she gave information to a magistrate. A posse of officers were forthwith despatched to seize both persons and papers. A great number of bills of the above bank were discovered. They were elegantly executed, and were drawn for various sums of $5 to $10,000. On their examination, the gentlemen were very indignant at being deprived of their liberty. They assured the magistrate that they had formed themselves into a regular banking concern, to be called the Ottawa Bank, and that it was their intention to carry on business under the above designation. As a reason for printing bills in this city, they said they could get it done much cheaper than in Canada . . . The first said he was director — the second had been appointed president — the third was cashier, and the fourth claimed to be a stockholder to a large amount. As it could not be shown that they violated any law, in thus starting a new bank, they were discharged. [Reprinted from the *New York Times* in Niles *Weekly Register*, vol. 52, May 13, 1837.]

George Macesich, "Sources of Monetary Disturbances in the U.S.," op. cit. See also Phillip Cagan, "The First Fifty Years of the National Banking System," Deanne Carson, ed., *Banking and Monetary Studies* (Homewood: R. D. Irwin, 1963) p. 21.

12. Ibid., p. 20.

13. Bray Hammond, "Banking Before the Civil War," Deanne Carson, ed., *Banking and Monetary Studies* (Homewood, Ill.: R. D. Irwin, 1963), p. 14.

14. See, for example, R. C. H. Catterall, *The Second Bank of the United States* (Chicago: University of Chicago Press, 1903); D. R. Dewey, *The Second United States Bank* (Washington: Government Printing Office, 1910); W. B. Smith, *Economic Aspects of the Second Bank of the United States* (Cambridge: Harvard University Press, 1953); and Bray Hammond, *Banks and Politics in America* (Princeton: Princeton University Press, 1957). The Second U.S. Bank operated from 1816 to 1841 with a State of Pennsylvania charter.

15. The money supply as defined in this study is specie held by the public plus bank deposits and bank notes held by the public.

16. H. R. 460, 22d Cong., 1st sess., p. 363, and H. O. Adams, *Gallatin's Writings,* 3 (Philadelphia: Lippincott, 1879), p. 336.

17. H. R. 358, 21st Cong., 1st sess., p. 18, and Niles' *Weekly Register*, 34, p. 154.

18. Hammond, *Banks and Politics in America*, p. 325.

19. Ibid., p. 304.

20. Ibid., p. 534.

21. Total goverment deposits amounted to more than $410 million during the entire period that the Second Bank held them. The importance of government deposits to the Second Bank may be seen from calculations made by the Secretary of the Treasury Taney, and R.C.H. Catterall. Average government deposits estimated by Taney for every month from 1819 to 1833 amounted to more than $6,717,253. Catterall computes the profits at 6 percent for the whole time that the Bank was a government depository. His computations indicate that the Bank was the gainer to te extent of $403,035.18 each year from 1818 to 1834 — a total of $6,448,562.28. S. D. 16, 23rd Cong., 1st sess., pp. 4–5, and R.C H. Catterall, *The Second bak*, p. 475.

22. For a more detailed analysis, see Macesich, "Sources of Monetary Disturbances," pp. 407–434 and Macesich, "International Trade and U.S. Economic Development Revisited, "*Journal of Economic History,* September 1961, pp. 384–85. See also Clark Warburton, "Variations in Economic Growth and Banking Developments in the U.S. from 1835 to 1885," *Journal of Economic History,* September 1958, pp. 283–97; J. Ernest Tanner and Vittorio Bonomo, "Gold, Capital Flows, and Long Swings in American Business Activity," *Journal of Political Economy,* January/February 1968, pp. 44–52; T. D. Willet, "International Specie Flows and American Monetary Stability," *Journal of Economic History,* March 1968, pp. 28–50; Peter Temin, *The Jacksonian Economy* (New York: W. W. Norton and Company, 1969); J. G. Williamson, "International Trade and the U.S. Economic Development, 1927–1843," *Journal of Economic History,* September 1961, pp. 372–380; D. C. North, *The Economic Growth of the U.S. 1790–1860* (Englewood Cliffs, N.J.: Prentice Hall, 1961).

23. Harry N. Scheiber, "The Pet Banks in Jacksonian Politics and Finance, 1833–1841," *Journal of Economic History,* June 1963, pp. 196–214.

24. Arthur M. Schlesinger, Jr., *Age of Jackson* (Boston: Little, Brown and Company, 1945), pp. 115–31.

25. L. H. Jenks, *The Migrations of British Capital to 1875* (New York and London: A. A. Knopf, 1972), chaps. 3–4.

26. Phillip Cagan, *Determinants and Effects of Changes in the Money Stock, 1875–1960* (New York: National Bureau of Economic Research, 1965). I am indebted to Leonard T. Elzie for a number of computations contained in this section. See also Macesich, "Sources of Monetary Disturbances."

27. See M. D. Bordo, "The Classical Gold Standard: Some Lessons for Today," *Monthly Review* (Federal Reserve Bank of St. Louis, May 1981), pp. 2–17.

28. H. Geoffrey Brennan and James M. Buchanan, *Monopoly in Money and Inflation;* and see especially the essays in Leland B. Yeager, ed., *In Search of a Monetary Constitution* (Cambridge: Harvard University Press, 1962).

29. Brennan and Buchanan, *Monopoly in Money and Inflation,* p. 65.

30. Ibid., pp. 59ff.

31. Ibid., p. 59.

32. Ibid., p. 62.

33. Ibid., p. 65.

34. James M. Buchanan and Gordon Tullock, *The Calculus of Consent* (Ann Arbor: University of Michigan Press, 1962); James M. Buchanan, *The Limits of Liberty* (Chicago: University of Chicago Press, 1975); James M. Buchanan, *Freedom in Constitutional Contract* (College Station: Texas A & M Press, 1978); Geoffrey Brennan and James M. Buchanan, *The Power to Tax: Analytical Foundations of a Fiscal Constitution* (Cambridge: Cambridge University Press, 1980), pp. 1–37.

35. Brennan and Buchanan, *The Power to Tax,* p. 22.

36. Buchanan, *The Limits of Liberty,* op. cit., p. 67. See also F. A. Hayek, "The Future Unit of Value" (Paper presented to Visa International, Annual Conference, Athens Greece, 14 September 1981); Richard E. Wagner, "Boom and Bust: The Political Economy of Economic Disorder," *Journal of Libertararian Studies* 4, no. 1, (Winter 1980), pp. 1–37.

37. See, for example, L. B. Yeager, "Exchange Rates Within a Common Market," *Social Research,* January 1959, pp. 415–38. Macesich's published material relevant to the topic includes Macesich, *Yugoslavia: Theory and Practice of Development Planning* (Charlottesville: University Press of Virginia, 1964); "The Theory of Economic Integration and the Experience of the Balkan and Danubian Countries Before 1914" (Paper delivered before the First International Congress on Southeast European Studies, Sofia, Bulgaria, August–September 1966), *The Florida State University Slavic Papers,* vol. 1, 1967; Macesich, "Economic Theory and the Austro-Hungarian Ausgleich of 1967, Proceedings of the Congress; Macesich, "Inflation and the Common Market," Review of International Affairs, 5 June 1964; Macesich, *Money and the Canadian Economy* (Belgrade: National Bank of Yugoslavia, 1967); Macesich, "Supply and Demand for Money in Canada," in David Meiselman, ed., *Varieties of Monetary Experience* (Chicago: University of Chicago Press, 1970); Milton Friedman, "The Case for Flexible Exchange Rates," in Milton Friedman, ed., *Essays in Positive Economics* (Chicago: University of Chicago Press, 1953), pp. 157–203; Harry Johnson, "The Case for Flexible Exchange Rates, 1969," *Review* (Federal Reserve Bank St. Louis, June 1969), pp. 12–24; Jacob A. Frenkel and Harry G. Johnson, eds., *The Economics of Exchange Rates* (Reading, Mass.: Addison-Wesley Publishing Co., 1978); Bluford H. Putnam and D. Sykes Wilford, eds., *The Monetary Approach to International Adjustment* (New York: Praeger Publishers, 1978); Macesich, *Money in a European Common Market Setting* (Baden-Baden: Nomos Verlagsgesellschaft, 1972); Macesich, *The International Monetary Economy and Third World* (New York: Praeger Publishers, 1981); Macesich and Tsai, *Money in Economic Systems;* Macesich, *Monetarism: Theory and Policy.*

38. See George Halm, "The Case for Greater Exchange-Rate Flexibility in an Interdependent World," and Albert G. Hart, "Commentary," in G. Pontecarvo, R. P. Shay, and A. G. Hart, eds., *Issues in Banking and Monetary Analysis* (New York: Holt, Rinehart and Winston, 1967), pp. 169–88.

39. See, for example, William Nordhaus, "Creeping Economic Constitutionalism," *The New York Times,* 27 December 1981; *The Impact of the Federal Reserve System's Monetary Policies on the Nation's Economy* (Second Report), Staff Report of the Subcommittee on Domestic Monetary Policy of the Committee on Banking Finance and Urban Affairs, U.S., Congress, House, 96th Cong., 2d sess., December 1980 (Washington: U.S. Government Printing Office, 1980). The report suggests that Congress is not solely a source of inflationary pressure in the Federal Reserve System.

40. Frankel, p. 85.

41. Thus Hayek writes:

Government, of course, could in justification of its policy use the pretext that a single uniform kind of money used in all transactions constitutes such an advantage that it was worth sacrificing potential improvements. Yet we recognize how much avoidable harm is done by the kind of money we now have. And not the least reason for not having better money is that there has not been enough experimentation to lead to agreement about what kind would be desirable. Selective evolution has been cut off by authority before we have been able to explore adequately the different possible solutions of the problem. That, surely, was too high price to pay for what may have been a temporary convenience. [Hayek, "The Future Unit of Value," op. cit., p. 2]

For a useful discussion of Hayek's major theme in his work on social philosophy, that the "unintended consequences of human action are both efficient and desirable," see Roger A. Arnold, "Hayek and Institutional Evolution," *The Journal of Libertarian Studies,* 4, no. 4, (Fall 1980), pp. 341–52; also Arthur M. Diamond, Jr., "F. A. Hayek on Constructivism and Ethics," ibid., pp. 333–65.

Index